The Book of the Year

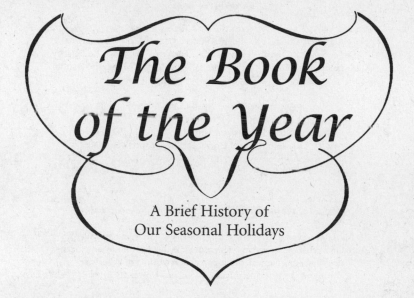

The Book of the Year

A Brief History of Our Seasonal Holidays

Anthony F. Aveni

OXFORD
UNIVERSITY PRESS

OXFORD
UNIVERSITY PRESS

Oxford   New York
Auckland   Bangkok   Buenos Aires   Cape Town   Chennai
Dar es Salaam   Delhi   Hong Kong   Istanbul   Karachi   Kolkata
Kuala Lumpur   Madrid   Melbourne   Mexico City   Mumbai   Nairobi
São Paulo   Shanghai   Taipei   Tokyo   Toronto

First published by Oxford University Press, Inc., 2003
First issued as an Oxford University Press paperback, 2004
198 Madison Avenue, New York, New York 10016

www.oup.com

Oxford is a registered trademark of Oxford University Press

Library of Congress Cataloging-in-Publication Data

Aveni, Anthony F.
The book of the year : a brief history
of our seasonal holidays / by Anthony F. Aveni.
p. cm.   Includes bibliographical references and index.
ISBN 0-19-515024-4 (cloth) ISBN 0-19-517154-3 (pbk.)
1. Holidays—History.
2. Rites and ceremonies.
3. Archaeoastronomy.
4. Biological rhythms.
5. Chronobiology. I. Title.
GT3930.A94 2002   394.26—dc21   2002067176

1 3 5 7 9 8 6 4 2

Printed in the United States of America

For Lorraine, who makes all seasons bright

There is a deep moral influence in the periodical seasons of rejoicing. . . . They bring out . . . the best sympathies in our natures.

Sarah Josephine Buell Hale

Halloween, Valentine's Day, Christmas, Thanksgiving, New Year's Day —these are but a handful of modern holidays descended from the red-letter days, seasonal celebrations we have invented and reinvented over more than five millennia to meet our changing human needs. When we explore their origins, the holidays begin to reflect not only who we are but also why, though oppressed by time and thwarted by the forces of nature, we never seem to lose the will to control the future.

Contents

Acknowledgments x

Preface xi

1 Creating, Organizing, and Transforming the Holidays 1

2 Happy New Year! But Why Now? 11

3 February's Holidays: Prediction, Purification, and Passionate Pursuit 29

4 Spring Equinox: Watching the Serpent Descend 47

5 The Easter/Passover Season: Connecting Time's Broken Circle 63

6 May Day: A Collision of Forces 79

7 Summer's Solstice: Feasts of Fire, Water, and Feminine Affairs of the Heart 91

8 Labor Day: Remembering the Great Time Wars 107

9 Halloween: Dead Time 119

10 Thanksgiving: Transcending Pilgrims' Progress 135

11 Christmas: From Resurrection to Rudolph 149

12 "What Goes Around . . ." 165

Notes 171

References 177

Index 183

Acknowledgments

Thanks to William Frucht, Robert Garland, Steve Lagerfeld, Dick Teresi, and Gary Urton for seasonal discussions; Diane Janney and Lorraine Aveni for editorial assistance, and Sonny Faulseit for his assistance in pictorial research; Joyce Berry and Helen Mules for fostering my continuing relationship with Oxford; and Faith Hamlin, fifteen years my agent and dear friend, for never ceasing to seek value in my work.

Preface

Christmas, Halloween, Groundhog Day, and St. Valentine's Day, Labor Day, May Day, Passover —where do our holidays come from? Why do we celebrate them when we do and not at some other time? The answers lie rooted in the quest to satisfy our deepest inner needs.

Food and sex are life's raw necessities. And, if you think about it, nutrition and propagation go together. We depend on the proliferation of other species because they lie at the root of our capacity to sustain ourselves—they guarantee our success. Deny us our needs and our passions become inflamed.

Our will to live transforms the fundamental things in life to subjects of veneration. Controlling the magical power of fertility that makes all plants and animals what they are (and us who we are) becomes the object of our desire. Harness that power and we can control the future! But as our ancestors recognized long ago, fertility waxes and wanes: abundance turns to scarcity as heat changes to cold, rain to drought; vegetation gives way to snow, blossoming to withering. The whole earth ebbs and flows. Global carbon dioxide levels rise and fall because of photosynthesis in the vegetation that covers our planet's surface. One "earth breath"—an inhale followed by an exhale—lasts a year, the same time it takes shadows cast by the noonday sun to shorten and lengthen over a full cycle.

The cycle of life, the death and rebirth of all things, operates by extremes, each component with its own turning point signaled by nature's visible cues: when the birds come, when the thistles sprout, when the leaves change colors, when the frost appears. We call this cycle the *seasons*, or "time due" in Greek—a word that turns out to live up to its meaning.

We punctuate the seasons with rites, formalities, or ceremonies. We fix each to its appropriate time in the cycle in anticipation of the outcome we desire—what we feel we are due. Why did our Paleolithic ancestors draw figures of bison on the walls of their caves when it came time to hunt? They donned the mask of the animal to impersonate its spirit. Then they ceremonially "killed it" because they believed rehearsal would lead to the act itself. Once our forebears became sedentary, the appropriate holy rites got fixed in the yearly cycle: rainmaking rites, irrigation rites, sowing, plowing, and reaping festivals. All were aimed at controlling the powers related to vegetation at crucial joints in the framework of the seasons.

The Egyptians, the Romans, the Aztecs, and other highly organized ancient agrarian civilizations keyed many of their communal celebrations to the birthdays of the gods (later the Christians replaced them with the saints). The religion of the state deemed them responsible for providing society's various necessities. Elaborate feasts and sacrifices were arranged to placate the deities, to cajole them, to plead with them, to pay the debt owed them. The Aztecs honored their rain god, Tlaloc, in early February in the midst of the dry season. Surrounding communities brought children to the hilltops around their capital of ancient Mexico City in tribute, hoping that the tears they shed prior to being sacrificed might serve as payment for the bountiful crop he had delivered the year before. When the low rays of the sun signaled the arrival of autumn and thoughts turned to the impending struggle with the forces of death and gloom, medieval Christians prayed to St. Michael, protector against the devil (formally on September 29, Michaelmas). Some agrarian holiday rites were extraordinarily specialized: the Roman Robigalia, fixed on April 25, was specifically dedicated to averting *robigo*, a kind of mold that developed on wheat. Celebrants would parade down Rome's Via Claudia to a sacred grave believed to be the birthplace of Robigus, the god of mildew. There they would offer animal sacrifices to him.

To map out the pattern of rituals that make up the seasonal round that we call the year, organized societies the world over created a device outside of themselves to set the pace of life—a kind of metronome to keep the beat of human activity tuned to the manifold overlapping cycles of life. Every culture has its own map. Creating it, as historian Martin Nilsson comments in the epigraph to Chapter 1, has a complex history all its own.

You have such a map near you—a common household article within arm's reach. It achieves for your long-term outlook what your wrist-watch does for the short run: it organizes your own personal life cycle. We call it a calendar. "Just a minute, let me get out my calendar" are words we utter every time we contemplate future action. For most of us the calendar is a bound, opened-out packet of a dozen pages, usually hung on a wall, that metes out our periods of wakefulness by compart-mentalizing them into a four- or five-by-seven grid. Often the facing pages are decorated with pictures reminiscent of the time due—sail-boats on a lake in July, brightly colored leaves in October. My desktop-pad version has 365 ring-bound pages. Each features a Far Side cartoon along with a miniature version of the relevant page of the twelvefold grid that appears farther away on my wall. I have a version of it that I wear on my wrist and my VCR harbors still another.

Calendar time flows just like the words on this page, from left to right. The leftmost days (we call them Sundays) used to be highlighted, like capital letters that start sentences, and were often numbered in red. Other red-numbered days are sporadically sprinkled about the neat little squares that make up the grid—25 is highlighted in December, 4 stands out in July, 1 in January. What coffee break, lunch hour, and workout time are to the 24-hour day, these special numbered days have come to be to the months and the year—points of collective recognition in the cycle of the seasons that distinguish who we are as a culture. First dubbed "red-letter days" by the eighteenth-century Church of England after the scarlet robes worn by judges who held court on those days (or possibly after the red ink used by medieval scribes to mark them on the calen-dar), all ecclesiastical holidays were so indicated to distinguish them from the ordinary days marked in black—to focus on them as a way of break-ing the monotony and sense of chaotic timelessness that comes from experiencing an otherwise uninterrupted chain of mundane events. Our modern holidays—the days we keep—descend from these archaic red-letter days. To be sure, we have jostled some of them around on the grid, even altered what they mean. We have made some of them obsolete and our changing needs have compelled us to devise new ones. The beat may change but, as we will learn, we never cease to keep the rhythm of the seasons.

The Book of the Year

Chapter

1

Creating, Organizing, and Transforming the Holidays

> The fusion of the various seasons into the circle of the year is arrived at only by degrees.
>
> Martin Nilsson

The schedule of rituals that we call our calendar emanates from the vast differences among the seasons that we all experience. Traditionally, we think of the seasons as four in number—summer, fall, winter, and spring. But this taxonomy turns out to be largely a nineteenth-century reinvention of the ancient habit of pivoting the year about the pendulum-like northerly and southerly migration points of the sun (the solstices) and their midpoints (the equinoxes). (Most Indo-European languages have root words for winter, spring, and summer only, which may mean that there once were only three seasons.) In stark contrast, the ancient Celtic calendar set four seasonal marking posts at dates that lie at approximately the middle of our four seasons. Halloween, Groundhog Day, May Day, and the now defunct Lammas, or the First of the Harvest Festival (August 1), once signaled the changing of the fourfold seasonal guard.

Cultures that grow up in tropical climes usually recognize a two-season year: the wet and the dry or, to judge by the changing skin color of the breathing earth, the green and the brown. There are exceptions: the central African Babwende, who experience a double rainy season, have five seasons; they call them "big rains," "little dry period," "little rains," "big dry period," and "burning of the withered grass." Native tribes of Virginia also once recognized a fivefold year: "budding," "caring of corn," "highest sun," "fall of the leaf," and "cold." If we strictly follow nature's cues—depending on where we live—some of us might set the commencement date for the "green" season at the March equinox, the official first day of spring. Northerners would likely place it closer to May Day, which has a long history of marking the explosive entry of life's forces into a dormant world.

Some calendars used the moon's phases as their unwritten pages, often basing the names of the full moons on the natural phenomena and accompanying human activities that occurred about them; so we could say their years had twelve or even thirteen seasons. Contrast this with the seasons we live by today, which begin on Labor Day (the start of the work/school cycle), July or June 1 (the start of the fiscal year), or the many "openers" in the seasonal sport cycle.

One of my major goals in *The Book of the Year* will be to trace the origins of the modern customs tied to the holidays that make up the seasonal calendar: what we eat (why the egg at Easter, chocolate on St. Valentine's Day?), the games we play (bobbing for apples on Halloween, football on Thanksgiving), the rituals we engage in (dancing around the maypole, making New Year's resolutions), and the *dramatis personae* we invent to go with each red-letter day (Santa Claus, the Easter Bunny, the demonic Halloween crew). Like loose threads in a fabric, once tugged at, our quaint customs separate into strands that allow us to peek through the calendar we fabricate to deeper layers of meaning. Our evolving calendar becomes a kaleidoscope of the modern collective soul.

I open with a chapter that celebrates beginnings. Just about every day of the seasonal cycle has functioned as Day One in one calendar or another. How did ours get to be January 1? We enter the round of the seasons on the "firsts" that matter to us—first rain, first planting, first flower . . . but "what's first" on our list changes with time. Why do we behave paradoxically at that timeless moment between successive cycles on the eve of the arrival of the New Year? On the one hand we solemnly recognize the spirit of the rebirth of gods, plants, animals, life; but on the other hand the self-examination and moral reckoning that underlies making New Year's resolutions abruptly interfaces with the reckless revelry, excess, and abandon that comes with taking license, at least momentarily, to become someone we are not.

In Chapter 3, I explore the unlikely connections between St. Valentine, the groundhog, and the Virgin Mary. We honor all of them at the beginning of a cold, light-deprived month named for the purification rites that once opened the old Roman (and later Celtic) season of great seasonal expectations. Driven by the need to see into the future, we make this a time to express our faith in the predictive power of animals. But where do expectations about our love lives enter the picture and how did today's version of the holiday for lovers come to be played out on the turf of the modern shopping mall where we buy elaborate valentines to consummate our love?

In Chapter 4, on the spring equinox, I offer answers to the question: Who owns the past? To judge by the groups of seekers, worshippers, and protesters who show up on special days at historic places from England's Stonehenge to the Mall in Washington, D.C., history has many claimants. At the ancient Maya ruins of Chichén Itzá in Yucatan, I personally explore the birth of a contemporary myth tied to the equinox. Those who stake claims to an ancient heritage there include native people, modern mixed-blood Mexicans, members of diverse New Age communities, and masses of tourists. All venture on pilgrimages to the ruins on equinox day to watch the unique interplay of light and shadow that takes the form of a giant serpent cast upon the stairway of a pyramid. They come today, as their Maya counterparts may have come a thousand years ago, in search of sacred knowledge that comes at a special season of the year and gives meaning to their lives. But whose serpent is it?

Who put the bunny and the egg into Easter? As we learn in Chapter 5, for the past 5,000 years more energy has been devoted to figuring out just when to celebrate this solemn, yet joyous festival than any other holiday. Why do we behave so ludicrously—as on a bawdy New Year's Eve—at Carnival and Mardi Gras that mark the inception of the Easter cycle?

May Day's old rituals include tree worship, and one of its hidden symbols is our Statue of Liberty, as we learn in Chapter 6. It is an excellent example of a holiday that emerged as a reinvented tradition. It carries a special irony because it arose out of rationalist movements that were hostile to the original rites once practiced on this day, which curiously seem to be undergoing a contemporary revival. But May Day was never intended to be a day focusing on workers' protests and the antiglobalization movement as it does today—not until antiestablishment forces seized it and turned it against those who observed established May Day rites.

The Book of the Year also heralds holidays long gone from our calendar. The June solstice (Chapter 7) was one of the most important days of the year to the ancient Chinese as well as the ancient Greeks, Romans, and contemporary polar Inuit—all avid sunwatchers. Neolithic people erected Britain's most famous ancient monument, the Inca built sun pillars, the Maya specially oriented temples—all to frame the sun god's image on the day of his annual northerly turnabout. But yesterday's solstice fires and fire-jumping rituals, though doused by our inherited puritanical mind-set, still lives on in our Fourth of July fireworks. And rites once rife with feminine magic still persist in the month of brides.

In Chapter 8, I revisit the problem of the ownership of time by exploring the origin of Labor Day (our modern version of the fall equinox). Although this holiday celebrating the partnership of capital and labor grew out of economic necessity in a changing nineteenth-century industrial world, its deeper roots necessitate telling the story of the great medieval "time wars," when the invention of the clock first pitted labor against management. But who would have thought that in the last two decades we would develop a curious need to work more—even on this saintly Monday—despite living in an age devoted to creating new technological devices to save us time?

With the odor of decay in the air the seasons turn—to Halloween, the subject of Chapter 9. There I trace the origin of Halloween symbols ranging from trick-or-treating to jack-o'-lanterns, and I also explore why a holiday connected for five millennia with honoring the dead turned into a day of controlled, socially condoned deviant behavior, and the number-two U.S. consumer holiday of the year.

As I follow the history of Thanksgiving proclamations (Chapter 10), I find that we haven't always been thankful for the same gifts on the fourth Thursday in November. What began as an end of the harvest period of giving thanks to God for enabling the Pilgrims to survive in a strange land was later recast to offer gratitude for the constitutional government that saw us through the Revolution, then again for unity in the midst of strife during the Civil War, and now for a way of life all Americans share despite our diversity.

Finally, Christmas (I trace its history in Chapter 11) is another good example of the invention-reinvention process that transforms our seasonal holidays. It began in prehistoric times as a set of rites aimed at persuading the dying winter solstice god of light to return to a course worshippers feared he was about to abandon. Christianity altered the pagan festival to symbolize the return of light to a dark and decaying world through the birth of a covenanted savior. Then, in the nineteenth century an industrial secular society refashioned Christmas yet again to resonate with the desires of a commercially driven, overworked society, guilt-ridden for not having paid sufficient attention to its children.

As I follow the sinuous history of each red-letter day, I also try to demonstrate how the rites behind the days change with our cultural and psychological needs. The calendar may look different, but our motivation for devising it remains basically the same.

We discover that the roots of our system for reckoning holidays are deeply immersed in the struggle over retaining one's own identity in the face of change. Anthropologist Charles Frake has compared the pages of a medieval calendar to the façade of a Gothic cathedral: both structures consist of intricate elaborations. Far more complex than our own, one version of the calendar reckoned no fewer than 126 days dedicated to local feasts and saints' days—marking not only their birthdates but also the days of their martyrdom and transition. But if we look at them closely,

the pages of fourteenth-century calendars look to be copies of Roman
calendars from a millennium or more earlier, with saints' names substituted for the gods of the Roman pantheon. The setting of the dates required elaborate calculations by specially skilled computists who worked
out the motion of the sun, moon, planets, and stars to be sure the calendar was kept in tune with the whirling spheres above (which they believed influenced what happened here below—astrology pure and
simple). The problem behind the gargantuan time machine, which led
philosopher Roger Bacon to write in exasperation: "The calendar is intolerable to every computationist," lay in consolidating the pagan Greco-
Roman and Hebrew traditions once held together under the umbrella
of the Roman Empire within the emerging symbolism of Christianity.
"The need to be identifiably different," writes Frake, "while retaining a
connection with past traditions, was the major force driving the calcula-
tory involution that marked the construction of the Christian calendar."

I think this applies to all calendars. Human invention makes and re-
makes the holidays to meet cultural and psychological needs that arise at
different times in the seasonal cycle. New demands prompt us to reinvent
the holidays, to alter their meaning—often substantially—to respond to
the climate of the times. For example, the celebrated Roman Bacchanalia,
the archetype of orgiastic Roman feasts depicted in so many films (and
the source of a lowercase adjective to describe wild parties in general),
started out as a foreign cult. It converted the sane and sober Dionysus, an
ancient vegetation god, into the licentious Bacchus. His cult, which included slaves as well as freemen, became a celebratory nighttime (rather
than a daytime) affair involving *both* men and women engaged in highly
ecstatic demonstrative behavior—the kind of emotional high that might
be found in today's Pentecostal ceremonies. The Bacchanalia's enormous
popular appeal developed out of a reaction to the hardening of social authority in third-century B.C. Rome. The senate reacted by putting an end
to the wild music, howling, ecstatic delirium, and (what they termed) lewd
practices, which they regarded as obnoxious to any festival portraying the
death and rebirth of life. Success was modest at best.

In complex civilizations, the renewal of nature is often likened to
the renewal of society as a whole; this is a major pattern of behavior

underlying the celebration of many New Year's festivals (Chapter 2), the revivified May Day (Chapter 6), and the renewal of moral behavior in rites of atonement such as Rosh Hashanah and Good Friday (Chapter 5), days devoted to lamenting society's wrongdoings.

As we course through the sequence of holidays that make up the fabric of the seasons, we discover still other patterns of behavior that characterize their evolution. For example, the willful substitution of one entity for another: I call it the *principle of substitution*—Bacchus for Dionysus, Christ for the sun—turns out to be one of the major attributes of practically all our holidays. The groundhog (Chapter 3) is not the original animal indigenous to the day that celebrates it; nor was the pumpkin the traditional autumnal vegetable associated with Halloween (Chapter 9).

The *inversion principle* is another kind of behavior that character-izes the way we choose to make time. How we behave at the office party is a scant reflection of the way we act in the workplace. The great turn-ing points in the yearly cycle bring with them moments of anticipation: the sun dramatically halts its southward movement, warm autumn days suddenly give way to frosty nights; in the dead of winter, the storehouse empty, a ray of warm sunshine offers hope of spring. Time mirrors life at these critical joints in its fabric. The elite let their hair down and ac-cord the unholy a temporary claim to status. Mardi Gras, New Year's Eve, ancient Rome's Saturnalia, and our Halloween are all examples of the inversion of time, and the role reversal that seems to accompany such pivotal moments.

All holiday rituals include a healthy dose of sympathetic magic— what we today might call simple superstitions; for example, wearing green on St. Patrick's Day or red on Valentine's Day will bring on the luck of the Irish or make your love life fortunate. We make up New Year's reso-lutions because we think that our behavior at the beginning of a cycle will determine what we'll do for the rest of the year: *performance equals outcome*. Finally, the idea that the future is contained in the past and can be acted out in the present also underlies our celebration of Groundhog Day and the twelve days of Christmas. Believers say weather predictions can be garnered for the entire year by watching the behavior of nature on a particular day or set of days. What happens in micro-time holds the secret of what will happen in macro-time—for what is the year but a drawn-out imitation of the day?

The holidays once spoke to us directly and without meta-phor. They were "reality based." But modern life has a way of blurring the old distinctions that once defined the pattern of the changing sea-sons. Our loss of direct contact with nature coupled with an ever deep-ening techno-immersion have dulled past customs. Still, we never seem to stop making and remaking the map of time we call the calendar. We still use our holidays to mark significant points in the yearly cycle. Whether they be highjacked versions of old ones, or new ones that we create (Martin Luther King Jr. Day, President's Day, Memorial Day, Flag Day, Independence Day, V-J Day, D Day, Columbus Day, Veterans Day, and Pearl Harbor Day are a few that have arisen since American nation-hood), we continue to reconfigure time; we make it conform to what we desire and deserve.

Our obvious need for patriotic identity connected with the creation of many of these holidays is coupled with attempts to redefine the con-temporary American holiday cycle to reflect the change in the ethnic makeup—not to mention the increasingly secular nature—of our cul-ture. And so we have created Kwanzaa adjacent to Christmas just as we have "Christmasized" Chanukah (Chapter 11). Our preoccupation with calamity and disaster causes us to keep days with negative connotations—lest we forget. For example, April 19 has become the anniversary of the expulsion of the Branch Davidians from Waco, Texas (1993), the bomb-ing of the Murrah Federal Building in Oklahoma City (1995), and the Columbine High School shootings in Colorado (1999)—a day both to honor the dead and to celebrate the senselessness of the moment. And in an instant, September 11 became the nation's first solemn day of reck-oning in the new millennium. Future versions of our red-letter-day cycle will continue to reflect events both sad and glad that have yet to tran-spire, for only when all segments of a culture are given their due can a society survive and thrive.

Why bother with a history of the holidays? Recovering our lost heritage is part of understanding the prevailing pattern of the seasonal calendar we celebrate. Abandon contact with the sources of our beliefs and practices—and many readers will probably conclude we already have—and we will only come to recognize the days we keep as mere diversions—excuses for time off from the work that occupies an ever-increasing segment of our life cycle. Worse still, we would lose hold of the sense of communal solidarity that comes with the active participation in celebrating a holiday.

So I offer *The Book of the Year* to elevate the innocuous desk calendar to a signature element in the continuous struggle between ordinary mortals and the forces of time and to dramatize the impact of seasonal change on individuals and the society in which we live. As we act out the history of each holiday we discover a drama played out in a universe that seems uncontrollable yet in which we still harbor an insistence on being influential participants. The old "red-letter" days are alive. They are the great moments of tension, key turning points in a microcosmic version of the whole earth's breathing cycle transformed into the cycle of life, death, and the hope of renewal—of all things. What our forebears did on such occasions would set the tone for their future course in the next cycle. Likewise, how we behave today reflects the dynamic nature of the process of calendar making for the future. By understanding how we organize and comprehend the passage of seasonal time, we realize just how profoundly successful human empowerment over the structure of time has been in assigning new meaning to each of its aspects: we put new spins on old holidays.

Happy New Year!
But Why Now?

Time present and time past
Are both perhaps present in time future,
And time future contained in time past . . .
Time past and time future
What might have been and what has been
Point to one end, which is always present.

T. S. Eliot

Where to begin? Basically I am a morning person, but shall I have that second cup to be sure I am totally awake before I start work? Should I clean up right after dinner or savor a quiet moment by saving the dishes for later? When am I going to restart my diet? Can I wait until after the weekend when I will be less tempted by the evil gastronomic missiles my hosts will likely hurl at me Saturday night? Or should I take the high road and test my mettle by deflecting delectable desserts directly in the line of fire? When to stop warming up and start exercising? When to take my vacation week? When to get out of bed—or back into it? Time and all the routines that fill it go round and round, the ending of one cycle immediately followed by the beginning of another. Days—months—years: they are all closed loops. Yet each requires a point of entry.

We break into the diurnal cycle when we wake, and day is done when we slip between the sheets and experience that longed-for period of dream sleep when we all exist outside of time—until we return to the merry-go-round the next morning. For poets, plants, and animals, sunrise signals the dawn of a new day and sunset brings down the curtain of nightfall. The National Bureau of Standards would have us begin the twenty-four-hour cycle at midnight, whose stroke resets all two-times-twelve-hour timepieces. In medieval times, noon was the start of a new day in Venice, but it was one o'clock in Basel. Can you imagine confused merchants traveling from city to city not knowing which page of their date books to use to enter their sales?

Before we tore off pages of our calendar every thirty (or thirty-one) days to mark the month, astronomers pondered where to start the lunar count. Should Day One coincide with a full moon (It did in Tibet, Korea, Japan, and Vietnam) or a new moon (as the Chinese calculate it). Or should it be the first crescent moon you spot low in the western sky after sunset, which is what the Babylonians, who gave their time-reckoning habits over to the Greeks, chose. Official moonwatchers once stood on the roof of the highest temple in Babylon to decide when citizens should pay the rent or money owed a creditor. The news of a new month's beginning would be broadcast from the mouth of a hired town runner with a booming voice.

When is the old year finished and what signals the rebeginning of the cycle of the seasons? If you run a business, July 1 is as important a beginning as January 1, for each date commences a pair of fiscal half-years. The quarters, marked by adding October 1 and April 1, are equally important. From a practical economic standpoint, April 16 is as good a beginning as any, because it follows the April 15 midnight rush of hastily filed tax returns at the post office—the final look back on the status of our financial fitness over the past solar cycle. Teachers, students, hockey and soccer moms and dads might choose Labor Day, the real starting point of most school years. And a host of New Year's Days connected with professional sports are sprinkled about the twelve months of the year. The baseball year begins when the spring training camps open in February, football in late July, basketball in early October.

"Happy New Year!" has been uttered across the globe on every imaginable date for every conceivable reason. In ancient Egypt, water was the deciding factor in a three-season year that consisted of Inundation, Germination, and Warmth. In the Old Kingdom (ca. 3000 B.C.), the flooding of the Nile around the summer solstice kicked off the agricultural season by bringing rich loam to the parched periphery of the green aqueous ribbon that meandered through the North African desert. Anticipating when the life-giving water level would start its climb up the Nilometer that calibrated its depth was as dicey as predicting next season's first Atlantic hurricane. Hydrologists looked upward to recognize a telltale sign in heaven: Sothis, the brightest star in the sky. Sothis was the messenger of Isis, sky goddess of love (our classical Venus), who was perpetually engaged in trying to awaken her lover, her brother (as well as her husband via an incestuous marriage) Osiris from the dead. Every year around the time of Inundation a cadre of royal astronomers assembled to witness the first predawn appearance of what we would later call Sirius, the Dog Star, which served as a convenient celestial indicator that coincided with the flood season. Once they glimpsed the brightest star returned to the sky, they would be assured that the "Dog Days" of sun-scorched drought were just about over. The attentive reader can easily pick up on the symbolic equation here: fertility of the land equals fertility in the human species, the latter tied to the sexiest of all female deities. Her messenger star flirts with the landscape by appearing close to the horizon, thus mimicking the frequent action of her own celestial counterpart, the planet Venus.

But over long intervals, celestial Sothis began to muddy up the waters of Nilotic time by slowly getting out of sync with the seasons. By 30 B.C. Alexandrians were forced to nail down the first of the Egyptian year to a fixed position in the seasonal calendar. They reset it for August 29, based on the rising of the Nile, the sun's position, and general agricultural operations. Like modern Wall Street moguls, the ancient Celts bifurcated their year. They based their pivot points on movement and stasis: one-half the year for cattle herding, the other for sedentary winter activity near the shelters of home. The half-New Year's Days May 1 and November 1, as we shall discover, live on in our modern calendar as May Day and Halloween/All Souls' Day.

New Year's Day came on the shortest day of the year for the Inca of Peru (June 21 in the southern hemisphere). For the Inca, the sun symbolized royal power and the ruling elite saw fit to lavishly display the sun's splendid metal on both the royal personage and his palace, aptly named the Qoricancha, or "Golden Enclosure." Spanish chroniclers tell us that on New Year's Day all fires were extinguished in the capital city of Cuzco, to be relit later in the day by a piece of cotton batting ignited by the rays of the sun god, Inti. (A cloudy New Year's Day was an evil portent because it necessitating kindling the new flame by friction instead.) The Inti Raymi festival commenced when the sun reached its turning point in the sky, which was marked by huge pillars erected along the mountainous horizon. When the sun arrived there the populace gathered in the city square; they brought out their mummified ancestors robed in gold and paraded them around the city and into the Qoricancha along with the emperor, who was similarly garbed. There the Inca placed a golden disk to reflect the sun's solstitial glow all around the courtyard. In today's version of the Inti Raymi festival, the effigy of St. John has replaced the emperor and his retinue (we will learn why in Chapter 7). The last time I witnessed the Inti Raymi festival, the Plaza de Armas in front of the great cathedral of Cuzco accommodated more than 100,000 people, and the parade went on for most of the afternoon accompanied by the playing of music, the drinking of pisco, and open-air dining upon countless plates of roasted guinea pig.

The ancient Maya of Central America rang in their New Year by observing the absence of a shadow. The passage of the sun directly overhead, a phenomenon that takes place only in the tropics (between latitudes $23\frac{1}{2}°$ north and south), was one of nature's cues that conveniently marked the beginning of a new agricultural cycle. Wrote one Spanish admirer of the Maya:

> To this day the Indians commenced the New Year on the 16th of July (in the most tempestuous days of the rainy season). Their progenitors, having sought to make it begin from the precise day on which the sun re-

turns to the zenith of this peninsula on his way to the southern regions, but being destitute of instruments for their astronomical observations, and guided only by the naked eye, erred only forty-eight hours in advance.

Incidentally, I think the chronicler has made an error here. There are actually two solar zenith passages per year and they vary with latitude. In most areas of southern Mexico, where the calendar was invented, one of them occurs close to the start of the rainy season, which begins the agricultural cycle, around May 1 (closer to May 25 in north Yucatan, where the text was written), which is probably the date that was initially chosen.

What calendar keeper would be foolish enough to create a seasonal reckoning scheme that did not respond to human needs? So entrenched was the native Mesoamerican habit of commencing the yearly ritual cycle on the shadowless moment that occurs at noontime when the sun passes overhead that the Spanish conquistadors, thinking it connected with idolatry and devil worship, systematically ordered the custom of celebrating it abolished. The Eastern Holy Roman Empire had an equally contentious time with the pagan Macedonian New Year's designation—November 18 after the birth of their sun god. One compromising Christian chronologist tried unsuccessfully to fudge the date of the Nativity to justify its continuation.

September 22, harvest day—and the autumnal equinox—became the new New Year's Day in the decimally-based calendar following the French Revolution of 1789. It ended abruptly fourteen years later, not because that particular day was a bad choice but because Napoleon intervened and restored the Gregorian calendar, which pivoted about the other equinox. (My own opinion is that the nine straight days of work followed by one of rest called for in the base-ten weekly time count did little to contribute to the calendar's longevity.)

In some cultures New Year's Days are based on the moon rather than the sun. Lunar anchor points have a habit of floating around in the framework of the seasonal year because cycles of full moons do not mesh evenly with the 365-day solar cycle. The moon takes 29½ days to go through its phases, which means you can fit either twelve of them into a year (with a remainder of eleven days) or thirteen (and run over into the next year by eighteen days). Our modern calendar avoids the problem by assigning twelve slightly longer phony months to the year. (I call them phony because not one of them has a count of days that corresponds to what the real moon does in the sky.)

The Jewish calendar is a familiar example of a moon-dependent yearly cycle. Like the French Revolutionary calendar, it starts with the harvest, but it is based on Old Testament designations of activities that took place in consecutive moons timed from the sighting of the first crescent: the month of fruits (ripening), rain, flowers, and so on. Every few years when the twelve moon months got out of kilter with the 365-day year (for example, people would notice that flowers didn't tend to bloom in their designated month because the temperature was still below freezing), they added, or "intercalated," an extra (thirteenth) month. Still echoing its fall equinoctial beginning, today's version of the Jewish New Year can begin anywhere between September 6 and October 5, a period that neatly brackets full moons closest to the September equinox. Rosh Hashanah, literally the "head" (of the body) of the year, is the first day of the month of Tishri. It begins a ten-day period of moral stocktaking that terminates on the Day of Atonement (Yom Kippur), when the Lord would abolish (literally "cover over" after "Kippur") the sins of the Jewish nation. Five days later, or one-half of a moon cycle into the new year, Sukkoth, the Feast of the Tabernacles or Rejoicing of the Law, completed the short cycle of moral cleansing that opened every year.

The Chinese calendar is based on the moon too, except it begins with the winter solstice. Oddly enough, though they call the first month the "new lunation," they begin the actual year count two months later, in late January or early February in the Christian calendar (likewise the month of Nisan, which envelops the spring equinox, begins the list of Hebrew months, though not the year). Shifts like this often happen when people tinker with their calendars. Chinese New Year's Day is Yuandan, a day to be spent in the company of extended family—and to shoot off lots of fireworks.

Many native North American calendars center on counting and naming moons after the activities that take place beneath their light. Our Harvest and Hunter's moons, the first and second that follow the fall equinox, are mileposts in the time band of the native people who inhabited the New England forests before the arrival of the pilgrims.

You can tell a lot about people and their interaction with the seasons if you compare old month lists of, for example, the Algonquin tribes from New England to the Great Lakes (left) and the Kwakiutl people of Vancouver Island (right) (both begin around March), as shown in the following table.

Table 1. Month Lists of Two Native American Tribes Contrasted

Algonquin	Kwakiutl
Worm Moon	No sap in trees
Pink Moon	Raspberry sprouting season
Moon of flowers	Huckleberry season
Strawberry Moon	Salalberry season
Moon of the buck	Southeast wind moon
Moon of the sturgeon	Sockeye moon
Harvest Moon	Elder Brother
Hunter's Moon	Pile driving (or sweeping houses)
Beavers' Moon	Fish-in-river moon
Cold Moon	Season of Flood
Wolf Moon	
Snow Moon	

Each season begins with the first of its kind: first flowers, first sap, first snow, and so on. Particular days within each of these months marked by different phases of the moon are set for performing the rituals connected with recognizing these firsts.

What about the calendar we keep today? Where did our New Year's Day come from? Originally, when it was set up two and a half millennia ago in Rome, the seasonal year commenced in March. Mars, to whom that month was dedicated, was more than the god of war. He also was called on to protect the land and its crops; so it made sense to worship him in the month when Roman farmers turned their thoughts to assisting nature in her annual process of renewal. To the months March, April, May, and June, which composed all of a 120-day year, the Romans later added a fifth month, Quintilis, and a sixth, Sextilis, each of which was adopted by a Roman emperor (they became July and August, respectively)—plus four more number-named months. Our September,

October, November, and December translate from Latin as months number seven (Septem), eight (Octo), nine (Novem), and ten (Decem), respectively. Originally there was no January (or February) in the calendar we inherited. Like the Kwakiutl year in Table 1, it consisted of just ten months. The Roman year totaled 304 days, a highly symmetric number if pastoral and other farming activities mark your seasonal round. It also approximates the gestation period of cattle and it is evenly divisible by eight, the number of days in a market week. Time rules life!

No work, no pay, no time. The only time that really mattered to the early Romans was when things were alive—when they grew and needed tending, when human action was a part of the picture. The rest was nature's "time out," temporal leftovers unworthy of even being counted. (Not shaving on Sunday is my way of paying respect to this time-honored custom.) Once things began to germinate again, the year would be restarted.

Things changed in 153 B.C. when a Roman emperor added two months to the ten-month count, the better to align the tally of the moon's phases with the sun's cycle. He also hit upon the notion of designating the month in which the sun could first be recognized making its way back from the southern climes as the perfect symbol to herald new beginnings. The New Year was reckoned by the first sighting of the crescent moon in the west after sunset following the winter solstice. Midwinter is the beginning of the new sun and the end of the old one, the first-century Roman historian Ovid tells us in his *Fasti*, a compilation of the holidays. Citizens reveled in celebrating the return of the *Sol Invictus*, or "Unconquered Sun," by eating and drinking to excess. (Pliny the Elder notes that he was forced to hide in a soundproof room to escape the noise of the revelers.) Because the Romans had initiated this custom, the Christian church, once firmly established, stubbornly clung to the spring equinox as the starting point of the solar cycle. Staid England and her colonies continued to designate New Year's Day as March 25 and refused to adopt January 1 until 1752. April Fool's Day is the remnant of the bogus new year created when Charles IX of France made the switch from spring equinox to January 1 in 1564. But because news traveled slowly, most rural folks continued to make New Year's calls and exchange gifts on the first of the month after the equinox. The situation gradually evolved into mockery and it became the custom to hook a *poisson d'Avril* (April fish), after the young fish more easily caught in streams at the beginning of the season, by offering up a silly gift.

As the sun god flexed his newfound radiance and emerged victorious from the world of death and darkness, both he and the landscape around him breathed life anew. More daylight and shorter shadows at noon brought promise of the nurturing warmth we desperately long for as winter shows signs of losing its death grip. Now was the time to kindle new fires in the temples, to drape them with garlands, to offer honey to the gods to make the year sweet—and money to the calendar priests to see to it that the offering got to the right place. To bring good luck, Roman citizens exchanged gifts of food and coins for three days in honor of Janus, the god of beginnings. "Omens are wont to wait upon beginnings," Ovid says. Janus was the guardian of doorways, who could look both ways in defiance of time's arrow. If you want to know what goes on inside the building, ask the doorman—for he who guards the threshold provides ready access to the gods!

Getting wind of a New Year's omen in old Rome was no mean task. An official member of the College of Augurs would camp out on New Year's Eve, rise early, and, facing east in the morning twilight, offer prayers. He would perspicaciously scan the sky in search of one of nature's telltale signs—a lightning flash on the left was particularly propitious. The news would be delivered to the Forum via a solemn procession of senators and consuls; there the public would witness the sacrifice of a white bull.

Today there is scarcely a vestigial remnant of the old omen-seeking ritual that opened the door to the New Year, but, if we look carefully, signs of survival are evident. Not to be outdone by our Roman forebears, we too celebrate our new beginnings with feasts. Instead of looking for signs from the gods, we make resolutions in anticipation of our own personal rebirth. We lust after that second chance we know we all deserve as we reboard the carousel of life for another circuit, another click to the zeroes on longevity's odometer in search of a smoother ride than the last one—Happy New Year!

Keeping track of New Year's Day in our calendar has been as consuming as the issue of deciding when to celebrate it. Back in Caesar's day the sun passed the spring equinox on March 25, which he designated the official New Year's Day in 45 B.C. His astronomer Sosigines calculated that about 100 days needed to be added to the previous year to realign the badly out of joint calendar with the actual course of the sun. But even though Caesar tacked on a leap-year correction, the real year still managed to slowly backslide through the seasons. Sixteen centuries later when Pope Gregory XIII re-reformed the calendar (as we'll see in Chapter 5, he did it to get a better handle on when to fix the Easter holiday), the equinox had fallen all the way back to March 11. Gregory promptly wrote a decree to make up for the long lost time by skipping ten days in the sun count. He declared that the day after October 4 of 1582 would be October 15. Imagine bills coming due on the 15th. Should your creditor offer a ten-day extension or collect on the spot? And what about birthdays and anniversaries that fall in the second week of the month? Chaos!

Historically, setting the instant of the arrival of New Year has bordered on a worldwide obsession. The ancient Chinese did it by precisely measuring the noonday shadow cast by a gnomon. Old texts tell us that the winter solstice shadow there was 3.14 meters (about 10 feet) long. Religious rules specified that jade must be used for the template or gauge laid out on the floor to fix the measurement. Unfortunately, jade does not come in 10-foot slabs. So chronologists worked out better techniques for measuring the much shorter shadow cast earlier in the season when the noonday sun is higher in the sky; then they performed mathematical calculations from that point to set the winter solstice New Year date. However, because they were not aware that all four seasons are not exactly equal in length (owing to the elliptical shape of the earth's orbit and its axial tilt), they frequently got the wrong answer. To add to the difficulties, pinning down any solstice day is difficult because the sun (and consequently its shadow) moves very slowly from day to day at turnaround time. Finally, because the sun is an extended disk rather than a point of light, all shadows are fuzzy. (Check out your own umbra sometime to verify this point.)

Today we have passed beyond the sun and even the stars in our quest for accuracy—9,192,631,770 beats of a cesium oscillator (one beat is timed by the transition of electrons between two favored orbits of the cesium atom) make up the international seconds we use to clock our year. And even though we can mark New Year to New Year with an accuracy comparable to measuring the distance to the moon down to the width of a human hair, we still find it necessary to add an occasional leap second to the year (usually at the halfway mark at midnight on June 30 so as not to mess up the ceremonial countdown to January 1). Our classical concept of the exact arrival of the great moment remains the dropping of the time ball at midnight in New York's Times Square, part of an old maritime tradition. (All port cities from Portsmouth, England, to Mystic, Connecticut, once had them. The ball usually fell at noon, serving as a visual time signal so that ships in port could reset their chronometers.)

Deciding when to jump on the seasonal carousel emerges as a collective, conscious decision, based almost always, as we have seen, on the resumption of human activity and its consequent "firsts," such as the opening of the farming season, or the coming of the rains that wash away all vestige of last year's marvels and miscarriages. Life follows death and if there is a single theme that binds the setting of these diverse New Year's Days together, it is resurrection. When the Egyptians held their festival of Isis to coincide with the rising of the Nile, they believed her tears of mourning for her dead husband/brother Osiris were responsible for swelling the river. Only the rebirth of his spirit would guarantee a bountiful harvest. It all emanates from the age-old myth of Osiris. He was the illegitimate product of the union of the male earth god and Isis, who had cheated on the sun god. It was Osiris who civilized the Egyptians and introduced them to the cultivation of grain. He had left the people in the care of his young wife Isis while he traveled the world over to bring the blessings of civilization to other wayward cultures. However he was done in by a conspiratorial brother who nailed him alive in a lead-sealed coffin and tossed him into the Nile. Isis spent her life searching for Osiris, but once again her brother-in-law managed to recover the coffin and, for good measure, dismembered his brother's corpse and scattered it about the land. Undeterred, the faithful spouse collected all the body parts (minus the penis, which had been devoured by fish, thus necessitating a wax replacement) and reassembled them by constructing the first mummy.

She dedicated one part each to the lands over which he had spread his teachings. Out of pity the jilted sun god revived Osiris, but confined him to rule over the dead in the underworld. Thus his worshippers acquire the promise of everlasting and bountiful life once they pass beyond the grave through the mummification process. Minus the mummy, doesn't this resurrection story have a familiar ring?

On New Year's Day in Babylon citizens resurrected their own god Marduk (Roman Jupiter) through dramatic plays they acted out in his temple. Jews believed that on Rosh Hashanah all creatures pass in review before the searching eye of God. The start of a new year is a serious time given over to self-examination. The Torah is read and a communal meal is shared. All of this seems a far cry from the secular abandon that comes with Auld Lang Syne.

Why is it that noise and revelry accompanied by excessive eating and drinking are the hallmarks of New Year's celebrations that come down to us? So little do some of us trust our behavior on New Year's Eve that we spend extra money to confine ourselves to the safety of a hotel room. Clanging bells, wailing sirens, piercing whistles, pounding drums, blaring car horns, loud fireworks, the crack of firearms, and general yelling—they are all survivals of New Year's Eve din once deliberately contrived to ring out the evil spirits of the old year by any means necessary. On New Year's Eve, late-eighteenth-century Scottish herdsmen would dry out a cow's hide and drape it over one of their young males. The lucky lad would then run three times sunwise (clockwise) around the outside of the barn, and everyone in the community would chase the stiff-skinned impersonator, beating the hide with sticks and shouting "Raise the noise louder!" Others pounded on milk cans, pans, and bread boxes; some hammered the walls of their houses with clubs, loudly chanting rhymes as charms against witches and demons. (Russians today still carry the beating ritual to every corner of every room of the household—prime hiding places for lingering evil spirits.)

New England colonists fired their muskets before making the round of taverns to beg for free drinks. The New York City of two centuries ago was as jovial and boisterous as it is today at midnight on December 31. One traveler describes drums beating and guns firing as he made calls for a dip into the wassail bowl at the neighborhood houses. Wassailing ("Good Health" in Gaelic) in essence means wishing health not just to one another but to one another's possessions as well. Toast begets toast, and every pass by the wassail bowl challenges the imagination of the well-wisher. Drinking in rural communities would often be carried on in the orchard as celebrants gathered around their prize fruit-bearing trees and drank a hard cider *sköl* to them while howling good luck rhymes:

> *Here's to thee old apple tree*
> *Whence thou mayst bud*
> *And whence thou mayst blow!*
> *And whence thou mayst bear apples enow!*
> *Hat's full! Caps full!*
> *Bushel—bushel—sacks full,*
> *And my pockets full too! Huzza!*

Others would encircle a particularly productive ox, splash its face with spirits, stick a plum cake on its horns, and wassail-toast it with a verse that might begin with "Here's to your pretty face…" and end with "And if we're all here next year we'll do it again." Then it was on to the apiary to perform a more perilous toast.

"Take out then take in, bad luck will begin; Take in then take out, good luck comes about" rings an old couplet. New Year's is a two-way street and bringing new things in is as important as letting old things out. The ancient Aztecs celebrated the New Fire ceremony first by destroying their household mats, then taking a fired pine stick from the sacred temple of the rain and fertility god and delivering it to their home hearth. More modest Brits brought a small piece of coal into the house. A more exacting ritual called for a silver coin, a hunk of bread, and a piece of coal to be laid on the outside windowsill the night before, then brought inside first thing in the morning. In the old Scottish custom called "first footing," the symbolic bread and coal are to be carried by a tall, dark man, who silently strides into the domicile. The tall, dark, and handsome—and masculine—quality reinforces the stereotype of the figure a woman keeper-of-the-house would desire most to bring good luck to the household by being the first to set foot in it on the New Year. Sometimes the first footer would make the obligatory three times sunwise round of the kitchen table and say a rhyme, like "God send you plenty, where you have a one pound note I wish you may have twenty." More demanding clients might require in addition food for the table, logs for the fireplace, perhaps even a bottle of whiskey.

These customs are all a part of the old English Yuletide tradition of *saining* or conducting rites to safeguard people and property against evil forces thought to be active during the vulnerable period of transition between the years. We may think of such rituals as harmless superstitions designed to bring good luck, but many of them really constitute rites of purification. You need to cleanse the environment, purge it of all remnants of the old cycle, before you can institute the new. New Year's Eve is to the year what midnight (the "witching hour") is to the day—a time of danger where past and future meet. This is why we need to take stock of ourselves, why we must realize our own vulnerability. We make resolutions because we think they have the greatest likelihood of coming true when Janus's doorway to the future momentarily lies open for us.

Every act of saining had a magical element. Although largely lost to our enchantment-purged world, each has its vestige in the modern age: never throw away anything on New Year's Day; put a sum of money on your doorstop on New Year's Eve. (Taking it in next morning assures you your incomings will exceed your outgoings in the coming year.) Putting money in all your kids' pockets guarantees money for all the family in the 365 days ahead. Pay your bills before January 1 lest you be guaranteed debt for the rest of the year. If you don't sweep out your house by midnight, the old year's dirt (and all the symbolic burden that goes with it) will be carried into the new. Toss the lucky log you've been saving all fall into the New Year's fire. Wash anything on New Year's and you wash a family member away. Whatever you are doing when the bells go off, you will do the same for most of the year—good reason to stay up late. Finally, on New Year's Day, put on your best clothes, settle your debts, fill your fridge, and indulge in a great meal.

Most of these popular magical folk beliefs are still practiced. Last New Year's Eve at a friend's house in Mexico City all guests were required to eat one grape at the sound of each of the twelve bells that tolled in the New Year and to simultaneously think of a wish for each of the twelve months to follow. I only got as far as seven. (Had the grapes been seedless, I might have successfully completed the cycle.) Many farmers' almanacs still predict the weather for the next twelve months based on the meteorological conditions that occur on each of the twelve days of Christmas, December 26–January 6, which neatly bracket New Year's Day. T. S. Eliot had it right: the future resides in the past.

Chinese New Year prognostications lie in the numbers. If in any given year the number of days between winter solstice and lunar New Year is fifty, then food for the people in the coming year will be adequate; every day under fifty means a deficit, every day over a surplus. Since Chinese New Year can happen anywhere between January 21 and February 20 (and the solstice falls on December 21 or 22), the arithmetic usually points to a fairly pessimistic prognosis. Observing clouds—the directions from which they come and go, their speeds, and their colors— provides further details. Why? Yang enters from the northeast, a safe direction. Red, the color of fire, signifies drought. Quite the opposite of the West, in China New Year itself is a time of repose—you dare not act to upset the balance of nature. You must fast, restrain yourself, keep your body at rest—but it is still OK to let it all out the night before.

The timeless in-betweenness of the moment of the New Year, like other pauses in the flow of seasonal time we will encounter throughout the holiday cycle, encourages us to let loose our inhibitions, to behave abnormally for a brief time. Role reversals are common at year's end— the replacement of Old Father Time with his scythe by a newborn baby in a diaper juxtaposes the beginning of life and the beginning of death personified by the grim reaper. As a child, I vividly recall our extended family acting out this ritual of transition at the annual New Year's Eve bash held in my paternal aunt's house. A few minutes before twelve one of my uncles, clad in "Father Time" attire—an old string mop for a beard, a bedsheet for a toga, and a discarded golf club doubling as a scythe— would suddenly materialize out of one of the back bedrooms. At the stroke of midnight on the grandfather's clock in the hallway, the front door would pop open and we would all confront a second uncle clad only in a diaper, screeching baby cries while lying in repose in a large mock cradle fashioned out of a cardboard carton, perched on the doorstep. The Old Year uncle would slowly bend over, pick up the New Year's baby (who fortunately weighed only 140 pounds soaking wet) off the welcome mat, deliver him out of the winter darkness into the warmth of the hearth, and plop him on the living-room sofa. Then, waving goodbye, he would disappear into the cold night air. What an unforgettable time play for a young child to witness!

If you think about it, many of nature's entities really do appear to reverse themselves at the end point of a cycle—a pendulum changes direction, the sun retraces its motion along the horizon, and the moon glides backward through its phases. No wonder the Greeks once spoke of a magical time when men would be born from their graves and gradually grow younger, when slaves and masters would exchange places, when all strife would shrivel away and disappear as time literally flowed backwards. Reversals constitute dangerous, even threatening times, for we must be careful not to go too far. At the end-of-the-semester Christmas party in my institution, teachers, administrators, secretaries, and custodians all come together in a communal environment quite different from the hierarchy-bound workplace. We talk of family and our personal lives; we laugh and we joke; we eat and we drink (usually in moderation). Rare occasions such as these, when we all suddenly become who we are not, can contribute to communal bonding by momentarily bringing us all to the same social level. On Monday morning when we resume our regular duties we may well remember that the "other" are perhaps more like us ordinary folks than we had previously thought.

Like Thanksgiving, the modern American New Year's Day (and more recently the week preceding and the few days following) is given over to sporting events, few without their own associated parade. Pasadena, California's Rose Bowl Parade may hold the spotlight today, but the Mummer's Parade in Philadelphia has the deeper tradition. It dates back to the thirteenth-century Swedish and English habit of donning masks (*mommo* in Greek), pretending to be someone you're not. Ordinary folks would dress up as knights, squires, the pope, or an emperor. Often mummers enacted comic plays (much like those from old vaudeville days) that poked fun at the establishment. They would feature the doctor who doesn't know the cure or the money collector who can't keep track of his

books. Like risqué behavior at the office party, such acts are social sta-
tus-levelers, the central theme of much good comedy. Nobody in society is beyond being the object of mild derision—not the boss, not our
president, not even our most revered religious leaders.

Many of us cocoon our way onto a private couch, cheering near the
TV on the day after the time ball falls, but some of us spend the first of
the year visiting friends and family. These visits are faint remnants of
the traditional open house that took root in early America when George
Washington initiated it officially at the national level. By the time of the
Jefferson Administration, hundreds of diplomats and officers spent the
afternoon at the White House toasting with punch and eggnog, dining
on roasts, pastries, and sweets. The idea caught on, particularly in the
East Coast cities. The higher the rung of the social ladder you stood on,
the more invitations you would receive. You would be expected to don
your best finery and dutifully attend every one of these functions, if
only briefly. And you would be sure to leave your calling card on the tray
in the entryway to maintain or advance your status. For the ambitious
social climber, Day One of the year was a marathon.

We all stuff ourselves on New Year's Day. Overindulgence is the sort
of misbehavior that, I think, derives from the feeling that at least occasionally we need to flaunt whatever we've got even if we haven't got much.
The guilt that comes with eating food is a recent development—it stems
from post-World War II prosperity. Before the war undernourishment
was the plight of democratic America, not to mention the rest of the
world. And so our special foods: turkey, ham, or roast beef for us, honey-
dipped apples for the Hebrews, salmon and acorns for the Native Americans, lucky black-eyed peas for the Texans, crepes for the French, pancakes
for the English, lutfisk and rice pudding for the Swedes, bannocks
(doughnuts) for the Irish, fish for the Germans, and ale or cider or whiskey or wassail for everybody.

We gave New Year's presents before we ever exchanged gifts at Christmas. Roman historians wrote about exchanging good luck coins with
Janus's head on one side and a boat on the other to protect all trades-
men. The Chinese sent New Year's greeting cards at least a thousand
years ago. In medieval Britain it was customary for members of the court

to send gifts to the king, queen, and high nobility. Elizabeth I was said to have owned hundreds of pairs of bejeweled gloves. British commoners exchanged fruit, nuts, candy, and cheeses; lemons were given in India, eggs (symbols of life's beginning) in Iran. A reversal of this process consisted of a householder giving gifts to his servants.

Whether we begin our festival cycle with an inundation, the sun arriving at a fixed point in the sky, or the first appearance of one of nature's cues for change, New Year's Day is, above all, a time when we remain open to the process of renewal. That's why so much of the activity we engage in symbolizes rebirth—the cycling of death back into life. What, after all, are our New Year's resolutions but promises to ourselves to write a fresh page in our book of life, to cast out the undesirable that keeps us from rising to greater expectations. In the human struggle against time, no day in the year carries a greater burden, yet at the same time, a greater hope, a greater joy for what we might yet make of ourselves. Thanks to rebeginnings.

February's Holidays: Prediction, Purification, and Passionate Pursuit

After they have been safely delivered of childbirth, and have lain in, and been shut up, their month of days accomplished; then are they to repair to church and to kneel down in some place nigh the communion table . . . (then) cometh Sir Priest; straight ways standeth by her, and readeth over her a certain psalm, viz. 121, and assureth her that the sun shall not burn her by day, nor the moon by night, [and] sayeth his Pater Noster, with the prescribed versicles and response, with his collect. And then, she having offered her accustomed offerings unto him for his labour, God speed her well, she is a woman on foot again, as holy as ever she was; she may now put off her veiling kerchief, and look her husband and neighbours in the face again. . . . What can be a more apish imitation, or rather a more reviving of the Jewish purification than this?

Henry Barrow

Everybody knows the North American tradition tied to what appears to be a purely secular holiday: if a certain rodent who spends most of the year living in a cage in Pittsburgh emerges on the second day of February and sees his shadow, back in the hole he goes and another six weeks of winter weather is in store for us. But should skies be cloudy when he makes his exit, spring is surely on its way. So out he stays and so do we. (Logic would seem to dictate the opposite: clear weather in winter usually means a high pressure system and colder air.)

Every great theme has its variations: some say that if a groundhog sees his shadow on February 2, he will return to sleep for four weeks, or that it will rain for the seven following Sundays, or seven weeks of rain are in the offing. First popularized in the United States by a late nineteenth-century western Pennsylvania newspaper editor, the archetypal omen-bearing woodchuck, Punxsutawney Phil, has his magical imitators, among them Canada's Wiarton Willy, Ohio's Buckeye Chuck, and western New York's Dunkirk Dave. In the South, Georgians have conjured up a fat fellow named General Beauregard Lee, while Virginians have Rebel Robert. The gender-blind, species-bending state of Indiana boasted Henrietta until she died a few years back and was replaced by Hilary the Hedgehog.

While northwest Pennsylvania remains the woodchuck's stronghold, the matter of local dominance is hotly contested among dozens of groundhog clubs. If being first has any cachet, the issue is easily decided. In 1898, a group of local businessmen in Punxsutawney formed the Punxsutawney Ground Hog Club. Their annual ritual called for a squadron of fancy-garbed groundhog watchers to head for the holes by trekking up to Gobbler's Knob in the Allegheny foothills, white signal flags in hand. First one to sight a groundhog would give a yell. Later they would all get together for the Hibernating Governors' official report. (I was crushed to learn, via the rumor mill, that today the whole process apparently takes place on a private estate twelve days in advance and that some of the groundhogs are possibly stuffed animals.)

Ten years after Punxsutawney, a gang from Quarryville in Lancaster County, on the other side of the state, created the upstart Slumbering Groundhog Lodge. They proclaimed their town the only authentic groundhog watchers' haven and declared their rivals mere pretenders whose only interest lay in selling books that tell how to cook and serve groundhog meat. The Lodge's official creed proclaims:

> *We believe in the wisdom of the groundhog,*
> *We declare his intelligence to be of a*
> *higher order than that of any other animal. . . .*
> *We rejoice that he can, and does, foretell*
> *with absolute accuracy the weather conditions*
> *for the six weeks following each day*
> *of February.*

The Quarryville clan also boasts the largest contingent of 'hogwatchers and holes to peek into, and they claim the highest rate—90 percent—of successful prediction. (The weather bureau disputes this claim, placing the figure at a rarefied 28 percent, which may be what prompted *National Geographic* to suggest the observance be abolished.) Not content to wallow in modesty, celebrants end each February 2 in a local pub where they perform their club song. Sung to the tune of "The Battle Hymn of the Republic," it goes:

> *Let the scientific fakirs gnash their teeth and stamp with rage—*
> *Let astrologers with crystals wipe such nonsense from the page—*
> *We hail the King of Prophets, who's the world's outstanding Sage—*
> TODAY THE GROUNDHOG COMES!
> *Glory! Glory! to the Groundhog,*
> *Glory! Glory! to the Groundhog,*
> *Glory! Glory! to the Groundhog,*
> TODAY THE PROPHET COMES!

Why do we pay attention to all of this, even bother to create a popular movie with the underlying theme of the repeatability of the groundhog cycle as a device for bringing salvation through love to an amoral TV weatherman? (Rumor also has it that most of the 1993 film was shot in Illinois.) Aside from having fun, which to judge from the behavior of the tuxedoed "Hibernating Governors" is clearly a major agenda item, Groundhog Day renews the age-old tension between magical divination versus hard science as a way of acquiring secure knowledge about the future.

Anyone who lives on a farm knows that you can reliably predict the weather by watching animals. Cows lie down in advance of coming rain, cats move their kittens and dogs their puppies to shelter, ants and prairie dogs bank up the earth around their burrows, a snake makes for higher ground. "When ducks are driving through the barn, that night the weather takes a turn," say the Scottish. "When swallows fly low expect storm or cold," warn the English. Animals also utter sounds to predict a change in the weather. If a deluge is approaching, coyotes howl all the more just after sunrise or just before sunset. But it's a sign of clear weather if they broadcast in the middle of the night. A rooster's crowing at sunset or midnight, and an owl hooting in the daytime also mean rain. A hoot from the hills means clear weather, from the pine trees not so good, goes an old proverb. Long-term predictions too—who hasn't heard of reading the banding on caterpillars to predict the severity of the coming winter? If your chickens molt in August, they say, winter will be severe; in October, mild. Could it be that when we were closer to animals we better recognized their wisdom?

Given our meteorological sophistication, thanks in part to the weather channel beaming up a multicolor radar view of moving cloud patterns every ten minutes, these old climate superstitions may strike many of us as nonsensical. But even if support stats for each proverb's validity may not be there, a fair share of the population continues to believe that weather wisdom extends far beyond the collective community of trained TV talking heads and that some people and animals are more weatherwise than others. At least this philosophy is more action oriented than "Everybody talks about the weather. . . ." So pay attention to your corns and don't step on an ant.

In the seasonal round, Groundhog Day represents our first formal anticipation of spring, a key point in the cycle with an enduring and fascinating history. But why the groundhog and why the beginning of February, traditionally a friendless, sawed-off month that for many of us really falls in the dead of winter? To begin with, a woodchuck (a corruption of its Cree Indian name *otcheck*) and a groundhog are one and the same. They aren't hogs and they don't chuck wood. And unlike lions and eagles, at least at first glance, these animals don't seem to offer us much reason to hold them in veneration. The squat and fat adults vary in length from 1½ to 2½ feet and weigh up to fifteen pounds. These slow-moving cousins of the squirrel and prairie dog inhabit the borders between timbered areas and open land. They feed on leaves, grasses, and our crops, and they often end up as messy roadkill. Before the eastern forests were cut down for farmland, groundhogs were relatively scarce, and in colonial times they were confined almost exclusively to Pennsylvania. So it is appropriate that any legends that might attach to this uninspiring animal would originate there.

But there is one groundhog trait well worth extolling, and I believe it lies at the root of the annual divinatory rites we perform at its doorstep. Groundhogs live in a part of the world where winter is very harsh, yet they manage to escape this most unpleasant time of the year by blissfully curling up in an out-of-the-way place and dozing the time away comfortably and inexpensively—which beats expending all the energy birds and people who flee southward consume. Those of us who choose to remain and endure winter's punishing blows while we go broke heating the nest can well admire the wise woodchuck who lies dreaming, oblivious to the freezing winds, ice, and snow storms that rage a few feet above his lair.

Mammalogists regard the groundhog as the least industrious of all his kind. He works like a beaver only for the day or two it takes him to dig his hole. That accomplished, he spends most of the spring, summer, and fall indoors. When dining out, he gives more time to sunning than to lunching. All the while he never ventures more than a hundred yards from home and unlike his prairie dog and squirrel cousins, he undertakes no remodeling of his modest quarters. By the time the leaves begin to drop he is comfortably obese.

Groundhogs suddenly disappear from the scene in late September or early October and do not reappear for an average of five months. Left to themselves they might choose to celebrate their day anywhere from early February to late March, depending on the local climate. They spend the whole winter in what experts aptly describe as "a state of profound torpor," curled up so tightly you could roll one of them down a bowling alley without disturbing its pose. While insensibly stagnant, their breathing and heartbeat are slowed dramatically (the latter from a normal 200 down to 5 beats a minute). Biologists who have somehow managed to insert rectal thermometers into hibernating woodchucks inform us that their body temperature never gets much above 60°F. During this prolonged sluggish existence in no-chuck's-land they subsist solely on stored body fat.

Groundhogs have evolved an uncanny knack of awakening if there is a sudden drop in temperature. If sleeping is your forte, then waking up has to be a major event in your life. When the time is right, the animals begin to twitch, blink their eyes open, and gradually emerge from the coiled position they've occupied in seeming death for months. Gasping to normal respiration, they violently tremble as they struggle to get back on their feet. How the return to life resembles birth!

"Pennsylvania Dutch" was originally "Deutsch," and the legend of Punxsutawney actually originated in Germany. There the predictive powers were attributed to the badger or, less commonly, the wolf or hedgehog, and still earlier to the bear. It's a case of superstition transferal: when you move to a new neighborhood and can't find the original animal responsible, you look for its closest relative. Except for the white median stripe and a carnivorous diet, an Old World badger isn't a bad prototype for a New World groundhog. The badger has about the same size, shape, and gait as a woodchuck. He occupies a similar edge-of-the-forest habitat, lives in a hole (where he also hibernates), and is just as timid and gentle unless you poke at him with a stick.

What I find interesting about Groundhog Day, in addition to our popular faith in the power of animals, is the persistent belief that events transpiring in a brief span of time foretell what will arise over longer periods in the future. This is a common feature of farmers' almanacs in many seasonal rites. Long before the idea was brought to America, weather prediction by animal watching became allied with the custom of lighting candles on the day of the Purification of the Virgin Mary.

"Wanns uf Aller Heil un Sél sché is bleibts noch sex woche sché; is 's wetter aber rau, dann is der winter dó." (If the weather is fine on All Saints and All Souls, there will be six more weeks of fine weather; if, however, it is cold and raw, winter is at hand.) This old German weather proverb predates both the groundhog and the badger and is thought by some to be the original source of filing major weather predictions at the beginning of February. But, as we will see, it may recall an even older pagan custom that was revised during the sixteenth-century Protestant Reformation, when Germans rejected the Roman Catholic saints.

The Gospel according to Luke (2:22) tells the story. In the last act of the birthing process, Hebrew tradition specified that forty days after giving birth all mothers were required to enter the temple to make an offering and be purified. When Mary went there with Jesus, a man called Simeon and the prophetess Anna recognized and publicly proclaimed him as the savior, not only of the Jews but of all mankind. The day was formally installed on February 2. The idea of a February feast of purification follows the old Roman tradition of such ceremonies, probably deliberately. February, whose name comes from *februa*, to purify, was for the Romans a time of cleansing in preparation for a fresh start to activities incumbent upon spring. It was likely grafted onto a heathen custom to take advantage of established tradition (the transfer principle works for superstition too). This is why Renaissance thinkers like Henry Barrow saw the purification ritual as a dangerous magical ceremony (see the epigraph at the beginning of the chapter). Lighting candles was part of the ritual, perhaps originally to permit the busy activity schedule to continue late into the night. And so it became a festival of lights, the blessing of candles— Candlemas: for Christ, says Simeon, is "the light to lighten the Gentiles."

Celebrating the return of light at this time of year would have been especially significant, given the long winter nights of the north of Europe. But despite the once widespread popularity of the Candelmas holiday, reformists regarded the idea of sanctification by lighting candles, and the omens that attended it (light the candle that the devil may flee; carry home fragments of the lighted candles to ward off evil spirits; take down all your Christmas decorations by Candlemas or suffer bad luck), as so much superstitious nonsense. When Henry VIII approved continuing the feast in sixteenth-century England he made it clear that the purpose of lighting the candles was to proclaim Christ as the retaining light of the world—not to shoo away Satan. By the mid- eighteenth century in most Protestant countries, Candlemas passed unrecognized.

The number of Candlemas omens dealing with weather prediction far exceeds animal proverbs. Here are just a handful of old couplets:

After Candlemas Day the frost will be more keen, if the sun shines bright, than before it has been.

If Candlemas Day is bright and clear,
there'll be two winters in the year.

If it neither rains nor snows on Candlemas Day,
You may straddle your horse and go and buy hay.

If the lanes are full of snow on Candlemas,
so the bins will be full of corn in autumn.

When the wind's in the east on Candlemas Day,
there it will stick to the second of May.

The badger peeps out of his hole on Candlemas Day and when he find it's
*   snowing, walks abroad;*
but if he sees the sun shining, he draws back into the hole.

The last one establishes the European version of the groundhog-Candlemas connection. From France and Spain comes an old verse that peels away yet another layer of the groundhog myth:

At Candlemas, cold in air and snow on grass;
if the sun then entice the bear from his den, he turns around thrice and
*   goes back again.*

In the Pyrenees, Candlemas was marked by the ceremony of the bear, one of the most ancient of all rituals tied to February 2. Before it became scarce over most of Europe, the hibernating bear antedated both badger and groundhog as the great inspiration for the rite of spring. His emergence from hibernation was actually thought to accelerate nature's awakening. Because of his strength, cunning, and intelligence, people thought the bear their equal—even their ancestor. Scandinavians believed people could change into bears (whence our word "beserk") and that donning a bearskin would help a warrior acquire the bear's power and stamina. To awaken the beast within them, men masqueraded in bear costumes and paraded through the village hoping to frighten away evil and incarnated spirits. The bear sat on a lofty pedestal to which both badger and groundhog could scarcely aspire.

All of these proverbs allude to the serious seasonal query: When will spring really begin? If by spring we mean plowing, planting, calving, and foaling, then any beginning is highly variable. In the north where I live, May Day might be an appropriate time to anticipate and prognosticate, for then the leaves sprout on my elms and willows. Further south in Washington, D.C., cherry blossoms bloom in early April, a time much closer to the March equinox, the traditional recognition of the beginning of spring in America. But by then spring is already well underway in most of the territory south of the Mason-Dixon line, not to mention other parts of the world.

Spring arrived in late February or early March in the calendar of ancient Greece. This is the time, wrote the poet Hesiod in his eighth-century B.C. poem *Works and Days*, to rouse your slaves to work, to prune and hoe the vines:

> But when Zeus has brought to fulfillment the sixty-day period after the solstice of winter, a period of stormy weather,
>
> then the star Arkturos, leaving sacred Okeanos brightly shines for the first time in evenings earliest darkness.
>
> Next the swallow, the lamenting child of Pandion, appears coming into the sight of man when spring is beginning.

(Arcturus in the constellation of Bootes, the Plowman, rising in the east after sunset still reminds every amateur astronomer that spring is here.)

England, warmed by the Gulf Stream, began its plowing season at the end of the Christmas season, often as early as the day after Epiphany (January 7), but according to ancient tradition the target date was *Imbolc*—February 1. (The word may mean "sheep's milk," in reference to the first spring milking of the ewes, a term that derives from an earlier Indo-European word meaning purification.) Imbolc once marked the official opening of the four seasons in the Celtic calendar. The day became popularly associated with St. Brigid, the Irish Mother Saint and likely successor of a pagan mother-goddess/provider.

Interestingly, there is a hedgehog connected with St. Brigid whose behavior on her day was said to predict the weather. Sky conditions are closely watched in general between her day and St. Patrick's Day (March 17), which lies close to the equinoctial starting point in the Gregorian calendar and symbolizes the Christian takeover of the seasonal calendar.

Now, the four cardinal points in the Celtic year (oddly enough, just like those in the Chinese calendar) are *not* the equinoxes and solstices that demarcate our seasonal year. Rather they are approximately half-way between. The first days of February, May, August, and November all survive, to varying degrees of obscurity, as holidays in our own calendar (we'll encounter the last three in later chapters). Imbolc, of course, falls at the same time as Candlemas a.k.a. Groundhog Day, if you allow a shift of one day. By this reckoning the English term "midsummer" begins to make sense. If summer starts on May 1 and ends on August 1, then June 21 is just about the halfway point. The switch to the equinox as spring's commencement is largely a twentieth-century reinvention, and as we will see in the next chapter, it is pretty much an American phenomenon—mainly because it works for us.

Moved by earth rhythms, our ancestors attributed magical powers to plants and animals that changed their behavior at key points in the year's cycle. February is no exception. In Ireland the blackthorn's black spikes yield to beautiful white blossoms that open on Imbolc, the change from dark to light providing as profound a contrast as that between winter and summer. Blackthorn is equally effective at Imbolc's seasonal antipode (All Souls' Day), the first of November, when the darkness of winter returns. Since the seventh century this shrub tree, which grows in hedgerows, has been touted for its healing qualities. Its fruit was cooked up into an astringent syrup used to heal stomachache and constipation and to induce vomiting. A weak tea made from its flowers offers a milder effect. The cleansing properties of the blackthorn also apply to the spirit. Today it enjoys a New Age resurgence. For example, you can use it to dissolve karmic energy blockages resulting from negative thoughts. A more practical magical formula asserts that if you have a friend who constantly throws negative vibes your way, carve a candle into the approximate shape of his or her body. Engrave the victim's name in the wax. Then take three blackthorn prickers and push them respectively into the image's head, heart, and abdomen. Next light the candle and, as it burns its way to the position of each thorn, recite the following spell:

> *Evil return to the one who sent thee,*
> *For me and mine are now set free.*
> *No hurt nor harm can enter here,*
> *For my life and way are now made clear.*

While old spells were directed at the outside world, new ones serve as palliatives for the human psyche.

Worshipping the cult of the Virgin Mary, lighting torches and candles, and using burrowing badgers and bears to divine by may seem worlds apart but all are linked to the anticipation of springtime. Historians tell us that later Christian conspirators invented a Roman goddess named Februa who they alleged was once honored, like the Virgin Mary, by a candlelight procession. Not so far ahead on the seasonal time line—and suspiciously close to Candlemas—lies a holiday given over to activity that on the surface offers a stark contrast, though a bit of torch bearing and the presence of one of our divinatory animals lies submerged in legends attached to it.

Why is it that the fourteenth of February causes us to think of love? If you can imagine a holiday given over to the ingestion of Viagra, you'll come close to the original intent of the Roman holiday that preceded it and may well have been connected to our modern romantic St. Valentine's Day (though some classical scholars have their reservations). The exceedingly popular Roman festival Lupercalia, held on the eve of the feast of Juno the Fructifier, was a time of lovemaking and licentiousness. It was also appropriate for taking cures for sterility.

On the ides of February, if you were a young Roman male, you would hasten to the grotto of the Lupercal, a wolf deity, on the southwest foot of Palatine hill. This was the place at which Romulus and Remus, Rome's founding twins, were washed ashore in a flood and later suckled by a she-wolf who lived there. There you would sacrifice several goats and, as in the Scottish New Year ceremony that likely was derived from it, don their skins as loincloths, and laughing loudly (this is important!) run a circuit around the hill. Along the way, you would be instructed to strike with thongs made from the goatskins every young woman you'd approach along the course. All this seminude frolicking may sound silly to us, but the Romans took it very seriously. The youths were imitating the lecherous Faunus (or Pan), god of cattle. (We all remember him in cartoons, prancing about the forest lusting after sexual favors.) The idea of covering the male genitals with the goatskin and using the same to strike the opposite sex is intended both to eliminate feminine barrenness and awaken the powers of fertility in all things whose reproductive faculties have been stultified by the deadening winter. And because it symbolizes the power of life, boisterous laughter helps.

All well and good, but who was St. Valentine, the celebrated saint of passionate pursuit? One story—and there are many, for there were at least a dozen Valentines, two of them from the third century alone—has it that Valentine was a Roman martyred for refusing to give up the principles of his newfound Christian faith. Third-century Rome was ruled by the emperor Claudius II, the "Cruel," as he was dubbed for his many bloody military ventures—which led to a fair share of draft dodging by otherwise eligible males. One could avoid the army by marrying (only single men were pressed into service), and so to boost his ranks Claudius temporarily outlawed marriage. In defiance, a young priest by the name of Valentine performed secret marriages by candlelight. Eventually he was caught, imprisoned, and sentenced to death. But so popular were his endeavors, goes the story, that young people came to visit him, offering him flowers and slipping him notes expressing shared feelings lauding love over war. These missives were the first "valentines." Later someone spiced up the story by suggesting that while in prison Valentine had a love affair with the jailer's daughter and left a farewell note to her with the message "From your Valentine."

Valentine's execution went off on schedule (he was stoned and decapitated), by coincidence on the day devoted to the old Roman love lotteries, February 14 (Old Style) in the year A.D. 269. It took two hundred more years for a Roman emperor, Gelasius, to officially proclaim his holy day. The Church later sought to cast his association with love in the Christian rather than carnal mode. After all, it was Valentine's love and charity, his work with the martyrs of the Christian faith, that provide the real incentive for sending messages of love to honor his memory. To abolish the lewd custom of boys drawing the names of girls from lots to honor the goddess Juno, zealous Christian prelates substituted saints' names on the tickets. This may have led to the much later nineteenth-century habit of calling them valentines after one of the prominent martyred saints. The little cards might equally well have ended up being called "Mariuses" or "Blaises" after other sanctified Christian martyrs of that age.

At least in the medieval world, St. Valentine, whichever one he was, became the one to pray to in times of emergency, say when there was a scarcity of food or a drought—a far cry from lusty Roman rites of fertility and pining lovers (more along the line of what we think about as we approach modern Valentine's Day). The big shift from martyr to matchmaker happened in the late fourteenth century.

In the mid-February natural environment of central Europe, no sign foreshadowed the forthcoming love rites of early spring more clearly than birds: "Let Men turn to the Birds, aerial philosophers of forever, safe from age, from change, from death," wrote Aristophanes, for it is they who give us warning of the passing seasons. The swallow was a harbinger of spring and sexual union in Greece from ancient to modern times. If a swallow builds its nest under your eaves or on your rafters, you'll be reproductively healthy and wealthy, goes one proverb. And you can appeal to the swallow for luck in love when young boys annually come to your house and rotate a swallow effigy made of wood in the four directions of the compass. [I'm no cultural diffusionist, but the same is true in China. At the beginning of spring in Han China, when the energies of yin and yang are in perfect balance, the Supreme Intermediary (Kao Mei), a sort of divine go-between, presides over the sexual outcome of a marriage between individuals from two different families. His earthly counterpart, the matchmaker official (Mei Shih), essentially a state recordkeeper who maximizes the institution of marriage, investigates which men and women are not married and formally brings them together. The process begins with the sacrifice of a bull to Kao Mei signaled by the arrival of birds returning from the south. Curiously, swallows again are the avian choice because they like to build their nests and rear their young close to areas of human habitation. Bows and arrows, symbols of wished-for male offspring, are offered and libations are drunk to all women who are pregnant, so that the Kao Mei might accord them special favor.]

The English romantic poet who exploited the universal amorous symbolism of birds was none other than Geoffrey Chaucer. He tells us that

Valentine's was the day the birds paired off: flights of ravens and crows commenced the repairing of the nest; the songs of thrushes and the clattering of woodpeckers signaled the reawakening of that old primal urge:

> *For this was sent Valentine's Day*
> *When every fowl comes to choose his mate*

Further propagating Chaucer's (and Cole Porter's) excuse that "Birds do it," the seventeenth-century poet Robert Herrick wrote:

> *Oft I have heard both youths and virgins say*
> *Birds choose their mates and couple too, this day:*
> *But by their flight I never can divine,*
> *When I shall couple with my Valentine*

Why Chaucer and other medieval courtly romantic poets decided to link St. Valentine with birds and lovers choosing their mates is as much a mystery as the identity of the original St. Valentine. But it doesn't take a wildly creative poetic imagination to seize upon the beginning of spring as an incentive for writing verses of love.

In Elizabethan England, anyone smitten by love was authorized to send a token of affection to the significant other of their choice on this special day. That could include anyone admired from afar—even a name drawn by lot. One custom considered appropriate to those not bound by holy wedlock decreed that the first person you saw on leaving your house that morning would automatically become your valentine. One Dorothy Osborne wrote in her diary (dated 1654) that she was up early on February 14th when, without being terribly bent on getting Valentined (changing nouns into verbs is another custom that predates modern times), she decided to take a short walk in her nightclothes. She met a Mr. Fish who was going out hunting, but did stop long enough to tell young Dorothy she was his Valentine. "I wouldn't have got rid of him so quickly," she writes, "had he taken the trouble to powder his hair." But if you play your cards right, you can work this magic to your advantage. "Mr. Blossom was my man," wrote another smitten lass, "and I lay abed and shut my eyes all morning (Feb. 14), till he came to our house; for I would not have seen another man before him for all the world."

Whoever it was, if you reached a mutual agreement on being Valentines, you would exchange names and write them on a long paper strip. Men would carry them in a hatband while women would wear the strip about the bodice. And unless time smoothed out the pulse of passion, the affair would continue at least to Eastertime with a formal exchange of gifts.

The holiday for lovers has always been filled with divinatory magic. After drawing lots, young people might proceed to a cemetery at midnight in search of an omen about their future mate, or place hemp seeds or bay leaves in bed to generate dreams about someone to love; or pull out alphabetic tabs from a hat to learn their future lover's initials. Women birdwatchers took special note: if the first bird you see is a blackbird, on this day you'll marry a man of the clergy; if a red breast it will be a sailor, a bluebird a poor man, a crossbill a quarrelsome husband. Yellow birds, the color of gold, net you a rich man, a wryneck no man at all. To tip the balance of nature, women would often employ a spell of magic:

> *A magic spell will bind me fast*
> *And make me love you to the last.*
> *Let Cupid then your Heart incline*
> *To take me for your Valentine.*

Such utterances could be accompanied by feeding your favorite Valentine an aphrodisiac. Carrots, eggplants, and bananas on the one hand, along with figs and oysters on the other hand, would be the natural comestibles of choice—their resemblance to male and female generative organs is likely not coincidental. The gift of chocolates represents a more contemporary way of paying homage to Cupid. Chocolate contains phenyl ethylamine, "the love molecule," so called because the high experienced during sexual intercourse is caused by its production and release in the brain and can be triggered by the touch of a hand or mere eye contact with the subject of your desires. A rational theory connecting chocolate buying with February 14 has yet to be worked out.

In America, the mid-nineteenth-century return to romanticism, combined with the rise of a consumer oriented culture, sparked yet another reinvention of Valentine's Day. Thanks to the ingenuity of booksellers and printers, Valentine gift giving rose to epidemic proportions in a country in which it had scarcely been recognized a generation earlier. Between 1840 and the outbreak of the Civil War, Valentine exchange grew into such a mania that post offices in major cities were forced to purchase wheelbarrows to get all the cards delivered.

I can still remember the homemade classroom Valentine's Day mailbox with its red heart on white crepe paper, perched on my first-grade teacher's desk. Through its slot passed one valentine from each member of the class to every other: 25×24, or 600 missives by my arithmetic. No wonder it took the bulk of the afternoon to distribute them all! Although the first commercial valentines appeared about 1800, it took Esther Howland, a student at Mt. Holyoke College in the late 1840s, to turn them into a craze. The daughter of a stationer, she developed a knack for creating beautifully sentimental messages that she hand painted on quality paper and trimmed with imported lace. Her well-marketed product netted over $100,000 a year by 1850. A forerunner of cards by computer, special books of verses called "Valentine Writers" (largely pirated from the British valentine industry) had already appeared on the market in 1823. These enabled enterprising individualists dissatisfied with preprinted phrases to write their own message on a decorated but otherwise blank valentine. Rococo valentines became heavily ornamented and demand created a cheap line of the same product. Garish cards, printed on inexpensive paper with terse, often comic messages, replaced sentimentality with farce. By the gay nineties, confectioners climbed aboard the commodity train by crafting the heart-shaped box of Valentine chocolates.

Insult valentines went a step further. They offered the opportunity to privately poke fun at those who might be a bit different from the rest of us. This exemplary verse, intended for a stay-at-home husband, captures the social climate of the turn of the century. (It accompanies a picture of a depraved-looking dandy holding a screaming baby):

> *You old henpicked wretch, you are quite a disgrace,*
> *Let your wife mind the baby and keep her own place.*
> *Be more of a man, don't allow her to roam,*
> *Make her leave off the breeches and keep her at home.*

Equally insulting is this verse for an "Old Maid":

> *If you'd lasso a real live man,*
> *and dope him, as you only can,*
> *then cut his throat and shoot him through.*
> *He might be coaxed to marry you.*

Ralph Waldo Emerson, an early critic of gift merchandising, complained in 1858 that our tokens of love had fallen to the level of the barbarous. He regarded shopping for Valentine gifts a cold and lifeless substitute for a personal offering from the heart. Few listened: by 1930 Valentine's Day ranked second only to Christmas as an occasion for retail spending. (I share Emerson's lament every time I receive an online greeting card.)

Valentine's Day commercialism is still well entrenched more than seventy years later. In 2001, eleven million people made a Valentine purchase on line. Married, middle income men aged 30–49 represented the largest segment of the clientele; fragrances, cosmetics and jewelry were the lead items of choice. The Japanese have taken so enthusiastically to America's Valentine's Day that they have created their own extra love day by dedicating March 14 to men to receive love presents from admiring women. And Valentine's Day divination devices still flourish. I plugged my name and that of my mutually adoring wife of over forty years into the Love Calculator's website and it instantly mathematized the probability of a successful relationship between us: 85 percent! Less convivial and communal, today's Valentine's Day celebrations are given over to couples or the immediate family and close friends; gift exchange is largely controlled by advertising and mass production. Sadly, the magical elements have almost thoroughly evaporated from this seasonal ritual.

Only the Victorian revival of Christmas and resurgent Halloween (which we will explore in later chapters) eclipse the dramatic transformation in popularity of the red-letter day we dedicate to St. Valentine. His is a day of many meanings, a rite transformed from lustful Lupercus to martyred St. Valentine, to cherubic Cupid, the love goddess's roguish little boy archer whose gold-tipped arrows can make even the gods feel sexy. We have witnessed its migration from the realm of the pastoral, to the religious, to the secular—from divine love to the inner sanctum of affectionate sentiment to the public world of the shopping mall. The fervent belief in romantic love remains alive in modern democratic American society—a necessary breath of air to fill the emotional vacuum that suffocates all restrained law-bound societies.

The anticipation of a cycle's beginning is the right time to divine for love, for good weather, good crops, blessings from the gods, or for that matter anything important you need to know about the future. Bears or badgers or groundhogs, emerged from winter's sleep, stir up life's juices redolent with good things to come. Imbolc, Candlemas, Groundhog Day, all once began the cycle, opening the season of great expectations. And if you do the arithmetic (February 14 minus the Gregorian correction of twelve days equals February 2 in the Old Style calendar), St. Valentine's Day is there too, right on time!

Spring Equinox:
Watching the Serpent Descend

Spring is a resurrection of all life, and consequently of human
life. In that cosmic act, all the forces of creation return to their
first vigor. Life is wholly reconstituted; everything begins afresh;
in short, the primeval act of the creation of the cosmos is
repeated, for every regeneration is a new birth, a return to that
mythical moment when for the first time a form appeared that
was to be constantly regenerated.

Mircea Eliade

Four o'clock in the afternoon, March 20, 2001—the first
equinox of a new millennium. Modern astronomers and timekeepers
recognize it as a seasonal dividing line, the date when night and day are
equivalent, when cosmic symmetry causes sunrise and sunset to transect
the north-south line precisely. For the rest of us the equinox signals the
rites of spring, a celebration of the return to life of all that has lain dormant in winter's icy grip. I stand together with 45,000 other celebrants,
in the ten-acre plaza fronting a pyramid they call the Castillo, or castle,
at the thousand-year-old Maya ruins of Chichén Itzá in the northern

part of the Yucatan peninsula. We have come by car, bus, train, plane, and cruise ship from all over Mexico, the Americas, Europe, and from all around the world—religious people, scientific photo-documenters, vacationing tourists, people in groups, families, solitary people. White people and black people have come to Chichén; mestizo people, people with goods to sell and ideas to trade stand alongside others looking for guidance, direction, or just a good time.

We are all here to watch the magical interplay of light and shadow on the side of an ancient Maya pyramid, for the zigzag shadow cast late this afternoon by one edge of the stepped seventy-five-foot tall pyramid on the outer balustrade of its northern stairway that leads up to the great temple on its summit will take on the shape of a giant snake. Those who come to the Castillo in search of the sacred say that when they glimpse the luminous serpent made up of seven half-diamond-shaped patches of light, they share a moment in time with the ancient Maya. Legend has it that they too witnessed the same image a thousand years ago alighting upon this most monumental of all their cherished architectural works, the one they also called the Temple of Kukulcan, the "Feathered Serpent," the God of rejuvenation whose effigy symbolizes the renewal of life. There we all wait, poised behind a chain fifty feet from the pyramid that prevents eager onlookers from ascending the steep steps and breaking the mood of anticipation that descends on all of us as the image takes on its serpentine shape.

At half past three the first hint of a pattern makes its appearance on the stairway. In the 90° humidity most shadow seekers haven't really settled in, though pilgrims who arrived in the early hours of dawn have already sat for hours on mats, towels, or pieces of cardboard cartons on claimed turf. Since early afternoon colorfully garbed native dancers from the Folkloric Ballet of the State of Yucatan have entertained us. We have listened to the orchestra play authentic Maya music and witnessed a dance aimed at drawing down the serpent from heaven so that his energy might rekindle the spirit of life within us. We have thrilled to a theatrical performance on Maya prophesy and the failed nineteenth-century Yucatan resistance movement against Spanish colonialism and then a showy speech by the governor of the state—all of it broadcast from a grandstand off to the southeast side of the Castillo. In the interim some have either raced back to the parador for a snack, or, fearful of losing their place, picnicked on their dusty prized square meter while dodging the footsteps of the interweaving pedestrian traffic that flows zig-zaggedly like the famous snake about Kukulcan's temple.

Four-thirty and the first few elongated diaphanous triangles that will make up the ophidian shape are now fully formed at the top of the balustrade. The muffled voice of archaeologist Alfredo Barrera Rubio, Director of the Regional Center of the National Institute of Anthropology and History (INAH), begins the official audio account that always accompanies the annual appearance of the equinoctial ribbon of light. He times the appearance of each of the lighted geometrical figures as they take shape one by one from top to bottom down the side of the stairway. By 4:55 all seven half diamonds of light are in place, the last one seeming to attach itself to the large open-mouthed serpent's head carved in stone at the base of the temple.

We are all transfixed. Crowd movement and sound abate as the luminous triangles link together and slowly begin to slide toward the upper edge of the banister. Late afternoon shadows lengthen and the air begins to cool just a bit. A puffy cumulus dims the sun for a few moments, but when dazzling sunlight returns the first of many collective oohs signals the appearance of an even sharper image of the feathered serpent deity. A half-dozen elderly New Agers collected together near the restraining chain chant in unison as the sound of a beckoning conch trumpet momentarily breaks the silence. Bare-chested, long-haired white men, eyes closed, raise their hands in the direction of the sinuous image. Guards drive back the one or two fanatics who cannot resist jumping the chain in a futile attempt to lay hands on the façade they deem holy. A fair-haired woman with Scandinavian features holds a naked year-old child over her head above the crowd and directs his countenance toward the pyramid, bathing him in serpentine energy while intervals between camera-shutter clicks wax to an almost continuous low-pitched rattle.

Five-fifteen and as the sun dives down to earth, Kukulcan's facade is all ashade but for the thinning illuminated undulating swatches that continue to rise upward. The oohs and aahs, the chants and mantras, reach a five-minute-long crescendo as the phenomenon fades from view. Well before the last luminous segment of slithering serpent has slipped off the balustrade and vanished into the sky some of the pyramid watchers begin to head for the parking lot. By 5:30 the show is officially over and what had been a trickle of exhilarated pilgrims exiting the ancient ruins assured of the continuation of the cycle of life now turns into a crush of tired tourists advancing like so much freeway traffic during rush hour. Guides wave signs of variegated color and symbol above the crowd to keep their tour groups together. More indefatigable sojourners pile into the gallery of shops outside the parador to collect their last souvenir T-shirt or ceramic idol, while dozens of bus drivers rev up their diesel engines in anticipation of the hour-long, one-mile traffic-clogged meander back to the main highway. The great equinox serpent hierophany of 2001 is history.

Records from colonial times tell us that the Castillo may well have been built in a place where spring rites of renewal were once actually performed. Bishop Diego de Landa of Yucatan who came with the conquistadors to civilize the Maya Indians says he witnessed such a ceremony not so far away in the town of Maní (where in 1555 he fueled a bonfire with Maya hieroglyphic books he thought to be works of the devil). Having fasted and abstained, people came from all the surrounding towns and joined in a great procession with other pilgrims to a diminished version of the Temple of the Feathered Serpent:

> . . . and having arrived there they placed the banners on top of the temple, and they spread out their idols below in the courtyard, each for himself, on the leaves of trees . . . and having kindled new fire, they began to burn their incense in many places and to make offerings of food cooked without salt or pepper or drinks made of their beans and the seeds of squashes. The lords and those who had fasted remained there without returning to their houses for five days and five nights of prayer, always burning copal and engaged in their offerings, and executing several sacred dances until the first day of (the next month).

This "New Fire" ceremony was one of the major seasonal rites celebrated throughout ancient Mexico. Dedicated to the completion of one time cycle and the start of another, it reenacted the sacrifice made by a

humble god who cast himself into the fire of creation in order to give
birth to the sun and life. At the spring equinox, the ancient Maya turned
over their new leaf by throwing out all their mats (seats) and breaking
all their dishware. They carved their statues and wove their banners as
gifts to honor the god to whom they dedicated the pyramid and the
ruling lords of the towns who were believed to be his incarnation. "They
said ... that Kukulcan came down from heaven on the last of these (days)
and received their services, their vigils and offerings," wrote Landa. Far
from the slimy evil creatures of Judeo-Christian biblical lore, snakes were
important to the Maya. As symbols of the rebirth of time, they shed
their skins to renew the seasons. When they die, they sprout feathers and
fly to heaven. They become Kukulcans, say their contemporaries.

I first started following the origin of the serpent of light myth
that would develop into Yucatan's celebrated springtime show shortly
after I came across an obscure 1970 note by an obscure figure in an obscure journal printed in mimeograph. I have had little success uncover-
ing who Jean Jacques Rivard really was, but, to judge by the precision
and style of his descriptions, I imagine he must have had some training
in science and engineering. In the only piece this traveler/photographer/
self-taught student of anthropology ever seems to have written, he quite
succinctly refers to the Castillo as "an architectural assemblage oriented
in such a way as to make use of the information gathered by the deter-
mination of the equinoxes." Then comes a statement that would guarantee the Castillo its "must see" status for decades to come (provided an
enterprising entrepreneur of Maya antiquity waiting in the wings would
seize the opportunity to shine the limelight on it—we'll meet him later):
"a spectacular *hierophany* ... is presented there which makes even modern man stand in awe and wonder" (my italics). It is the lifting of this
term hierophany from the 1968 writings of the celebrated historian of
religion Mircea Eliade that steals the reader's imagination. It invites participation and evokes a feeling of sympathetic causation. It is as if the
very presence of the viewer creates an emotional tension that brings about
the event itself: "Man becomes aware of the sacred because it manifests
itself, shows itself, as something wholly different from the profane," wrote

Eliade. "To designate the act of manifestation of the sacred we have proposed the term hierophany." After describing the event and documenting it photographically, Rivard adds his own interpretation of the meaning of the phenomenon: "To the ancient peoples who worshipped at this site a manifestation such as this must have seemed a most awe-inspiring hierophany since the serpent was one of the meaningful aspects of their religious experience."

Little did Rivard know that he would be party to the creation (or recreation?) of one of the great myths of seasonal time about the ancient Maya that would span the last decades of the old and the first of a new millennium. Although Rivard may have captured the dazzling serpent, the Mexican journalist and amateur astronomer Luis Arochi is singularly responsible for unleashing it on a late 1970s upswinging Mexican tourist industry primed for a hierophany. Arochi is the enterprising entrepreneur who pied-pipered the masses then beginning to flock to the newly created Miami-like touristic mecca of Cancun, one hundred miles west to inland Chichén.

I remember my first meeting with Arochi quite vividly. It was March 20, 1973, and I and a few of my students were perched with our surveying equipment at the top of the Caracol, Chichén Itzá's round tower observatory. We had been engaged on and off since 1970 in making a survey of astronomical alignments through the three narrow horizontal windows that lead out of a once enclosed six-foot-square chamber in its turret. Among the sight lines were some orientations I thought had been deliberately designed to mark the setting sun at the equinox and I had come to the site to document them. Poised to shoot the equinox sunset through one of the windows, I was suddenly elbowed out of the way by a slight Mestizo man sporting a long focus lens. Clad in leather-soled wingtips, he had quietly crawled up to the turret via the slippery snail-like coiled accessway after which the structure gets its modern name (*caracol* means snail in Spanish). After he shot his image of the solar disk descending through one of the windows, I elbowed him back, shoved my Nikon through the horizontal shaft, and added a frame to my own film sequence. As we planted our feet and staked out the disputed turf, Arochi complained, "I am Mexican and you are a *gringo*. I have more rights to shoot these photos than you," and he wedged a shoulder in front of me as he pointed his instrument through the window. "You may be Mexican but you're no more Maya than I am," I retorted as I flashed my official permit at him and landed another photographic blow in return. We engaged in this cinematic tit for tat, exchanging mild insults leavened with tension-relieving jest until the last vestige of the reddened solar disk slipped below Yucatan's flat horizon. And then he too vanished.

A year later while browsing in a Mexico City bookstore I learned where Arochi had found the cosmic event he was seeking. It was in that other famous Chichén building four hundred yards to the northwest. Titled *La Pirámide de Kukulcan—Su Simbolismo Solar* (*The Pyramid of Kukulcan—Its Solar Symbolism*), the book's dazzling red-and-purple cover with a picture of the serpent of light descending the balustrade darted out at me. Arochi's book would develop into a perennial best-seller in Mexico, netting six editions by 1987. Between its colorful covers, Arochi claimed discovery of the phenomenon, grandstanding the snake theme as he documented the similarity between the triangles made by the sun and those that appear on the back of the diamondback rattler. He added dozens of photos of other serpent sculptures at the site along with scores more of the phenomenon taken from every conceivable angle. On his many geometrical diagrams of the ground and site plans of the Castillo, he circumscribed dotted circles, triangles, and octagons, conveying the impression that the building, in addition to encoding calendrical information, also comprised a catalog of lost Maya geometrical wisdom cast in stone—"Marvelous pyramidal geometry," he called it.

The next spring equinox a few hundred curiosity seekers appeared at the ruins to watch the serpent ramble down the Castillo's banister. Arochi, a dynamic public speaker, showed up at the site to explain what was happening. The *Diario de Yucatán*, the capital city of Mérida's daily newspaper, featured a front-page piece accompanied by a photo advertising the serpent of light. By 1980, the crowd had ballooned to some twelve thousand, thanks to a host of new guidebooks plugging the event.

Self-styled Castillo experts soon began to thrive in a Barnumesque atmosphere rife with amazing archaic revelations handed down directly from antiquity's hierophany. Two enterprising Yucatecan amateur astronomers produced a popular pamphlet (still sold in the Chichén Museum) purporting to show (via a series of complicated diagrams) exactly how the Maya had calculated and planned the whole architectural arrangement centuries ago. Another laid claim to the discovery of the first nocturnal Maya lunar hierophany by showing that the full moon nearest the equinox would produce a paler version of the zigzag spectacle on the Castillo.

In 1982, when Mexican president José Lopez Portillo showed up to experience the Chichén serpent, he took advantage of the opportunity to use the phenomenon to promote Mexican cultural patrimony. He saw to it that the event, which happens to coincide with the birthday of Mexico's heroic reformer and Lincolnesque president, Benito Juarez, would achieve wider acclaim. (Juarez was born March 21 and the equinox can occur either on March 20 or March 21.) The 1982 equinox event fell on a Sunday and it drew close to twenty-five thousand weekenders from all over the peninsula and beyond.

In 1984, the first staged recognition of the event, which had by then become a national holiday, took place. Heralded by ads in the *Diario*, the attendance swelled to an estimated thirty thousand. Stalls were set up to dispense T-shirts, miniature stone idols, and a variety of Mexican street foods. Indigenous elements crept into the equinox event as colorfully costumed "voladores," or "flyers," performed the ceremonial pole dance native to the Totonac Indians from faraway Veracruz: four costumed men plummet from a seventy-five-foot high perch and descend spirally to ground level executing thirteen revolutions as their flight unwinds four ropes tethered to the top of the pole, each one tied to a performer's leg. (The calendrical significance of the dance is reflected in the $4 \times 13 = 52$ turns, the same as the number of years in an ancient Maya sacred time round.) Arochi, then annually monitoring the serpent hierophany's play-by-play, excitedly noted the appearance of each diamond of light from top to bottom, right down to the very last one that vanished off the edge of the balustrade and into the sky as the equinox sun approached the horizon.

By 1987, attendance had soared to thirty-five thousand, as the gates were thrown open and the normal six-dollars-per-person admission fee was waived on Serpent Day. (As far as I can judge, the gate receipts at Chichén have yet to make an impact on the impoverished masses who still live in the nearby town of Pisté in the shadows of the great Temple of Kukulcan.) Millennial New Age fever now began to impinge on the serpent. Chicano art historian José Argüelles had just published his popular book *The Mayan Factor: The Path Beyond Technology*. Applying a space age spin to the old Kukulcan myth of eternal return, Argüelles explored a complex numerology he claimed reveals that all the cycles of Maya time would soon come together in the dawn of a new era. Then the feathered serpent hero of ancient Mexican mythology would return from a distant galactic world to announce the beginning of a new era for all humankind. Argüelles argued that the collapse of the ancient Maya civilization happened when their priests, led by Kukulcan, realized it was no longer the appropriate time in the cycle of the universe to spread their knowledge. Instead they transformed themselves into "light beings" and removed their philosophy to a distant region of the Milky Way Galaxy.

But a new utopia is just around the corner. A post-technological phase of history with lost writings of the ancient Maya as its keystone will descend upon us in the year 2012 (December 23 to be exact), when the Maya cyclic day-count odometer is due to turnover. This received wisdom from far out in space and far back in time, Argüelles contended, will offer us a pollution-free technology, regional harmony, and more leisure so that we can all get to know one another collectively. As a way of showing solidarity among believers in his philosophy, Argüelles called for a Harmonic Convergence, a kind of preparatory mass gathering, on August 16, 1987. According to his calculations, this date marked one of the pivotal points in the last cycle of the old era, which is headed for apocalypse thanks to our environmentally impactful, high-tech, suburban, existence. Mildly reminiscent of the rendezvous of the Hale-Bopp comet with the Heaven's Gate cult, pilgrims convinced by the convergence came by the several hundreds to the appointed place, the top of a mountain in Colorado, to concentrate their collective cosmic energies in an effort to avert the Armageddon script.

The sun played a primary role in Argüelles' utopian vision for, as he puts it, it is only by matching solar with psychic frequencies that human action can be deployed to skirt disaster. So I was not surprised to find many of Argüelles' disciples showing up at the Castillo on equinox day in 1988 to invoke their god of the future at precisely the time when he would be expected to make a Virgin Mary-like appearance along the side of the temple dedicated to him. One group of Americans led by a California woman and a Maya spiritualist named Hunbatz Men, from a town near Chichén Itzá, had come on a pilgrimage tour to undergo spiritual training in Maya knowledge that would lead to their becoming Maya themselves. The Harmonic Convergers were but one of four gnostic groups to join the many thousands who assembled in front of the Castillo that afternoon. These included the Neo-Aztecs, countercultural urban mestizos (largely from Mexico City) who had turned to ancient Mexican wisdom as a way of creating a new anticapitalist, naturalistic community. The two other groups were more international and heterogeneous in character.

A discussion among various members of these groups who had gathered in Pisté the day before resulted in an alliance that led to a plan to perform a ritual on the steps of the pyramid shortly before the image of the serpent was due to materialize on the roped-off side of the stairway above them. Anthropologist Quetzil Castañeda, who witnessed it all, describes the assemblage of pilgrims at the pyramid. Signaled by the sound of four conch-trumpets, the celebrants formed a human chain and executed four clockwise turns about the building. Accompanied by music, they invited bystanders to join the circle, thus harmonizing with the energy of the universe embodied in the sacred serpent hierophany on this special day. The ritual intensified, with the pilgrims swaying back and forth and chanting. Then all hell broke loose when the celebrants were confronted by officials who were concerned that the diversion might spoil the official, government sanctioned proceedings for the onlookers. Castañeda describes what happened next:

> It was just before 4:00 P.M., during the intermission between parts one and two of the government program, that the master of ceremonies included in his lost-child announcements the authoritarian proclamation

that the brothers, the persons who are doing this religious practice, do not have any permission whatsoever. "We ask you to stay seated so that everyone can see." Intended, no doubt, to impose order on the chaos of a pre-Columbian revivalist performance, this comment had the contrary effect; an aggressive faction of the audience, upset at the police and the Boy Scouts for having imposed the New Agers literally on top of them as they sat in the front, began to push back against the Aztecas, Maya pilgrims, and even the police and the Boy Scouts as they shouted and cursed with increasing threats of violence. The police, for their part, were getting ready to use force to assure compliance with their vision of order. Tensions were explosive, when all of a sudden the aggressive members of the audience and the authorities lunged forward toward each other. Caught between these antagonistic forces, the spiritualists' response was to shout, in Spanish, "Mejico! Mejico!"—A shout that within twenty seconds became mixed in with persons English shouts of "Mexico! Mexico!" (pronounced with English "x"). This general shout quickly intensified as the pronunciation converted in to an explosion of "Meshico! Meshico!" (Nahuatl pronunciation) together with loud blasts of the caracol, drums, flutes, shells, and rattles. All the while, the master of ceremonies continued with his messages in the background. Up front near the pyramid, this blast of energy occupied everyone's attention and lasted for ten minutes or so. Then all fell silent as the serpent began his descent.

As the last decade of the millennium closed, Mexico turned into a breeding ground for equinoctial manifestations of the sacred. Arochi offered up several other temples at a variety of sites as potential light and shadow showcases. For example, several hundred spectators make the short ten-mile trek from Mérida to the ruins of Dzibilchaltun to watch the first light of spring pass through the square windows of the House of the Seven Dolls. Portals and other apertures in the miniature temples of Tulum by the sea near Cancun also draw enthusiastic hierophants. A thousand miles away in suburban Mexico City over a thousand spectators show up at the Pyramid of the Sun at Teotihuacan to ring in the equinox, though no particular certified solar phenomenon actually takes place there on that day. My good friend, anthropologist William Breen Murray informed me that a group of 300 showed up at Alta Vista (Chalchihuites) near Durango, Mexico, an ancient colony of Teotihuacan that happens to be located almost precisely on the Tropic of Cancer. Back in the 1980s, archaeologist J. Charles Kelley had discovered what appear to be a pair of calendar counters carved on a stone nearby. He and I published a report suggesting several alignments to the equinox and solstice sunrise horizon points. Evidently this proved sufficient reason for a modest audience to turn out for a ritual sunbath at this relatively remote ruin on equinox day. I haven't kept figures, but Breen informs me that in more recent years a thousand—maybe as many as fifteen hundred—have spent the afternoon of March 20 at Alta Vista.

What calls forth these seekers of the grand illumination on the spring equinox? In Teotihuacan, as at Chichén, the idea of a "sun-pyramid" as a universal symbol of seasonal renewal seems to be at least a part of the answer. Teotihuacan was the place where time began, where the gods were born (as its very name implies), and the sun was made to rise by the sacrifice of one humble member of the pantheon who willingly hurled his body into the cosmic fire. It is a place where we need to be at the right time to reenact creation, as Eliade's words in this chapter's epigraph suggest.

But did the ancient Maya *really* see the serpent at Chichén descend? Or was it, even in its own time, a manifestation of Chichén Itzá recreating itself once again as a pilgrimage center? Did pilgrims come from far and wide to experience the religio-astro-engineering phenomenon of the age? Were they like today's pilgrims, spiritually transformed by their equinoctial engagement with it? If so, did the Maya contrive the pyramid to make it happen or was it just a coincidence? Maybe they saw something else? And even if they did see an effigy, what did it mean to them? Did it remind them of the passing of the seasons—of the voyage from death back to life through apotheosis? Was it the age-old universal symbol of the Stravinskian Rite of Spring?

But are these the issues that really matter? I think that over the years the Temple of the Feathered Serpent has become the contested ground over the ownership of time and place between native and foreigner, between scientific expert and New Ager, between local commoner and national bureaucracy. Perhaps the deeper questions attending the sinking serpent have more to do with how we create the myths that lie submerged beneath our holidays, how we alter them, how we make use of the past. Who really owns the archaeological record? Who turns the key to the past that lies in the present? Whose serpent is it, anyway?

Archaeologists have long argued that the builders of the great monuments of the world—Khufu's Egyptian pyramid, Monk's Mound at Cahokia, Britain's Stonehenge—sought to convince both citizen/subject as well as themselves of their right to rulership. Succeeding rulers would often take over, modify, even demolish and rebuild the works of their predecessors to alter an existing ideology or to validate their imagined bond with the deities who founded their sacred place. In ancient Egypt there was no better manipulator of people through the medium of architecture than Ramses II. Egyptologists attribute half of what remains in the Nile Valley to the power of his extended hand. Likewise, Eighteen Rabbit, one of a dynasty of more than a dozen Maya rulers, stamped his mark on 50 percent of Copan's architecture. Just as those who followed after them changed the written historical image of Jefferson, Kennedy, or Stalin, the monument builders of antiquity reflect the past they desired to project into the future through the physical remains they have left behind for us to ponder.

Sometimes those who manipulate the past are not the official bureaucrats who run the establishment, but citizens, partisans, or patriots who seek to install an idea of their own. Thus the Druids claim Stonehenge as their temple of worship despite the denial to their precedence offered by the official archaeological record handed down by a scientific cadre of excavators. In his book *Stonehenge Complete*, archaeologist Christopher Chippindale gives an amusing tongue-in-cheek account of the archaeological myth building that helped transform the Druids from shamanistic diviners in early medieval Gaul to Renaissance scholars and teachers to the alleged founders of the Anglican form of Christianity. The temple-computer-observatory theory of Stonehenge that created so much controversy in archaeological and astronomical circles back in the 1960s was, according to modern-day Druids, a testimony to the wisdom of their ancient ancestors.

Looked at historically, the search for distant origins in the Americas has taken many curious turns. Before Columbus came to the New World, religious philosophers debated the existence of "antipodal man"—a race of beings not of the seed of Adam and therefore beyond the possibility of redemption, people who lived on a vast continent on the other side of the ocean sea. Once the discoverers demonstrated the existence of an "Indian" race on an isolated continent, the Church found itself arguing against proposed alternative Adam and Eve pairs and in favor of the peopling of the Americas by seafaring Phoenicians, itinerant Mongols—even the Lost Tribes of Israel. To prove their point, serious historians of the seventeenth century drew up long lists of similarities between Hebraic and Native American customs: sacrifices of the firstborn, feasts of harvest and ceremonies involving the purification of the body, not to mention parallels in architecture, language, and writing.

But being non-Christian societies, and therefore incapable of self improvement, such cultures wallowed in a degenerate savage state. The high civilizations, the Maya, the Aztecs, the Incas—they were a different story. Having acquired the Old World skills of masonry and goldsmithing they fell from power. How else to explain why descendants of the builders of Chichén Itzá still live alongside the impressive remains of their ancestors, yet seem totally incapable of reproducing such great architectural works? This age-old idea of a past superior to the present, of the decadent fall from a distant Golden Age, is very much in tune with the gnostic philosophy that pervades contemporary New Age thinking. The nineteenth-century visitor to the Maya ruins was well disposed toward believing that although man fell because of Adam's sin, the human race nonetheless could be redeemed by discovering lost knowledge buried within the ruins.

Running cross-grain to this view of savage degeneracy was the later romantic idea that the Indian, shielded from contamination by the European vices of industrial capitalism, war, pollution, and the rape of the landscape, was, in fact, the highest form of humanity. Here was the noble savage who roamed free in nature's wild Utopian landscape. Emerson wrote of "His erect and perfect form. . . . Master of all sorts of woodcraft, he seemed a part of the forest and the lake, and the secret of his amazing skill seemed to be that he partook of the nature and fierce instincts of the beasts he slew." The image conveyed here is that it is the present "we" and not the distant "other" who live in a state of decline. Seek the ancient truths that still live on in these people—accept them and you will find individual salvation! This century-old secular formula for eternal happiness lives on today in the neoromantic visions of the mysterious Maya expressed by writers like José Argüelles and Luis Arochi.

The modern millennial manipulation of the Castillo on equinox day—the collective quest for revealed knowledge in a thousand-year-old faraway pyramid—is part of a pop cultural movement to get back in touch with the power of nature. And like all seasonal rituals in the round of cyclic time, it is also a way of rediscovering and renewing the lost values we all desire by sharing what those of an imagined past might also have experienced. (A 1997 Yankelovich poll showed that in twenty years the number of Americans who believe in astrology had doubled, in fortune-telling and reincarnation it had tripled, and in faith healing and spiritualism it had quadrupled.) The serpent hierophany is really about hope—the return of a desired past that elevates the present above the humdrum. The descending serpent offers food for a spiritually starved society possessed by a longing to recreate a glorious past superior to an unfulfilling present.

For the Mexican participants with old Aztec and Maya blood in their veins, like the famous Aztec sun stone and the Pyramid of Teotihuacan, the old god Kukulcan's temple comes to life once a year evoking a feeling of Indianism; it repudiates the European conquest. In our never-ending search for distant origins, it recognizes that the power of their proud ancestry still lives in the otherwise mute stones. Different pasts for different people and different meanings behind the days they celebrate— these are the histories we make and mingle together on equinox day on the vast dirt field that surrounds the Maya Castillo.

Voltaire once said that history is really a pack of tricks we play on the dead. What happens at Chichén on the equinox seems to suggest that he, too, hit the nail on the head. Yet another visit to the Castillo on a hot dusty March afternoon bolsters my belief that how we interpret the past will always be tainted by the ideas and attitudes of the present. I wonder whether my planned return to this sacred place next March will change my mind about what I am seeking?

Chapter
5

The Easter/Passover Season: Connecting Time's Broken Circle

This cute idea is courtesy of Bernadette from Virginia. You'll need small candies, like chocolate covered raisins, whoppers, mini marshmallows, jelly beans, etc. wrapped inside a baggie or saran wrap tied with ribbon. This can be placed inside a miniature Easter basket. Attach the following poem:

> *The Easter bunny came last night*
> *And left this little scoop,*
> *Because you weren't so good this year*
> *You're getting bunny poop!*

> Bunny Crafts and Ideas

Chinese, Indians, Africans, Mexicans—all have looked at the face of the moon. In the patterning of the dark lava plains against the stark white highlands, they have discerned the figure of a rabbit. Like kids on the beach who trace out animal figures at the rims of brightly lit cumulus clouds, not everyone agrees on how the rabbit is represented. Some see a frontal image, the rabbit's ears outlined by the Seas of Fecundity and Nectar, his round face marked by the Sea of Tranquility, site of the first lunar lander; the Seas of Serenity and Showers constitute the rodent's round body. Others view a rabbit in profile—the Sea of Humors and the Sea of Clouds mark the front legs, Nectar and Fecundity the back legs; the huge Sea of Storms is its head, the bright crater Kepler marks an eye, and swept-back ears are outlined by the Bay of Rainbows. But still the figure is a rabbit.

How did a rabbit get onto the face of the moon? One Sanskrit text tells the tale of a fox, a coot (water fowl), a monkey, and a hare. (We tend to lump rabbits and hares together, though there are significant differences between them: the American rabbit is smaller, has less powerful hind legs, and lives in a burrow; the hare lives in the open. The young of the hare are born with hair and their eyes wide open. Rabbits are born hairless and blind.) The four traveled together as hermits, pledging never to kill a living thing. The god Sakkria tested their faith by appearing to each of them in the form of a Brahmin (a member of the highest Hindu caste) begging for alms. The monkey immediately brought him a bunch of mangoes plucked from a nearby orchard; the coot offered him a row of trout left at the riverside by an unknown fisherman; the fox brought a pot of milk forgotten by a herdsman. When the Brahmin approached the last of the hermits, the hare responded, "I eat only grass which surely can be of no use to you." "But if you are a real hermit you can offer me your own flesh," replied the Brahmin. The hare consented and the Brahmin built a cooking fire into which the hare would jump. "That will save me the trouble of killing you and dressing your flesh," said the Brahmin. Again the rabbit consented. He climbed to the top of a rock above the fire and leapt off. But just before he reached the flames they were miraculously extinguished. The Brahmin returned to the form of the god Sakkria, took the hare in his arms, and drew its figure in the moon so that every living thing everywhere in the world might see and remember this noble character.

A Chinese version of the moon story has the hare picking lice off its body just prior to taking the fatal leap. Before he jumps he tells the insects: "I may sacrifice my body for the Holy One but I have no right to take your lives." A Hottentot spin on the tale from South Africa tacks on a bad news ending that finds the hare sent from the moon back to the earth to inform everyone that just as the moon goddess waned and died away and then waxed back to life, so too would humankind die and rise again. But the hare botches the last part of the message, saying instead that humanity shall arise no more. The goddess, enraged by the hare's blunder, grabs a hatchet and attempts to split its head open. The hare dodges the main thrust, but catches a glancing blow on the lip. Harelips remain as a reminder to all of us not to neglect our duty to our superiors.

On this side of the ocean the rabbit in the moon story is told by the Spanish chronicler Bernardino de Sahagun. Having interviewed members of the Aztec nobility in the aftermath of the conquest, he writes (in 1585) that they believed that once the moon and the sun were equal in brilliance. The gods had been discussing who would bear the burden of causing the sun to rise. One named Tecuciztecatl volunteers. He does four days of penance in preparation for the self-sacrifice, in which he will plunge into the great fire in order to make the sun rise; but then Tecuciztecatl hesitates. He is shamed by an older, more humble deity who takes the plunge. Both become suns. "But how can this be that they will both follow the same orb?," argue the gods. Then one of their number came out running. With a rabbit he came to wound in the face this Tecuciztecatl (the moon); with it he darkened his face; he killed its brilliance. Thus doth it appear today."

Although the Asian-African versions of the rabbit/hare story likely originated in a Buddhist parable, the congruency between the Asian and American fables of the rabbit in the moon remains pivotal in the age-old debate over whether mythologies from Asia diffused across the ocean to the Americas. That issue aside, the moral lesson central to all these stories resides in the element of sacrifice—undertaken (in the Eastern version of the story) by the most humble of characters, who, unlike those who would offer to god that which costs them nothing, is ready to give up his own flesh. He becomes a living sacrifice to be consumed as a burnt offering in service to the divine.

This story lies at the root of our modern association of rabbits with the most important Christian festival in the seasonal calendar, whose date is still fixed by the moon. Why is the Easter rabbit in the moon an ideal choice to exemplify the theme of death and rebirth associated with that holiday? Rabbits are symbols of fertility. (Hugh Hefner's choice of bunnies to adorn *Playboy* magazine was not fortuitous.) They are also nocturnal animals. On clear moonlit nights they gather together in play as if entranced by the moon. Their gestation period of twenty-eight to thirty days (the same as the human female menstrual cycle) is a near-perfect fit to the cycle of the phases of the moon. Like the moon, the rabbit never shuts its eyes (it really does if you sit and watch long enough) and, so they say, it always gazes at the moon when it gives birth. So, continues a Chinese proverb, they call her "The One Who Looks at The Moon," and by the intensity of the light of the moon on that occasion they determine the abundance of rabbits to be born in the coming year.

The rabbit's foot, that infallible gambler's talisman, must be obtained by an animal killed at the time of the full moon by a cross-eyed person in order to be truly effective. Bad luck too if a rabbit crosses a pregnant woman's path, she will have a breech birth—unless she makes a slit in her undergarments to break the spell. The rabbit lives in dark places, and if it comes into your home—bad luck, say the modern descendants of the ancient Aztecs, who still inhabit the mountains surrounding modern Mexico City.

Like the Easter bunny, the Easter egg, that other ubiquitous Easter icon, became very popular in the late nineteenth and early twentieth century as yet another old religious holiday (see Chapter 11 on Christmas) was converted to a family-centered festival focusing largely on children, thanks to the efforts of romantic middle-class home-centered Victorians who had a fascination with old traditions. If today's mass-produced chocolate confection version of the egg has any real roots in the distant past, I find them difficult to trace. Akin to the young Easter bunny, the baby lamb, or chick, the egg is an apt symbol of the season that celebrates resurrection because it symbolizes new life and spring in general. Spring is the time when we first see eggs in the nests of robins. On the other hand the egg is also the shell or tomb that imprisons the seed that holds the promise of new life—whence the chicken–egg problem. When Geb, the Egyptian earth god, united with sky goddess Nut in an illicit cosmic affair, the result was the fabulous Bennu bird, the peacock-like phoenix who came to symbolize the sun. Christians adopted the bird as a representation of their savior after the unique way in which it died and came back to life. Imitating the last flash of sunset, the bird died by setting fire to its own nest. But among its ashes lay an egg from which a new phoenix would hatch—every fourteen hundred years. Like the second coming of Christ, who is often represented by figures of peacocks in stonework, paintings, and engravings in churches, the resurrection, at least since early medieval times, has been regarded as a millennial phenomenon, each stage in the evolution toward perfection taking place at intervals of about a thousand years.

In American folklore, the egg is not the product of a bird but rather of the hare, a tradition brought over by the Pennsylvania Dutch who, we recall, were also responsible for the groundhog. It seems that the hare was once a bird—until Eostre, goddess of dawn, changed it into the four-footed creature noted for its prolific fertility. The corn spirit tied to the cutting of the last corn sheaf (see Chapter 10) is often called "the hare" and lopping it off, "cutting the tail of the hare," the seminal event that brings an official end to crop production. In parts of nineteenth-century Germany and Hungary an effigy of the hare was often placed in baskets of eggs given as gifts during the season. People were prohibited from eating them during Lent so that the luxury of devouring eggs on Easter Sunday might better be appreciated. In more wasteful late nineteenth-century times, they took to rolling them on the ground in a race—a vague reminder of the rolling away of the stone from Christ's tomb. Czarist Russia developed the custom of decorating the eggs with gold and jewels, fabricating yesterday's version of the Fabergé egg. Unlike the consumable gift intended for the mouths of those who could scarcely aspire to the luxury of protein, the jeweled egg of the wealthy class sits on a shelf or table—a feast solely for the eye.

The earliest hint of any seasonal holiday like Easter that I could find descends from the twenty-fourth century B.C. Babylonian Akitu festival. It was celebrated in the city of Ur—and, sure enough, it was dedicated to the moon and the equinoxes. The Babylonians recognized two six-month half-years, or semesters, each with its own moon feast, celebrated on the first and seventh months. Nisannu (March/April) and Tasritu (September/October) were denoted by full moons. During the period of Babylonian captivity (sixth century B.C.) the ancient Hebrews picked up the idea of the equinoxes as the turning points of the year: "You should observe the Feast of Weeks, of the first fruits of the wheat harvest, and the Feast of the Ingathering at the turn of the year," reads Exodus 34:22. The Feast of the Unleavened Bread at the turn of the year "when the kings do battle" came to be tied to the first of the two holidays, which was emphasized in particular by the Israelites. When Moses received instructions from God that the Israelites were to flee captivity by the light of the full moon, he told each family to sacrifice a lamb and sprinkle its blood over the doorjamb as a sign to the angel who would pass over their homes not to kill their first born. In haste they would be forced to bring unleavened bread with them to sustain their long journey.

Setting the date of the feast would turn out to be an obsessive and complex problem that would occupy calendar keepers for centuries. (We owe it at least a page or two of historical digression.) The Hebrew calendar first used to set the date was based on the cycles of the sun, but especially the moon. The Hebrews were well aware of the Metonic cycle (235 full moon cycles are equivalent to nineteen seasonal years). The biblical injunction of Passover (or Pesah, whence our word Paschal) stated that the feast was to be eaten on the fourteenth day of the month of Nisan, the day of the full moon nearest the equinox. The start of the month had been fixed in the Hebrew calendar with the appearance of the crescent of the "spring moon," the one nearest the equinox. With the rise of Christianity, the emphasis of unity in the Roman Empire came to be placed more and more on the Christian Church. By the fourth century A.D., pagan cults and rituals, along with the old Roman calendar, had been abolished and in their place a new calendar was instituted based on ecclesiastical reckonings and the commemoration of saints. Once second-century Christians adopted the holiday, which they viewed as the culmination of the Passover following the Feast of the Last Supper, they felt compelled to celebrate the anniversary of the Paschal date close to the time of year when the resurrection of Christ was documented as having occurred, and furthermore to fix it on a Sunday. Above all, church law dictated that Easter must not fall on the Hebraic equivalent. The computists, specialists in charge of Christian calendrical computations, believed a conflict could be avoided if they selected the first Sunday after the full moon that followed the vernal equinox. Now, since it already had been recognized that the equinox was falling earlier and earlier in the calendar year (it had shifted backward about three days in the four centuries since the Julian reform), the religious problem of determining Easter Sunday became tied to the astronomical problem of fixing the place of the vernal equinox in the zodiac—the first day of spring. One goal of the Council of Nicaea (Iznik in Asia Minor) held in A.D. 325 was to set a single date for the celebration of Easter by Christians in both the Eastern and the Western Holy Roman Empires and to resolve the opinions of arguing factions over whether the date of celebration should be reckoned from the fourteenth or fifteenth of the month of Nisan.

Since a Sunday, a full moon, and the equinox are all involved, given the set of rules for determining the movable feast, the computists were called on to reconcile three periods that do not readily mesh: the 7-day week, the lunar synodic month or month of the phases of 29½ days, and the 365-day solar or seasonal year. It turned out that Easter could occur any time between March 22 and April 25; and it would take over five-million years before the dates of the Paschal observance would recur in the same order. Having discovered the impossibility of devising a mathematical formula to set dates infinitely into the future, the computists created complicated tables based on averaged full-moon intervals. These tables of *epacts* listed the age or phase of the moon on January 1, from which the Easter date could easily be computed for that year. But they gave only approximate information about the phase of the moon on New Year's Day (the error could amount to two or three days); the true motion of the moon was far too complex to be formulated precisely in tabular form. One of the calendrical debates that followed after the Middle Ages centered around the extent to which religious festivals really needed to be calculated with astronomical accuracy. On this issue the German astronomer Johannes Kepler is reported to have weighed in: "Easter is a feast, not a planet."

Five centuries later, Easter calendar machinations are still not at an end. From time to time, business and industry, bothered by the floating nature of the holiday, which has persisted for nearly sixteen-hundred years, have sought to nail down Easter Sunday in the seasonal cycle. Today we seem to be in a quiescent phase, but when *Nation's Business* magazine ran a poll on the question in 1972, 52 percent of respondents were in favor of making Easter a Sunday late in April. "The practical arguments in favor of a fixed Sunday are impressive. The emotional arguments against it are not so impressive," wrote one supporter. "Not one person in a thousand knows how the date is set anyway," argued another. On the practical side, an early Easter is especially bad for Easter vacationers in the North and for retailers who use the season to trot out fashions for the warmer weather. That it can fall in either March or April has a complicating effect on month-by-month market analysis.

"Moving George Washington's birthday was one thing . . . Christ's Resurrection is another," complained an opposing member of the ministry. Hoping to unify Orthodox, Roman Catholic, and Protestant celebrations, ecumenical efforts joined the business world's push toward a fixed Easter in the late 1980s, but that effort, like the contemporary drive to go metric, petered out. Was it a result of a mounting public concern about government rubber stamping all our ways of reckoning things? As one opponent wrote, "I think commercialization of all holidays, religious or otherwise, has gone far enough."

Easter is more than a feast. It is a *season*—a time of some continuance, a cycle with open ends. If "All the world's a stage," then time is life itself. The seasons segment the numbered pages of a script that we players in the drama of life act out. In a famous passage from *As You Like It*, Shakespeare likened life to a seven-act play:

> *. . . At first the infant,*
> *Mewling and puking in the nurse's arms.*
> *Then the whining school-boy, with his satchel*
> *And shining morning face, creeping like snail*
> *Unwillingly to school. And then the lover,*
> *Sighing like furnace, with a woeful ballad*
> *Made to his mistress' eyebrow. Then a soldier,*
> *Full of strange oaths and bearded like the pard,*
> *Jealous in honor, sudden and quick in quarrel,*
> *Seeking the bubble reputation*
> *Even in the cannon's mouth. And then the justice,*

In fair round belly with good capon lined,
With eyes severe and beard of formal cut,
Full of wise saws and modern instances,
And so he plays his part. The sixth age shifts
Into the lean and slipper'd pantaloon,
With spectacles on nose and pouch on side,
His youthful hose, well sav'd, a world too wide
For his shrunk shank; and his big manly voice
Turning again toward childish treble, pipes
And whistles in his sound. Last scene of all,
That ends this strange eventful history,
In second childishness and mere oblivion,
Sans teeth, sans eyes, sans taste, sans every thing.

And then . . . ? Winter and old age shrouded in darkness, cold and death, at least in the Christian view, offers the promise of resurrection and redemption that will follow in the next round of time. Easter tells the story of the resurrection myth, a tale not unlike that told by the ancient Egyptians of the life of Osiris or by the Greeks of Apollo or by the Aztecs of Quetzalcoatl. In the West, vivid seasonal imagery is made meaningful by paralleling significant episodes in the life of Christ, from birth to resurrection, with those in the year, from Christmas to Easter, when the cycle of life, broken by death, becomes reconnected. The devout Christian lives the life of the Saviour in microcosm each year by acting out its main events. The beginning of the cycle is easy to follow because it is based on the fixed Roman calendar, which, as we discovered in Chapter 2, is centered about the dead of winter—the solstice. It commences with anticipation at Advent, beginning the fourth Sunday before Christmas, which opens a period of penitence and recognition that Christ is near. Christmas celebrates the birth of Jesus and January 6 (the twelfth day following) his Epiphany or earthly manifestation as a deity, an event marked traditionally by his baptism.

The portion of the life cycle based on Easter Sunday is more complicated because depending as it does upon both the sun and the moon, it moves about the seasonal year. It opens with the Lenten season (after the old English word "long," signifying the lengthy days of spring), a forty-day period during which Christ was said to have sacrificed by fasting. Ash Wednesday, the first day of the cycle, is a reminder of our mortality; ashes dabbed on celebrants' foreheads serve as a reminder that we all come from and return to the earth. The Easter season proceeds through five weeks to Palm Sunday, which symbolizes the occasion of Jesus's triumphant entry into Jerusalem. This begins the Holy Week commemorating the last days of Christ's life on earth. Maundy Thursday is the evening of the Last Supper, when Jesus reveals the news that amid the tumult over his appearance in the city one of his disciples has betrayed him. Good Friday marks the Crucifixion, Holy Saturday the day Christ lay in the tomb; finally Easter morning witnesses the grand apotheosis that leads to the salvation of all believers and their relief from a long period of penitence.

The springtime resurrection of Christ and the bringing of light into the world resonates with the American and Asian idea of gods or animals needing to make the ultimate sacrifice in order to ensure the sun will rise. Our word for Easter derives from this very concept. In the Teutonic tradition, Eostre or Eastre was the sun goddess of dawn and consequently the East. When Baldus the sun god is slain by an arrow and condemned to spend half the year in the underworld it is she who tends the gates of Valhalla. She opens them in the spring when he reenters the world. Those who rise early on Easter morning can see him perform his dance as he returns to us over the eastern horizon. Sunrise services are still deeply ingrained in the modern church celebrations of Easter.

> The afternoon and evening was devoted to the magnificent tooling of the Carnival. . . . Nosegays were thrown to the donnas who honored the cavaliers with the same attention. Devils walked the street, arm in arm, harlequins with blown bladders banged passengers between the shoulders indiscriminately. One figure was in scale armour of laurel leaves, another as Hercules in a flesh coloured light suite, apparently quite naked with a club and a garland of flowers, and an Indian chief. All were mingling together in the same spirit of unrestrained hilarity. . . .
>
> The farmer holds high a fat white chicken. The band plays louder. The shouts rise like ugly thunder. The old man tosses the bird above the outstretched arms of the men. It struggles to fly, but lands less than ten yards from the frantic (the troop of masked riders), who pounce upon the poor, doomed fowl and send a cloud of feathers floating off into the heavens. . . . Carl LeBlanc, dressed himself like a chicken, rips the bird's head off and stuffs it in his kewpie doll shorts. "Poule grasse," he shouted, "poule grasse." Fat chicken, fat chicken.

How do we reconcile the wild self-indulgence and rowdiness of Mardi Gras or Carnival in Rio with the reverence that ought to accompany the

start of the Lenten season? The answer, which takes us back over familiar ground we have already encountered (and will encounter again), resides in the necessity of people to move time forward, to make things
happen in the universe—a far cry from our modern attitude of fatalism
that often gives way to passivity in the face of the daunting forces of
nature we perceive around us. But to fully grasp the reasons for the weird
behavior described in Rome's Carnival in 1843 (my first quote) or 1984's
Mardi Gras in Cajun Louisiana (the second quote), we need to stretch
time back to and even beyond the Roman world.

"Between maturity and birth, between the erected phallus and con-
ception, between the Terminus of the Terminalia and the New Year of
the March Kalends, is that timeless moment of orgasm—and this is the
essence of carnival." The "time-out" Roman historian Michael York describes is made up of the extra days once inserted at the terminal point
of the old year to make up the gap between the twelve-month, thirty-
day-per-month (after the phases of the moon), 360-day year and the
cycle of the seasons, which follows the 365-day circuit of the sun among
the stars. Although the Romans may have picked up this idea of interca-
lating (literally making insertions into the framework of time) five days
into the time count from the Egyptians (who invented this scheme in
the third millennium B.C.), there is no other way to account for why the
ancient Maya of Yucatan did almost the very same thing. Their full circle
of the year consisted of eighteen months of twenty days onto which five
nemontemi, "barren days" or "days of evil fortune," were tacked. For the
Maya the bad fortune associated with this critical turning point in the
year could be avoided only by inactivity.

Not so the Egyptians. For them being outside of time meant being
"beyond the curse." They say that when Ra, the sun god, cursed his
mother, the sky goddess Nut, for having had an affair, he had contrived
five epagomenal days or "days upon the year," enabling Nut to give birth
on each of them to one of the deities (Osiris, Horus, Seth, Isis and
Nephthys) who founded the Egyptian race. This quality of nonnorma-
tive behavior on the days that lay outside of the year (the Egyptians considered them unlucky for work) was most likely passed on to the Romans
and came to be most profoundly reflected in the end of February's most

famous festival, the *Regifugium*, or Flight of the King, celebrated to honor the expulsion of the foreign rule of the tyrannical Tarquins. On this occasion the real ruler would temporarily shut down the government and give over his crown to a mock king who was accorded nominal authority for a short period of more or less farcical rule before taking to his heels or perhaps being symbolically sacrificed. (We'll see this theme resurface when we discuss the December Saturnalia, which also falls at a cyclic end point—the winter solstice.) Originally, the intercalary king may have been called on to mediate between the conflicting forces of the sun and the moon, who had caused the problem in the first place.

Festivals like the Regifugium, accompanied by drunkenness, debauchery, and general party mischief presented to us in storybooks and cinema, are largely responsible for giving the ancient Romans a bad reputation. Nonetheless, such stereotypes emanate from vivid descriptions of the mock king's rule by Roman writers, who tell us that before he abdicated, the real king put out the fire that burned in the forum during the normal year, thus exposing everyone to the underworld deities. The intercalary period demanded a festive attitude among the people who participated in restoring the imbalance that occurs among the forces of nature at this time. They organized chariot races, the forerunners of our float parades, and costume balls and dances to imitate the way the carnival mock-king would disguise himself so as to resemble the real king and possibly a camouflage for the vacuum produced by the epagomenal days in the year cycle.

Our pre-Easter behavior still retains a remarkable resemblance to the old Roman customs. In the modern Christian calendar, Shrove (confession) Tuesday, set as the Tuesday before the beginning of Lent, is the last day for fooling around before the dietary, recreational, and (especially) sexual restrictions that come with the forty-day period of sacrifice by denial set in.

The idea seems to be that if you want to go into the holy season with a clear conscience, all the better to do your misbehaving before the clock expires. (Today precisely at the stroke of midnight the New Orleans police department immediately calls a halt to all Mardi Gras partying and sanitation workers commence washing down the streets.) How many of us have treated ourselves to a rich dessert on the eve of a new diet? Looked at from the point of view of the pastoralist (or, for that matter, the psychologist), the tension underlying all the emotional release that accompanies Mardi Gras originally stemmed from the realization that winter stocks of food were running low. What once looked abundant in winter's store at the start of the Christmas season of feasting had by now been reduced to almost nil. What would the next cycle bring? What better time to abandon your woes, release yourself into freedom, and live for today—at least for awhile? Shrovetide became the "time to make merry" in seventeenth-century England. Historians describe it as a period of gluttony and drunkenness—of eating up all the salted meats stored for the winter. The word carnival originates from the Italian *carne levare*, or "to take away the meat." (The savage butchery of the Cajun chicken described earlier has some practical meaning, for the chicken is eaten.) It was also time to deplete all the eggs, milk, and suet before fast time by concocting greasy pancakes, "flap-jacks," or "turnovers"—our first pancake breakfast. All of this naturally necessitated a strong, palatable beverage to wash it down.

London satirist John Taylor gives this gustatory off-putting description of a 1621 Shrove Tuesday pancake breakfast that offered "ballast for the belly" of hellish proportions:

> . . . then there is a thing called wheaten flour, which the sulphury necromantic cooks do mingle with water, eggs, spice and other tragical, magical, enchantments, and they put it by little and little into a frying pan of boiling suet, where it makes a confused dismal hissing (like the hemean snakes in the reeds of Acheron, Styx or Phlegeton) until at last, by the skill of the cooks it is transformed into the form of a Flap-Jack, which in our tradition is called a Pancake, which ominous incantation the ignorant people do devour very greedily.

Cockfighting, cock-throwing (hurling lead-weighted sticks at flocks of the birds—which often maimed throwers instead), and that paragon of misrule, football, were among the more brutal sports indulged in on Shrove Tuesday in medieval England. Modern football—even rugby—are tame when compared to their medieval ancestor. Variously described as a devilish pastime and a murdering practice, the game consisted of a rule-free, teamless, goalless, uninterrupted fight for possession of a stuffed animal bladder. You triumphed by kicking or carrying it all the way to your village, sometimes miles away from the point of origin.

The European version of Carnival was brought over as Fat Tuesday (probably after the fat ox once killed to accompany the pancakes) to New Orleans, one among several southern cities free of puritanical condemnation of its incumbent naughtiness, in 1827 by a group of wealthy young men who had participated in the then-popular custom of being shipped off to Europe to round out their education. In the American version of the season of disorder, pageants were followed by the parade custom when in 1857 the "Mystic Krew of Comus," the Mock King, first led a torchlight parade. Attended by a masked entourage, he ruled the French Quarter until the stroke of midnight while people from every walk of life—debs and dowagers, bankers and beggars, and college students—reveled together in the crowded streets.

Thus have we continued for centuries to set aside a time in Easter's cycle for excess feasting, burlesque, frenzy, and spontaneous delirium—a time to bring out the beast within us. But of the chaos of this varied and extreme carnival behavior comes the desired harmony that describes the flow of normal seasonal time. But still, how can organized societies allow such extreme disorder, in which people behave exactly the opposite of what characterizes "the civilized"—even sanction it?

Anthropologists who have pondered this question think that in large part the kinds of reversals of behavior I have described stem from genuine everyday conflicts that lie at the roots of all social organizations—conflicts about the roles of men versus women, family and friends vs. strangers, the living and the dead, humans and animals, and so on. The peaks of erratic activity we discover in the seasons of the year correspond to smaller bumps on the curve of social behavior throughout the yearly cycle. If you think about it, there is a little nonsense time in most days of our lives; for example, compare the formal rule-bound way we behave while on the job with the relaxation of our good manners at a backyard picnic. Or consider the language we use when we talk to members of the opposite sex or to our parents or our children as opposed to the more callous discourse we may carry on with our pals in the locker room.

Pre-Easter Carnival remains a collectively unconscious remnant of what once was a huge time-out between winter solstice and spring equinox, a long undefined stretch of time in the dead of winter, when fields lie fallow and the potential of the ungerminated seed can only be hoped for. Carnival is a break in the circle of the year, a temporal vacuum that signals a realization of the difference between the perfection that time might be in the ideal case, and the fact of what it really is—a round that cannot complete itself without our helping to connect the ends of its broken circle together. We assist time so that it can achieve its potential perfection.

The message of Easter, then, is that life does indeed emerge from death, provided we help stitch together these oddly paired existences. We need to tug at the ends of the open circle of time and pull them taut during the prolonged period of waiting and hoping and praying—and acting: for it is human action, played out in the rites and rituals we conduct in the Easter cycle, that tie Christmas and Easter together.

Easter was never much of a holiday in early America, but with an increase in the Episcopalian and Roman Catholic sects tied to the flood of immigrant population to the United States after the Civil War, Paschal observances suddenly began to increase in popularity. Elaborately decorating churches and homes with Easter flowers and donning one's Easter finery—especially the ladies' Easter bonnet—became an American postwar fad. Even Europe and particularly Great Britain willingly indulged in this American export.

Christianity converged with consumption as the merchant class quickly responded by developing Easter cards stressing friendship, family affection, and love of home life as a way of embracing more secularly oriented celebrants. Retailers helped convert religious Easter into the fashion season as worshippers paid more visits to clothiers and milliners than to church during Holy Week, knowing the public eye would focus on them in next Sunday's Easter parade following church services. Today's Easter parade has lost much of its Victorian gentility. It looks more like a street fair filled with fun and frolic perhaps more akin to holiday mumming.

Easter may have begun as a result of humanity's deeply rooted wish for life everlasting, the turning to a new page of life filled with greater hope following the demise of the last. Nearly extinguished from the calendar, its old spark has been fanned back to life by nostalgia overtaken by inventive consumerism (check my epigraph). Except for the devout, eggs, bunnies, and fancy hats now veil Easter's deeper meaning, but its persistence and its ultimate conversion into the calendrical pivot of a two-month season of remembrance of lives lived reflects the continuing tension between sacred and secular time in our contemporary culture and the persistent American penchant for transforming one into the other.

Easter in our modern calendar begins a season devoted to recognition of love for all members of the family. In 1907, the Philadelphia activist Anna Jarvis reinvented the old British custom of Mothering Sunday. On this fourth Sunday of Lent gifts were brought to all mothers in observance of Feeding the Five Thousand described in the Book of John (6:1–14), when loaves of bread were distributed to the poor by the more wealthy citizens of Jerusalem, "the mothers of us all." Jarvis chose the day to honor her mother Anna Reeves Jarvis who had organized mothers' days during the Civil War to care for the wounded and to work for better sanitary conditions. Just as Lincoln responded to Sarah Hale's plight to create Thanksgiving Day (see Chapter 10), President Woodrow Wilson was so moved by Jarvis's efforts that in 1915 he declared the second Sunday of May to honor all mothers, both living and deceased, by sending messages to loved ones on this day. Father's Day (the third Sunday in June), though first celebrated in 1910, was not officially proclaimed until Lyndon Johnson decreed it in 1966. The much older Children's Day (the second Sunday in June), which dates back to 1856, is now largely defunct—probably a result of the centrality of children in most other seasonal holidays.

This curious progression of springtime family-centered holidays gives way to a parade of patriotic ones that trickle into the summer, but not before our seasonal and social tensions are heightened by the arrival of a day of discontent, a day that serves as a bookend that caps the windward side of the long, hot season of leisure: from May Day to Labor Day.

Chapter
6

May Day:
A Collision of Forces

The budding generations
Will see their rosy babies flower
Like briars in the spring.
It will be the season of roses . . .
That's the people's future.

Eugene Pottier

May Day. Where did this now relatively obscure holiday identified with a distress signal and the once dreaded specter of world communism come from? And what could a political philosophy once deemed threatening to democratic society have to do with dancing around a florally decorated vertical log?

Every year on the first day of May in eighteenth-century German and Swedish towns, the citizens put on a kind of seasonal passion play. A pair of troops consisting of young men on horseback would enter a settlement from opposite ends of the main street. One group wore animal furs and boisterously threw snowballs at their foe. The other, clad in leaves and flowers drove them back, hurled them from their mounts, and ripped the straw packing out of their undergarments. The script of this mock battle dramatizes the clash between summer and winter. The outcome is never in doubt: summer emerges victorious.

We can trace May Day back to Beltane, the warm weather feast that once opened the second half of the Celtic year—the reciprocal in time of Halloween or Samhain (pronounced sáh-wen). If Candlemas and the Passover cycle are filled with anticipation for the renewal of life, the true essence of May Day centers around the explosion of activity that unfolds when the forces of summer arrive full-blown to claim victory. Those of us who share in the northern European climate where May Day originated are well aware of how 40° gloomy dark days can suddenly turn into 80° cheery sunny ones. People who reside in more southerly temperate climes experience their "May Day" somewhat earlier, but it is always dramatic.

Beltane means "luck fire." Originally, Bel (probably a corruption of Baal, a pagan god of the old testament) was the god of fire and of purification. To honor him (and bring good fortune on yourself), you needed to build a pair of bonfires and drive your cattle between them to rid them of winter disease—so says a mid-eighteenth-century text. Other sources hold that the purifying heat of the fire kept the milk from being stolen by evil spirits who roamed the woods. "Fire! Fire! Blaze and burn the witches" went the shout accompanying the farmers as they spurred their herds through the conflagration, whipping them with switches. Like Halloween, Beltane was a time when the swinging doors of seasonal change were wide open—when evil forces were active and fire was all that could combat them.

May has always been regarded a dangerous month. It can be a time when even good people have the power to do mischief—when the malignant forces of the evil eye are more effective. "March will search, April will try, but May will tell if you'll live or die" goes a British proverb. Isn't it paradoxical that a month traditionally associated with the optimistic burst of spring foliage would come to be fraught with peril? But all change—even the wisp of a breeze that breaks a silence—can bring with it an air of concern: is this the calm before the storm?

Like an uplifting morning wind after a still night, May signifies movement. The word means "the first motion"—of summer—and it has all the properties of a verb. In ritual parlance, "Maying" meant taking action to bring on the summer's forces in the battle of the seasons. When people went into the woods to "bring home the May," they acknowledged the fully regenerated powers of Nature now beginning to be evident in the environment. Young people awoke as early as midnight and made for the woods to gather garlands of flowers and greenery. They would convey the fertilizing powers of nature back to the village and decorate the doors and windows of their houses with them. For those whose thoughts turned toward making love, May Day was a time when the sexually aware could inquire about their future. On May Eve yarrow clippings placed under your pillow will guarantee you a dream of your sweetheart. Another charming May Day superstition calls for preparing a syllabub out of warm cow's milk, sweet cake, and wine. A wedding ring is stirred into the concoction and the lucky youth who gets it in his or her portion will be the first to marry. Not content with transporting boughs and branches, fourteenth-century Welsh celebrants established the tradition of uprooting an entire tree from the woods, dragging it to their settlement, setting it erect, decorating it with flowers and herbs, hanging streamers from the top and dancing around it—the first authentic maypole.

The magical Hawthorn tree (*prunus spinosa*), a craggy shrub with black thorns that suddenly blossoms perfect white flowers around May Day, lay at the core of a fair share of supernatural powers that came with the great May transition in the seasonal clockwork. The Hawthorn symbolized the divine tree that connects the human and heavenly realms, and people would circle about it to bring on the same good luck Bel's fire once brought to their ancestors.

The idea behind all vegetation rituals is that by allying ourselves with the plant world, whose return to life we experience every year, we can regenerate ourselves. But, more than this, our participation in the process is founded in the belief that the re-creation of all living things requires human action. This idea is not so far removed from the philosophy of modern environmental conservation—except that the actions we would undertake today to invigorate the cycle of life might differ considerably.

The American author Washington Irving, who visited England in the mid-nineteenth century, nostalgizes:

> I shall never forget the delight I felt on first seeing a Maypole. It was on the banks of the Dee, close to the picturesque old bridge that stretches across the river from the quaint little city of Chester. . . . The mere sight of this Maypole gave a glow to my feelings and spread a charm over the country for the rest of the day. . . . One can readily imagine what a gay scene it must have been in jolly old London, when the doors were decorated with flowering branches, when every hat was decked with hawthorn, and Robin Hood, Friar Tuck, Maid Marian, the morris dancers and all the other fantastic makers and revelers were performing their antics about the Maypole, in every part of the city.

Exalting trees is still a common practice. When was the last time you witnessed someone knocking on wood? The likelihood is that it was only a matter of a few weeks or a month ago; the custom is very common. People usually knock wood to avoid bad luck. The custom derives from a form of primitive tree worship that still resides in the old wooden maypole. Although urban dwellers might not get the connection, anyone immersed in nature is well aware that trees protect the toiling farmer from rain and sun, nurture his family with their fruit, and drop their leaves for a resting place. By living on for generations, the tree becomes nature's role model for the immortality we all desire. A tree's branches were once thought to connect all earthly creatures with the heavenly abode of the gods.

In the ancient Hebrew wisdom known as the Kabbalah the human body is likened to a tree that maps out the ascent of the mortal soul to heaven as well as the descent of God downward to the earthly realm via twenty-two paths. These branch out at key points of the body that represent god's attributes or emanations—endurance, love, beauty, intelligence, and so on. Other May Day rites that link tree and body include the Bavarian "Walber," the (Carinthian) "Green George," and the English "Jack-in-the-Green." All are variants of the maypole ceremony, except that the pole is either accompanied or substituted by a young man garbed in vegetation to symbolize the human aspect of the regenerative process.

Some poles got to be so huge they required several yokes of oxen to tote them into town. Needless to say, there was a negative side to pagan tree worship: "thorn means scorn," "holly is folly," "briar marks a liar," and "brooms brought in May sweep the family away"—the witches' broomstick is a negative spin on the maypole—are just a few nineteenth-century schoolchild sayings.

Like Beltane and Halloween, adolescence is a tenuous transient state, bringing with it certain pitfalls. We all know what mischief can come of a gaggle of mixed gender youths prancing around all night in the greenery with harps and lutes in hand, their senses piqued by the intoxicating emanations of fertile Mother Earth. Dancing around an erect log was thought to carry all the subtle undertones of a ploy for whipping young damsels into a sexual frenzy.

Nearly every segment of society, including most of all the Christian Church, has weighed in on the significance of the maypole's phallic symbolism. Generations before Freud, Thomas Hobbes contended (without very much in the way of documentation) that maypoles were the remains of the Roman worship of Priapus, god of male potency; however, historians haven't been able to establish anything more than coincidental links with customs falling at this time of the year in the calendar of the classical world.

The closest candidate is a spring festival called Floralia in honor of Flora, the goddess of flowers, ripening fruits, and consequently of youth and its pleasures. Featuring games and dances, this second-century B.C. analog of the Rose Bowl Parade consisted of marchers scattering beans (fertility symbols) among the crowd. Lovers would bring back blossoming branches to decorate their houses. In Rome, worshipping a goddess of fertility led to charges of indecency. Prostitutes claimed it as their holiday, performing naked in mock gladiatorial exhibitions. Cato the Younger was so shocked by a striptease act in a theater performance that he left the place in disgust.

One suspicious seventeenth-century Evangelical Protestant pastor reported threescore maids going into the woods overnight accompanied by "men of great gravity" with "scarcely the third part of them returning home undefiled." Another declared nine out of ten to be in a state of pregnancy following one Maying. It wasn't long before the youthful rite became a source of scandal. The maypole, which had already been pronounced a "stinkyng ydol" in the puritan manual *Anatomie of Abuses* (1583), was consequently abolished—even though historical records show no such rise in pregnancies during that particular season.

A sixteenth-century spoiler characterized the maypole dances as "riotous assemblies of idle people" who chop down all our healthy trees and set them up in front of town where they revel in their drunken Bacchanalia: "I think it were better to be quite abolished amongst us, for many reasons, besides that of occasioning so much waste and spoil . . . to adorn their wooden idols." (We will see a contemporary replay of this sort of community overreaction in connection with so-called sadistic Halloween pranks in Chapter 9.)

In 1644, British Parliament officially banned all maypoles, declaring them "a heathenish vanity, generally abused to superstition and wickedness." In the colonies the Anglican Thomas Morton created a scandal by setting up a pole on his Merry Mount Plantation. (He is described as having loved cakes, ale, and the gay life—which apparently included dancing with Indian women.) Governor Bradford of Massachusetts Bay witnessed one maypole dance and once was enough. Bradford railed against the dancing and "frisking together" and other "beastly practeses of madd Bacchinalians" that accompanied the May Day celebrations. He righteously reveals how he sought a court order from England to have them done away with (Morton was deported). The aftermath of maypole seizure, however, did result in some benefit to the emerging world of empirical science. In 1717, Sir Isaac Newton purchased one of the decaying English poles and used it to support a 124-foot-long telescope, then the largest in the world.

Games, some of them quite raucous, would traditionally follow the maypole dance. All these competitions were aimed at stimulating the forces of nature. In eighteenth-century southern Germany for example, two-man horseraces were popular. The loser's penance was to eat thirty loaves of bread washed down with four liters of beer. If he succeeded, he got to toast the king of the Maypole parade with yet another liter. But if he failed, he was suited up as a buffoon and marched at the head of the parade—where he begged for gifts of money and goods.

The eve of every change of season always seems to be accompanied by weird behavior. The Morris Dance is to May Day what New Year's Eve parties are to January 1. Detractors say the energetic Morris dancers (probably after the pagan "Moorish") initiate the devil's heathen ways. They ride hobby horses and dragons, play the pipes loudly, bang on their drums and ring their bells, all the while swinging their handkerchiefs wildly about their heads. Mummer plays in which elaborately costumed performers told stories of woodland spirits and licentious pleasures were another feature of the May holiday, especially in sixteenth-century England. Both have been revived in the last century.

Today Massachusetts rebels sneer at their puritan ancestors who had once dispatched a small army to chop down Thomas Morton's maypole. They rise on May Day morn and take to the bank of the Charles River just as dawn's rosy fingers mingle with the fading glow of streetlamps to set up their own maypole at the site. They even do a Morris folk dance around it.

As Washington Irving observed, Robin Hood, that loveable anti-establishment rogue who haunted the Sherwood Forest—and whose legendary actions symbolize a leveling out of society's unfair pecuniary hierarchy—was a logical box office attraction for celebrations on an eve of change. (From Douglas Fairbanks Sr. through Errol Flynn to Monty Python and Mel Brooks, Hollywood persists in reincarnating this ever popular character.) But was Robin a real man and, if so, was he a hero or just an outlaw? Or was he a woodland spirit, perhaps the beneficent resurrected deity of vegetation or the evil horned satyr worshipped by witches' covens? These were the sorts of questions that rolled around in the minds of kids who sat close to the stage on the village green to watch live recreations of the story or close up to the movie screen as I did as a youth. We would fantasize our own roles among an eccentric cast of characters: Friar Tuck (who got his name from turning up the hem on his robe for convenience in battle—though a man of the cloth he was not above knocking an enemy on the head with his staff), Little John (whose inverted name parodies his girth if not the subtle mixture of brawn and gentleness that goes with the character), and Maid Marian (a kind of half-man, half-woman character who is anything but the stereotypical girl next door), or the romantic swashbuckler himself. The collision of social forces immersed in the May Day tale of Robin Hood would prophesy things to come.

Like putting new wine in old bottles, we are forever changing the meaning of our seasonal holidays. But the timing is crucial. If an event coincides with a date already symbolically charged with meaning, it can often give a new twist to an old set of customs—the *invention of tradition* as anthropologist Eric Hobsbawm calls it. Recall how the ancient Maya descending equinox serpent was converted to a modern patriotic symbol. Likewise in revolutionary France the maypole was made over into the "Tree of Liberty," even though peasants continued to dance the same dance around it.

When India was a British colony, the end of the maypole ceremony got grafted onto an old Hindu custom that called for burning last year's maypole before erecting the new one. They used the ashes to regenerate the body and applied it to infected areas to ward off sickness; then they scattered what was left on the newly planted crops to help them grow. But sometimes the changes in the meaning of a holiday can be so profound that its original purpose becomes almost completely lost. The connection between May Day and communism is a good example of an invented tradition—one in which the new version played on the anti-establishment element of the old.

Little did those who paraded in Moscow on May Day during the Soviet period realize the irony that their major holiday first took root in conservative nineteenth-century mid-America. If eighteenth-century America boasted of the dignity of a hard day's work, the generations that followed began to recognize the deteriorating condition of the working person in the industrialized state that America was fast becoming.

Our modern concept of employer-employee relations was far from what actually took place in early America, where much of the household workload was carried on the backs of indentured servants. For us, a worker is one who performs tasks and receives money in return. But then, to *owe* and to *own* formed two sides of a social equation in an age rife with slavery. And in the private world of the elite estate the owner could conceal abuses doled out on lax employees. One of the earliest labor dispute cases from Maryland in 1659 details a complaint lodged by a twenty-year-old runaway, Sarah Taylor. Signed to a contract of seven years labor in return for passage to the colonies from England, she charged her masters with beating her black and blue with a stick for burning a batch of bread. Although she produced raw wounds as testimony, Sarah was nonetheless found guilty of breach of contract. She was punished by whipping and required to beg for forgiveness on her knees.

The nineteenth-century industrial labor market was no different in favoring management. After the Civil War, work loads and working conditions of textile laborers and tobacco growers were still appalling by contemporary standards. A typical seamstress, for example, might work six twelve-hour days at a closely scrutinized table and, if she was lucky, she might be permitted to do household sewing for her employer's wife on the seventh day—all of it formally unwaged. Workers were literally driven in gangs like cattle to and from work sites as poor white northern European immigrants squeezed freed blacks down to the bottom of the competitive workpile for the lowest of the lowly jobs. Poets and writers directed attention to poverty-level wages and filthy working conditions that plagued the life of the laborer. For example, Louis Untermeyer's "Caliban in the Coal Mines" vividly expresses the hopelessness of the mine worker.

> God, we don't like to complain;
> We know that the mine is no lark.
> But—there's the pools from the rain;
> But—there's the cold and the dark.
> God, You don't know what it is—
> You, in Your well-lighted sky—
> Watching the meteors whiz;
> Warm, with a sun always by.
> God, if You had but the moon
> Stuck in Your cap for a lamp,
> Even You'd tire of it soon,
> Down in the dark and the damp.
> Nothing but blackness above
> And nothing that moves but the cars . . .
> God, if You wish for our love,
> Fling us a handful of stars!

The inhumanity of the Industrial Revolution was no less tempered on the continent. Eighteenth- and nineteenth-century European cities swarmed with organized gangs of out-of-work beggars, each assigned their pitches and beats. "Young children were stolen from their parents and their eyes put out or their tender limbs torn and distorted, in order, by exposing them thus maimed, to excite the pity and commiseration of the public," wrote the American loyalist Benjamin Thompson (Count Rumford) of conditions in Munich in 1789, where 5 percent of the population lived out on the street. A social reformer, Rumford had set up Munich's first "Poor House" in 1796 in an abandoned factory. He called it a "Military Workhouse," intended to rehabilitate poor families whose males could then be inscripted into the army. Although many regard Rumford's beggars-to-workers project a complete success, his efforts did not escape criticism by later social reformers, Karl Marx among them.

On May 1, 1867, the Illinois legislature enacted the first eight-hour workday. On that day workers antagonized management by celebrating the demise of the ten-hour day with a parade and a mass meeting. They were protesting a clause in the legislation implying that the rule should apply only to workers with written contracts. Strikes and scattered riots followed. Some twenty years later, led by socialist forces, the now more powerful trade unions organized a mass strike—a day of revolt rather than rest they called it, choosing, appropriately enough, the anniversary of the Illinois date. This time more violent riots were accompanied by numerous deaths, arrests, and the imprisonment of leaders of the radical wing of the labor movement who were branded immigrant social anarchists. Out of the "Chicago Martyrs" cause, May Day came to be recognized by conservative elements as the temporal epitome of all socialist movements hell-bent on the destruction of American democracy.

May 1 was always the traditional date for ending hiring contracts, a time in the annual labor cycle as emotionally charged as any in the fertility cycle—especially if one happened to be an itinerant worker. Even though mid-nineteenth-century America was highly industrialized, the old date in the agricultural calendar was nonetheless adhered to. This turned out to be a fortunate development because many of the traditional May Day antiestablishment customs of the day, by pure coincidence, made sense even if the protesters (labor unions) and the authority (the organized nation state) took on different roles. In the 1890s, as the international solidarity of the worker became a broader goal than the length of the workday, the socialist labor movement gathered strength, particularly in Europe, where reformists Friedrich Engels, Arnold van Gennep, and Victor Adler all pushed for a workers' festival that would absorb and transform many of the old May Day rites. When Lenin spearheaded the movement to its ultimate success in 1917, he abandoned Russia's traditional calendar and installed May Day in order to be in step with the rest of Europe. Red flags and red-colored flowers (recall the roses in the epigraph) became the symbols of struggle, while plant growth provided the confidence for a hoped-for brighter future. The traditional parade became the centerpiece of May Day. Garlands and branches were replaced with a procession of products created by the hands of the industrial working class. The feminine symbol of fertility was recast in bare-breasted, garlanded Liberty carrying the banner of the plebeian worker and later the proletariat (our Statue of Liberty is a tidied-up version of this transformed icon of revolution).

Today America sets aside its first Monday in September to glorify the dignity of the worker. But everywhere else in the world organized labor gets its due on May Day, the once widely celebrated quarter-year post, famous for its festival of fire and new greenery. Paradoxical May Day, shared by both flower gatherers bringing in a new season and protesters who herald the coming of a new society, not only lives on but also its polarity has also been intensified. The World Anarchist Federation, a loose amalgam of forces formed to celebrate diverse struggles against capitalism, exploitation, and the destruction of the planet, declared May Day 2000 as an "International Day of Action Against Capitalism," with protest marches scheduled in cities all over the world. London's version of the event promised maypoles, mayhem and mass action. The "Battle for Seattle" protest that focused on antiglobalization wasn't the only venture that turned violent. May Day protesters and police also clashed in Krakow, Berlin, London, Karachi, Sydney, and Zurich as well as Minneapolis, Portland, and Phoenix in the United States. Once again on May 1, 2001, workers all over the world rioted and protested against globalization.

While all this was taking place, schoolchildren were celebrating a festival of happiness, joy, and the coming of summer with organized activities to spice up the curriculum—like reading Robin Hood stories, adorning trees in the schoolyard with scraps of yarn and colored paper, decorating shopping bags with May Day flowers and pinning them to the board, and taking home notes asking parents to contribute coins to be placed in the May Day wishing wells for donations to the poor. Meanwhile, conservative elements of the Roman Catholic Church instituted a take-back May Day movement featuring the Virgin Mary as an alternative to socialism: Ma(r)y's Day.

What once signaled the war between the seasons now focuses on a battle between social ideologies. If there is any connection between the May Day of old—a day on which people participated in ceremonies dedicated to stimulating the regeneration of life's processes—and modern May Day as a holiday that anticipates the rebirth of a better world community, maybe it has something to do with the idea that human action is a necessity in the reinvigoration of life's processes. If God acted in the first chapter of Genesis to make the world, why shouldn't we work to remake it?

Chapter 7

Summer's Solstice:
Feasts of Fire, Water, and
Feminine Affairs of the Heart

Today thousands of native people from across South America
converged on the ruins of Tiahuanaco to protest the injustice of
the European invasion of this part of the world.

> Dateline: *El Diario*, Potosi, Bolivia,
> June 21, 1998

From Paraguay, Argentina, Chile, Panama, Ecuador—from
all directions they came to reclaim their natural birthright, present their
flags, and honor their ancient ancestors at the site of the sacred temples
located on the outskirts of 12,000-foot-high La Paz, Bolivia, that they
had dedicated to the Earth-Mother Goddess a thousand years before the
Spaniards came to their shores.

The seasonal timing of this native rite of protest was conceived both
in history and in nature. Behind it lay the vision of a new reality, the
restoration of a multicultural, multinational, democratic state free of
oppression, segregation, and racism out of the neocolonial hodgepodge
that now stitches the South American continent together. This vision is
patterned after the last great unification that took place in the high Andes

over five hundred years ago in the time of the Inca, a mere fifty years before gold-thirsty Pizarro and his conquistadors landed on the coast of what is now Peru and quickly overran it.

Even if the old Spanish chroniclers and today's disenfranchised indigenists speak with the same tongue of its "Buen Gobierno" (good government), the Inca Empire was anything but democratic. Sole power was vested in the ruler and his offspring (the name Inca, like Tudor and Bourbon, was a family designation). Its history rested on the belief in a timed rebirth of the empire every five hundred years with the advent of a new Pachacuti, the name of their first (mythical) king. Ordained by their sun god Inti, who gave him ample justification for the conquest of the Chancas and other tribes up and down the valley of Cuzco, the ancient capital city, the Inca king would reenergize the entire empire.

The seasons conspire in the political drama that binds the native people of South America to the visible remains of their ancient ruins (just as it does with Yucatan's Maya at Chichén Itzá on the spring equinox). The day of the great 1998 convergence from all points of the compass was deliberately set to coincide with the June 21 festival of Inti Raymi, New Year's Day in the Inca calendar and a holiday dedicated to the newborn sun—the one they call Inti. Spanish chroniclers tell us that on this special day five-hundred years ago the Inca made a pilgrimage from the Valley of Cuzco up the Vilcanota River toward the northeast in the direction of the rising solstice sun. The route led to Lake Titicaca, where they say that both the sun and the Inca race were born. Contemporary Indian and Mestizo Bolivians, Panamanians, Ecuadorians, and Argentinians converge on the central square of Tiahuanaco to reignite the sacred fire their Quechua and Aymara ancestors once kindled. They call themselves "the new Inti" for they rise to proclaim their destined new beginning: "And the Inti who rises today brings with him the ascendance of a new civilization," say the disenfranchised claimants, for "nothing is eternal under the sun." New Year's Day 1998 was proclaimed a special "Pachacuti New Year," a new year that portended national reconquest and the return to a lost zenith.

Changes in the mood of nature never fail to kindle feelings in all sentient beings. The June solstice is a turning point—and what a grand turning point it is! The sun, having climbed ever higher in the noonday sky and having risen and set ever closer to the northern limit on its annual pendulum-like swing along the horizon, now slows its course to an imperceptible pace. It stands still, giving visual meaning to the word "solstice." (I have tried marking sunsets by sighting distant features on the horizon to see whether I could determine the exact day the turnaround actually takes place. I have yet to succeed.) Then, like a roller coaster at the peak of one of its summits, it begins ever so slowly to retrace its steps along the heavenly highway.

Pinpointing the sun's crucial turning point has preoccupied a number of ancient cultures. Some have even gone as far as incorporating the direction of the rising and setting solstice sun into the plans of their cities. No classic ancient Maya city was complete without a special sun observatory to mark the solstices. Maya lords converted the land- and cityscape into virtual sundials by erecting specialized architecture to demarcate the annual solar swing along the local horizon. For example, rulers of the ancient city of Uaxactun in northern Guatemala positioned a large pyramid on the west side of a perfectly north-south-east-west-oriented open plaza. At the east end of the plaza they built a low structure surmounted by three small temples. On the turnabout days, the sun would appear over the northern and southern temples in the triad; they would also mark the sun's arrival over the middle temple at the equinoxes. From a platform built into the large pyramid, a *hmeen*, or "daykeeper" (as the contemporary Maya still call the calendar specialist) would sit and sight the sun. They called him Kinich Ahau—literally Lord Sun-Day-Time all rolled into one. Over the years I have measured and carefully mapped architectural complexes like the one at Uaxactun at more than two dozen Maya ruins deep in the Yucatan peninsula's southern Petén rain forest. I can vouch that the ancient pan-Maya calendar housed in stone still works. Seasonal standard time ran uninterrupted even among warring city-states.

The Inca also paid strict attention to the sun's turnaround points. They converted the landscape around their highland capital into a natural, self-operating year clock powered by the movement of Inti himself. Their skilled stonemasons erected pillars to mark the course of the sun;

they placed a pair at each turning point to frame the position of the sun when it plunged below the distant high Andes' horizon. The June solstice pillars were perched on a hill north of the city known as Quiangalla. These two markers, writes a hemispherically biased Spanish chronicler, "they regarded as an indication to sunwatchers that when the sun reached there it was the beginning of summer." Official sunwatchers observed the event from an elaborately carved rock complex north of the city. It consisted of sculpted boulders, caves, building ruins, terraces, stairways, and a canalized stream. There the king is said to have spent his time celebrating the solstice rituals, while his subjects made offerings: " . . . and the sacrifice which was made there was directed to the sun, asking him to arrive there at the time which would be appropriate for planting, and they sacrificed to him sheep, clothing, and small miniature lambs of gold and silver." A similar sunwatcher's temple situated in the southern half of the city served as the backsight for marking the sun's entry in between a pair of December solstice pillars—a clever scheme because each half of the moiety (the dual kinship-based segments that made up the population of Cuzco) thus acquired a sense of responsibility for keeping track of the passage of time. Each segment of the citizenry would shepherd the sun through its own region of the empire, offering safe passage to Inti by tending to the observations and offering the prescribed sacrificial necessities that propelled him along on his course.

Far north of the tropics and eons backward in time, precise June solstice watching was a key item on the architectural agenda of the unnamed Bronze Age chieftain who oversaw the construction of Stonehenge in the south of England five millennia ago. Having studied it close up there is little doubt in my mind that Stonehenge was intended to be a sun temple from its very inception. It seems to have been arranged deliberately so that a viewer who stands in the center of the great stone ring could capture the rising sun's disk in the Heel Stone gateway to the northeast on June 21—the day the sun reached its northern standstill. Although the sun god they honored remains unknown to us, Stonehenge was surely built to celebrate his entry into the circular sanctuary at a very special time of year.

The Stonehenge tradition lives on. Because they regarded summer as the quarter of the year when the sun resides nearest its northerly extreme, the English, at least since the eighth century, have been calling June 21 "midsummer." Recalling that the old Celtic calendar marks the quarter segments of the year on the firsts of May, August, November, and February, we can also think of June 21 as more or less the halfway point between two seasonal markers, rather than the beginning of a season.

For us, architecture has a singular function: Joe's Garage is just a garage. We hardly think of it as a place where men gather on a Monday morning to rehash a weekend of football, though it does serve that function. A local church is considered only a place of worship, even if Bingo games are played in its basement on Friday nights. Likewise, Stonehenge was not erected solely for the purpose of gaining access to information from the sky and using the data to set up a calendar in the landscape. It was a multipurpose work of architecture that brought seminomadic people together at the right time to conduct religious rites, to see the sky gods in their places, to convene a market, to tell stories, to socialize. The great achievement of Stonehenge is that the genius of its inventors encapsulated all of these functions into a single monument.

Culture imitates nature. Like the old churchbell that calls to worshippers, the built-in timer keyed to the sun's turning points became an organic part of so much ancient architecture. Imagine how impressive the rites to the sun god would have appeared to viewers of a morning sun shining down the Stonehenge accessway on Britain's Salisbury Plain, framed by massive Inca pillars on a mountainside in the Peruvian Andes or perched in the doorway of a sculpture adorned Maya temple in Yucatan.

If you watch the sun wheel high across the sky on Midsummer's Day, you can well imagine why we might share the historic dictum that the ruler of the day and the conqueror of the night is now truly at the height of his strength. Daylight is longest and everything nurtured by it promises to blossom to its fullest. Summer solstice was the great turning point in China as well. In the Han dynasty lunar calendar the June solstice was clocked to the fifth day of the fifth month—they called it the "double fifth." They reckoned the day by the shortest noontime shadow cast by the gnomon of a sundial. Solstice rituals in China focus on the interchange of yin-yang forces, which feistily contend with one another at this critical time of year. They say that now the elements that make up life shift and move. And we must respond by desisting all human activity to await the return of the ethers to a more settled state. We relinquish our weapons; merchants do not travel; the government does not function; no fires are lit—lest yang will grow too powerful; no charcoal or metal are prepared; all wells are dredged so that their waters will be renewed, for water is to yin what fire is to yang—a stimulant.

When all living things finally function at peak, the yin ether has kicked in, bringing with it the watchful concern that if yang becomes too powerful all creatures might not continue to prosper. Now is the time for human action. To ward off destructive insects, string together your worst smelling vegetables—garlic, onion, cabbages. Peachwood strips with the appropriate words written on them nailed over your doorway will drive out pestilence from the home that originates in poisonous creatures that carry strong yin. Only then, after people sweep the house and purify themselves, can offerings of wheat and fish be made at the table of the ancestors. Like Christian and pre-Christian seasonal magic, to acquire efficacy the rites need to be carried out to the letter—no exceptions.

Far north in the land of the midnight sun the summer solstice brings even more drastic change. In polar regions, the sun's motion is strange: the great luminary corkscrews weirdly around in parallel daily circles, keeping his head above Arctic waters twenty-four-hours-a-day for several weeks—depending on how far north of the Arctic circle (66½° north latitude) you venture. The Iglulingmiut of Canada's Northwest Territories call it the "turning of the year." They say that when the sun achieves its high point during Egg Month (when they raid the nests of seafaring birds—late June to early July in our modern calendar), they gather formally to divide themselves into hunting and fishing groups. The Laborador Inuit make summer solstice a major ceremonial festival. This entry in a Moravian missionary's diary makes us painfully aware of the passionate disinterest of early visitors to America in the apparent richness (now largely lost) of native folkways:

The mark of time endures. A carved piece of bone from an eagle's wing, found in a cave in France's Dordogne Valley, has been dated by archaeologists to ca. 34,000 B.C. The markings, originally thought to have been made by someone sharpening a tool, were later interpreted to be a calendar based on the phases of the moon—the first evidence of a human record of celestial events. Each mark stands for a day; the turning points coincide with new and full phases of the moon. (A. Aveni, *Ancient Astronomers*. Washington, D.C., 1999, 23)

An eighteenth-century wooden calendar-ruler from Sweden. Pictorial symbols mark the holidays as well as the signs of the zodiac. (© Museum of the History of Science, University of Oxford; photograph by Gerald Howson)

DECEMBER hath 31 days. 1999

We've had some pleasant rambles,
And merry Christmas gambols,
And roses with our brambles,
Adieu, old year, adieu!
– George Lunt

D. M.	D. W.	Dates, Feasts, Fasts, Aspects, Tide Heights	Weather ↓
1	W.	Rosa Parks refused to give up her bus seat, Montgomery, Ala., 1955 • Tides {9.7 9.6 •	*Pack*
2	Th.	☾ on Eq. • ☌ ♇ ☉ • ☿ Gr. Elong (20° W.) • Maria Callas born, 1923 •	*the*
3	Fr.	☌ ♀ ☾ • First successful human heart transplant, 1967 • Tides {9.9 9.3	*malls*
4	Sa.	**First day of Chanukah** • 70° F, Boston, Mass., 1982 • Tides {10.0 9.3	*with*
5	**C**	**2nd S. in Advent** • ☌ ☿ ☾ • {10.2 9.3 •	*hours*
6	M.	**St. Nicholas** • First issue of *Ladies' Home Journal* published, 1883 •	*of*
7	Tu.	**St. Ambrose** • New ● • Pearl Harbor attacked, 1941 • {10.3 9.2	*folly.*
8	W.	☾ at apo. • Reagan and Gorbachev signed the INF treaty, 1987 • {10.3 9.2 •	*Get*
9	Th.	*If December be changeable and mild, the whole winter will remain a child.* • {10.2 — •	*ready*
10	Fr.	☾ runs low • First Nobel Prizes awarded, 1901 • Alfred Nobel died, 1896 • {9.1 10.1	*for*
11	Sa.	☾ at ☋ • ☌ ♆ ☾ • King Edward VIII abdicated, 1936 • {9.0 10.0 •	*a*
12	**C**	**3rd S. in Advent** • ☌ ♂ ☾ • ☌ ♅ ☾ •	*storm,*
13	M.	**St. Lucy** • The "Mona Lisa," missing for 2 years, was recovered and returned to The Louvre, 1913 •	*by*
14	Tu.	☌ ♂ ♅ • Halycon Days • Nostradamus born, 1503 • {8.8 9.4 •	*golly!*
15	W.	Ember Day • *Gone with the Wind* premiered at Loew's Grand Theatre in Atlanta, Ga., 1939 •	*Even*
16	Th.	*From error to error, one discovers the entire truth.* • Tides {9.2 9.2 •	*Santa*
17	Fr.	☾ on Eq. • Ember Day • William Lyon Mackenzie King born, 1874 •	*loses*
18	Sa.	☌ ♃ ☾ • Ember Day • Divorce became legal in Italy, 1970 •	*focus*
19	**C**	**4th S. in Advent** • ☌ ♄ ☾ • Tides {10.7 9.9 •	*in*
20	M.	Bus boycott ended, Montgomery, Ala., 1956 • Sacagawea died, 1812 • {11.3 10.2 •	*pre-*
21	Tu.	**St. Thomas** • ♃ stat. • Beware the Pogonip. •	*millennial*
22	W.	**Winter Solstice** • ☾ at perig. • **Full Long Nights** ○ • {12.3 10.7	*hocus*
23	Th.	☾ rides high • Bell Labs announced the invention of the transistor, 1947 •	*pocus.*
24	Fr.	☾ at ☊ • Kit Carson born, 1809 • Howard Hughes born, 1905 • {12.4 —	*Snow*
25	Sa.	**Christmas Day** • *Peace on Earth, Goodwill to men.* •	*descends*
26	**C**	**1st S. af. Ch.** • **Boxing Day (Canada)** • Tides {10.5 11.5	*as the*
27	M.	**St. John** • **St. Stephen** • Marlene Dietrich born, 1901 •	*century*
28	Tu.	**Holy Innocents** • William Semple patented chewing gum, 1869 • {10.0 10.2	*ends:*
29	W.	☾ on Eq. • Massacre at Wounded Knee, S.D., 1890 • Tides {9.8 9.6 •	*Ready!*
30	Th.	First color TV sets on sale, 1953 • Simon Guggenheim born, 1867 • {9.6 9.1 •	*Set!*
31	Fr.	*Fill your life with experiences, not excuses.* • {9.5 8.8 •	*Oh-oh-oh!*

Farmer's Calendar

If you want to know what the future has in store in any field, you ask those especially concerned. Is your interest sports? Ask a player. Is it loan rates? Ask a banker. Is it elections? Ask someone who has to run for office. Skip the experts and find a witness whose own life will be affected by the course of events you're inquiring about; find someone on the ground, so to speak.

This principle, no more than common sense, is part of the reason people hang stubbornly onto folk weather lore in a scientific age in which that lore ought to be obsolete. Most of us, no doubt, get our weather forecasts from TV and radio — that is, from broadcasters who pass on the conclusions of meteorologists. We have confidence in these scientific forecasts for the best possible reason: We have found them to be generally accurate. Nevertheless, the prescientific indicators of weather — the acorns, groundhogs, woolly bear caterpillars, and so on — are not forgotten. Though they survive mainly as humor, they do survive.

Why don't we let the old weather signs go, at last, and put all our faith in meteorology? Because meteorology isn't on the ground. Those likable, attractive people on the TV, even the scientists whose findings they report, aren't concerned with the weather the way a deer mouse, say, is. If the former get it wrong, they may have to find a job in Sioux Falls. But for them, that's the worst thing that happens. The deer mouse has a different stake. If he underestimates the winter to come and fails to provide in his nest, he starves.

This page from a contemporary Farmer's Almanac retains the old habit of highlighting Sundays and capitalizing holidays, such as Christmas (The so-called "Dominical Letter" for 1999 was C, the third letter of the alphabet, because the first Sunday of that year fell on the third of January). Modern secular calendars tend to label all days the same way. (*The Old Farmers Almanac 1999* by Robert B. Thomas. Dublin, N.H., 63)

Janus, the two-headed Roman god, who was a familiar figure on coins of that era, was still presiding over the New Year's feast in fifteenth-century England. This is the illustration that heads the month of January in the Fastolf Hours, 1440–50. (Bodleian Library, University of Oxford, MS Auct. D. inf. 2 II, fol. 1ʳ)

A similar Janus-like figure, featuring back-to-back Chaacs or raingods, occurs in this calendar in the Dresden Codex, a Pre-Columbian Maya document. They are positioned at the spring equinox, the end of the dry season, when worshippers heralded the coming of the rain and a new planting season.

You old henpicked wretch, you are quite a disgrace,
Let your wife mind the baby and keep her own place.
Be more of a man, dont allow her to roam,
Make her leave off the breeches and keep her at home.

Insult Valentines such as this one were popular in the mid-nineteenth century, "You old Henpicked Wretch," ca. 1850. (Norcross Collection, Smithsonian Institution Archives)

The anticipation of Spring is a great time to turn over a new leaf. "Groundhog Day," the movie, starring Bill Murray, offers a modern parable on how to break out of the rigors of cyclic time by acquiring a better attitude toward humankind. (© 1993 Columbia Pictures Industries, Inc. All Rights Reserved Courtesy of Columbia Pictures)

A rite of Spring or a figment of the contemporary imagination? Forty thousand people cram the open plaza fronting the Castillo in the Maya ruins of Chichén Itzá to watch the light and shadow serpent descend on March 20. (Photograph by E. C. Krupp; Griffith Observatory, Los Angeles)

A cartoon spoof of the great hierophany. (Drawing by Robin Rector Krupp)

The ubiquitous Easter bunny in the Moon. (Drawing by Peter Dunham)

Moon rabbit in East Indian folklore. (J. Collin de Plancy, *Dictionnaire Infernal*. Paris, 1863)

Rabbit in the moon in stylized iconographic representations in ancient Maya art (Linda Schele, "Palenque, the House of the Dying Sun," in A. Aveni [ed.] *Native American Astronomy*. Austin, Texas, 1997, 55)

May Day was once celebrated in Medieval Great Britain with the gathering of flowers, the crowning of the May Queen, and a march around the Maypole. The custom survives in America: "Maypoles in Motion on Bascom Hill, Wisconsin," ca. 1917. (University of Wisconsin Archives)

In the eighteenth- and early nineteenth-century Romantic period, the bare-breasted female emerged as a revolutionary May Day icon. In Delacroix's celebrated painting *Liberty Leading the People* (Musée du Louvre, Paris), she represents Liberty who points toward the desired utopian society of the future.

Labor Day, 1908 in Chicago finds meat cutters from the stockyards joining the parade of garment workers, tin cutters, and other union laborers. Their red, white, and blue garb signals the patriotic nature of this summer-ending holiday, which stands in marked contrast with the more anti-establishment May Day at its beginning. (Chicago Historical Society, negative no. DN-53253)

Decorations throw a party at the Louisiana home of William Joyce, a children's book author.

The role of the dead in today's version of Halloween isn't taken quite as seriously as it was in ancient and medieval times. This decorated Louisiana home belongs to children's book author William Joyce. (Philip Gould/Corbis)

Mexican-American Day of the Dead celebrations feature an altar decorated with photographs of the ancestors. This one from Ventura, California (1996) sports a saint's candle and a skeleton bottle. (Photograph by Juan Carlo; courtesy of the *Ventura County Star*)

"Home for Thanksgiving" (1945) by Norman Rockwell, the epitome of
Rockwell's many portrayals of the values of hearth and home that attend
each season. (By permission of the Norman Rockwell Family Agency;
© 1945 the Norman Rockwell Family Entities)

A Christmas tonic for the Depression Era. Of all the popular portrayals there was perhaps no better vocal Scrooge than actor Lionel Barrymore. (An advertisement in the *Saturday Evening Post*, December 28, 1935, 25)

Christmas consumption. Long before he arrived in the mall, Santa made his appearance in nineteenth-century department stores, a handy location for the parental procurement of his promised favors. (An F.A.O. Schwarz advertisement, 1881; Smithsonian Institution Archives)

Coca Cola Santa in *National Geographic Magazine*, 1955.
(Courtesy Coca-Cola Bottling Co.)

A

B

C

Unlikely greeting cards revivify ancient holidays keyed to the sun's seasonal course: A. Midsummer's Day (June 21); B. *Imbolc* (February 1); C. *Lammas* (August 1). (Artist: Janet Moses)

This afternoon the Eskimos began their heathen Diversions or ceremonies. They began two or three evenings ago during a couple of hours but as the weather had not been favourable they could not go on. But today as the weather was clear they continued their Diversions for seven hours without ceasing. The Diversions had their purposes and mysteries which are too tedious to mention.

A midsummer sun promises grain growing, cicadas chirping in the fiery heat cooled by thunder, refreshing vacations beside cool waters—leisure time. Even if he places blame on the stars for his seasonally diminished masculinity, the eighth-century B.C. Greek poet Hesiod captures the midsummer mood, signaled by nature's behavior:

> But when you see the scolymus flowering and hear the cicada sing in the
>   tree, sending its beautiful, vibrating song
> pulsing from under its wings in the season of scorching-hot summer,
> then you will find that she-goats are fattest, wine most delicious,
> women most desirous of love but men most enfeebled,
> for now the dogstar Sirios parches their heads and their knees,
> and in the heat their skin becomes dry.

And how should we respond to nature in this season?

> Then would I have a shady retreat in the cool of the rocks,
> and Bibline wine with milk-leavened bread and milk of goats that are
>   starting to go dry,
> and meat of cow that has fed in the woods, one never in calf, and
> that of the newborn kid. And then would I drink of the red wine,
> as I relax in the shade, my appetite sated completely,
> turning my face to enjoy the cooling breezes of Zephyros,
> and would pour from a clear and ever free-flowing stream
> three parts of water to mix for my drink with one part of wine.

Good advice—except for diluting the wine.

Greeks of the later Classical Age would be horrified at what most of us think leisure implies—a far cry from what Aristotle wrote of it in *The Politics*: "As peace is the final end of war, so too is leisure the final end of occupation." The Greek philosopher thought of leisure as the highest form of action, a time when we engage in activity for its own sake, not the amusement, recreation, or play that we usually associate with rest after a long period of occupation—summer vacation. A modern American version of Aristotle's Academy of Leisure Sciences (c. 386 B.C.) has been reinvisioned by a group of former presidents of the Society of Parks and Recreation educators. In 1928, they elected eighty candidate members whose "exceptional scholarly and intellectual contributions" supported the study of leisure and proposed a charter that called for a return to "advancing the intellectual understanding of leisure."

Fire ruled solstice day in much of the world. People moved it around, jumped over it, and gazed through it. Midsummer night bonfires could be seen dotting the Irish countryside well into the nineteenth century, a remnant of the old Celtic fires that opened the summer season. Medieval pagans rolled a flaming wooden wheel downhill into a river—not only graphically imitating the sun's high passage across the firmament, but also stimulating the great luminary to complete a successful passage on its downward course. In the Moselle Valley of sixteenth-century Germany, the men in charge of the fire would pass the morning collecting a bit of straw from each household. They would spend the afternoon using it to decorate a huge wooden wheel to mock the shape of the sun. It had a hip-high axis extending three feet out on each side, which served as a handle to move the symbolic sun on its course. At dusk the mayor of the town would give the signal to light the wheel. A shout would go up as two young men, accompanied by just about every other male in the burg, began to run the wheel down the hill to the river, each with a flaming torch in hand. Getting the fiery wheel through the vineyards on the slope of the hill to its aqueous destination was no mean task.

Magic followed in the wake of the fiery sun wheel's course. If, as it descended along the symbolic path toward autumn, it remained lighted all the way down the slope, a bountiful fall harvest was portended; if it went out: bad luck. Neither haste nor waste characterized all the activity surrounding the great solstitial conflagration. In the aftermath young men removed the hot char and reassembled the pieces in the village to prepare for divining omens from the sun now set. They would strip to the waist and run forward and backward—the way the sun oscillates across the seasons—through the glowing embers several times. Whoever did it the greatest number of times without getting singed was declared the victor over the powers of evil.

As in all male-dominated sports, young women would do the same, but only after the fire had died down a bit more. At stake for them were prognostications about the number of children they would bear. In some areas young couples leaped the fire hand in hand. As high as they leap, so will their crops grow. And, if they can accomplish the feat scorch-free, they will not get a backache at reaping time. To culminate a successful courtship nascent couples look at each other across the fire through straw wreaths or bunches of larkspur. Then, reminiscent of a ritual still practiced at most wedding receptions, the girl throws the wreath across the fire, hoping that the object of her affection will catch it.

Other fire jumpers included married women and young cattle. Herdsmen drove cows through the hot ashes with lighted hazel twigs, which were kept and later used as instruments of power on cattle drives (shoots and twigs of hazel are still widely believed by many to have the power to indicate the presence of water, which is why they are frequently employed as dowsing rods). When all the accompanying songs, dance, and general merrymaking were done with, everyone would dip a pine stick into the remains of the conflagration and carry a bit of the new solstice fire that they had helped to ignite with their contributions of straw back home to reignite the hearth to certify continued good luck.

To nurture and protect their crops, farmers generally kindled the solstice fire near their own fields, then walked the periphery of the flames holding lighted torches—or along the riverside where cattle could be driven through to protect them from witches who craved their milk. Ashes from midsummer's fires were then tossed on the crop to make produce abundant.

Sympathetic magic abounds on the solstice. Cut an ash tree on midsummer morning and place chips of it in your pocket to harmonize with nature and protect yourself against disease. If your herd is diseased, sacrifice a cow to the midsummer bonfire to protect the rest of the herd. Wear coal dug up beneath mugwort on the eve to protect from fever and acne.

If we look at the European summer solstice rites more closely, they turn out to have more to do with the affairs of women than men, for crop fertility and human fertility verge upon one another to assure good luck in their future together. June is wedding month for a good reason. The door is open. Nature's beneficent signals come through loud and clear as summer solstice becomes an ideal time to enter into dialog with her to learn her secrets of fertility. I find it interesting that holidays honoring family all fall in the season leading up to the solstice. Mother's Day (the second Sunday in May, begun in 1907) and Father's Day (the third Sunday in June, begun in 1910) culminate on the solstice (in fact, the latest possible Father's Day falls exactly on the solstice). The now defunct Children's Day, dedicated to the product of their union, lay close by.

Echoing from a time when getting a man was a major priority and preoccupation, feminine love magic culminates during the solstice season. It is aimed exclusively at proliferating the species. In seventeenth-century England, young women set out pots of orpine or sedum (also called the midsummer man plant) in pairs. Whether the herbs inclined toward or away from one another was supposed to indicate love or aversion in response from a sweetheart. Specialists in plant divination would lay out several pairs on the eve of June 21, each representing a couple/client. Next morning the pairs that kept together betokened a happy marriage while those that fell apart implied unfulfilled love affairs.

Sisters would place pieces of "dumb cake" under their pillows to determine the future love of their life by dream selection. The recipe for these "dreaming bannocks": 1 cup flour, 1 cup salt, water to thicken (some added a sprinkle of soot). Before ladeling them onto the griddle, carve your initials in one sector. Let everybody take a turn flipping them while they cook, adding a sprinkle of salt with each inversion. These unpalatable treats are called "dumb cakes" not because of the sound of the recipe, but because of the most important of all its rules: not a word must be spoken during the entire process.

Midsummer Night's Dream-induced visions for the lovelorn female can be enhanced by placing your shoes in the form of a T next to your bed and reciting:

I place my shoes like a letter T,
in hopes my true love I shall see,
in his apparel and his array,
as he is now and every day.

As in many magical rites, reversal and repetition are vital: next you switch the positions of the shoes and repeat the lines, then reverse and repeat yet again. Say anything else during the process and you break the charm. Once you've hooked him, you next discern his livelihood. So break an egg into a bowl of water at high noon just at the spot where the sun's zenithal image is reflected. The fantastic shapes of the flowing whites will indicate the profession of your destined paramour (the rigging of a ship: a sailor; the form of a desk: a school teacher; a book: a parson). With a bit more effort, you can do the same by pouring molten lead through the hole of a door key—this offers a permanent fix. But be sure to wear the lead ball in your shoe the day before you smelt it.

Check the old Roman calendar just after the Ides of June and you will find the undoubted source of much of the retentive power of the medieval folklore practiced from Spain to Siberia that I have just described. Rome's celebration of the solstice renders our twelve days of Christmas a brief time-out. It commenced with the *Vestalia*, the polar opposite, calendrically speaking, to the December *Saturnalia* (see Chapter 11). On this day, the vestal virgins officially opened the terrestrial storeroom to the abundance of consumables that came with the season. Likewise they stood guard at the central larder of the traditional Roman house and ceremonially swung open the gates so that women of the house could bring offerings to the temple of Vesta. She is forever guarded by virgins for, as the only unmarried daughter of Saturn, her sacred things are allowed contact only with chaste hands. She is as pure as the eternal flame that burns in her temple. "Vesta is the same as the Earth," writes the Roman historian, Ovid, "under both of them is a perpetual fire; the earth and the hearth are symbols of the home. . . . Conceive of Vesta as naught but the living flame."

Next in the Roman solstice season came the festival to Mater Matuta, another form of the feminine goddess—this time she is the goddess of dawn. To her, married women offer foods cooked in earthenware vessels. The feast honoring the sun's entry into the constellation of Cancer follows. It is dedicated to Jupiter Fulgur, hurler of lightning bolts. He represents the highest place or supreme dawn, the bright light that encroaches relentlessly on the darkness at the time of the summer solstice.

Now Roman bakers busied themselves, filling their ovens with the round-shaped cakes that honored Fortuna, another goddess of dawn (and luck). Rome dedicated several oracles to her—special sites with divine inhabitants delegated to resolve the uncertainties (or "fors") that beset human life at every turn. It is said that a wheel on Caesar's chariot fell apart just outside the doorway of Fortuna's temple bringing (in this case) bad luck—whence our wheel of fortune that turns like the sun. Water played a major part in the celebrations as young revelers tippled their way up the Tiber in flower-bedecked boats to celebrate the rites of the maternal cult in her temple.

Religions survive best that adapt to the old customs of the convert—by taking sympathetically to them and giving them renewed meaning. Historians call this largely unplanned process religious syncretism. Early Christianity acquired much of its success from making over the Greek planetary gods of antiquity, transforming them into symbols of Christian morality. Take Venus, the voluptuous image of fertility derived from the ancient Babylonian Ishtar, whose ethereal side is represented by the evening star that hovers over the setting sun, while her carnal flip side reveals itself in the love goddess's fiery morning star aspect. Renaissance thinkers recast this duplicitous celestial Venus to express their rather complex theory of love: one side of her is contemplative, divine, and immaterial—the sort of love we still call platonic and to which only prophets and saints can aspire. The other Venus is tangible and terrestrial; she tempts the male imagination through visual, then tactile sensation—all the way to debauchery if she is not controlled. Christian thinkers took advantage of this ideology and turned paintings and poetry depicting the old pagan deity into platforms for expounding on the sins of temptation and the battle between good and evil.

Assigning the summer solstice, exactly six months away in the seasonal calendar from the birth of the Savior, to fete St. John the Baptist, is another brilliant example of religious syncretism. Baptism is the principal rite of admission into the Christian Church. It offers both the washing away of sins and a rebirth, and it grew out of an older Jewish practice. Who better to incorporate the idea of purification once associated with cleansing by fire to bathing at sunrise than he who consecrated the rite of purification upon Christ himself.

With that delicate stroke, midsummer, a pause in the breath of the seasons when the sun makes its seasonal turnabout, became a festival of water as well as fire—a time when the quenching power of springs and holy water took on medieval virtue as sick people fled to the baths to heal their maladies. Wash yourself in three wells on the eve of St. John and your dreams will reveal all who are to die in the coming year, goes an old Austrian saying. Say the Irish: your soul can leave your body on St. John's Eve and wander to the spot where body and soul will ulti-mately experience earthly parting.

The magic of midsummer lingered on despite its Christian step-mother. St. John became the protector against witches. And anyone who carries St. John's wort is guaranteed that the devil will not approach within nine paces. It "mightly drives away all phantastical spirits and helps melancholy," according to a seventeenth-century anatomy text. Three nails made on St. John's Eve deeply driven on the spot where a person was stricken with falling sickness (epilepsy) will drive the disease away forever. Today this popular herbal enjoys a resurrection of its own as a remedy against depression (despite health officials' recent claims to the contrary).

Anthropologists still debate the meaning behind the old solstice holiday fires. For some the word "bonfire" denotes a fire fueled by bones. Others argue that the root word is boon-fire, which connotes a gift (neighborly goodwill) or a blessing from nature at a most auspi-cious time. Or is it a *baun* (beacon) fire or perhaps a *bane* fire for ban-ishing all things evil? The wondrous paradox of fire is that on the one hand its warmth creates and fosters growth and fertility, but on the other hand it possesses a fierce destructive power capable of consuming all living things—not a thing to play with. Like the radiant sun at its turn-ing point, fire has a tantalizing power worth harnessing and controlling. To judge from the samples from folklore mentioned earlier, the idea of good vibrations and blessings from nature weigh heavily. Because fire cleanses and purifies by burning up harmful influence, so we tap into its

forces precisely during the season the cosmic fire rages at its peak—
when the accompanying violent weather or blight hold the greatest potential to destroy crop or cattle, and when insect-borne disease can decimate
those who tend to them.

The powerful dualism of sun/fire lives on in us. The greatest of all
fires in our universe awes us just as much now as it did then. We still
speak in one breath of the nuclear forces buried deep in the sun (the
equivalent of one hundred billion megaton bombs detonated every heartbeat at a distance just eight minutes away by light beam) and in the next
breath of the quiet, clean, pure source of energy we might attain from
the great cosmic bonfire if we could only harness it. Our solar paneled
roofs are but a distant echo of the ritual of the rolling wheel of fire—a
lasting sign of respect and wonder at the paramount lifegiving source to
our planet.

We no longer build bonfires, roll fire wheels, nor envision fairies
and witches on June 21. My hometown of New Haven, Connecticut, fixes
its International Festival of the Arts, and Hamilton, New York, the town
where I now live, celebrates its Chenango Valley Music Fest on the solstice. The many communal markets-on-the-green and arts and crafts
fairs held circa the third weekend in June are a far cry from their forebears. Our inherited puritanical mind-set, traceable all the way back to
Oliver Cromwell's England, is as responsible as anything else for dous-
ing the fires and purging the pagan rites from the summer calendar.
Except for Hesiod's optimistic advice on the best way to spend a summer day, contemporary summertime ritual is remarkably free of communal holidays that even remotely resemble those our ancestors once
vigorously celebrated. The days we mark in the seasonal quarter that
follows the Christmas to Easter crescendo are all civic and patriotic in
nature: Memorial Day, Flag Day, Independence Day—not a one of them
has roots that tap very deeply into old tradition.

The Fourth of July has become America's solstice. Less attentive to
patriotic sentiments, except for the waving flag on the front porch, its
grand picnics and dazzling fireworks signify the full-blown arrival of
vacation time—a two-month season of leisure. Far less contemplative

than its Greek counterpart, our leisure consists of vigorous activity: outdoor sports and games, camping, boating, swimming, hiking, climbing. Even though the document that gives rise to this major American holiday was drafted two weeks after the June solstice of 1776, I had always wondered why the signers of our Declaration of Independence failed to seize on the connection between the official recognition of the blossoming of their new nation, conceived in liberty, and the arrival of the great luminary at its culminating point in the sky—the perfect celestial metaphor gone aglimmering. Or did they? Perhaps such a connection was deeply embedded in the brain of a Hancock, Adams, or Jefferson better in tune with the environment than we.

Solstice time is still heavily charged with the politics of the disenfranchised. Juneteenth (June 19) has been proposed as a national day of reconciliation from the legacy of slavery. It marks the anniversary of the day the last slaves learned they would be freed. Hands Across America, Live Aid, and the Cosmic Convergence in the 1980s, the Million Man March and the Mother's March for Gun Control in the 1990s, and the precisely orchestrated indigenous solstice marches that took place in five South American countries in 1998—they all happened in the same season. The practical half of my mind tells me that outdoor mass action against the forces of the establishment has a better chance of success if you conduct it in a suitably warm climate; but my less rational, more imaginative cerebral sector causes me to wonder whether such activity might not be conditioned more by a longing to return, like the sun, to a lost zenith—to a preferred (even if somewhat romanticized) communal way of life. Sadly, all that remains of the old midsummer rites—ceremonies of conjugal union, pilgrimages to ancient archaeological sites like Stonehenge and Tiahuanaco, and maybe even the fire in our Fourth of July fireworks—is a distant reflection of activities that once stood front and center on the day we all helped the sun to turn around.

Chapter 8

Labor Day:
Remembering the
Great Time Wars

I hear America singing, the varied carols I hear,
Those of mechanics, each one singing his as it should be blithe and strong,
The carpenter singing his as he measures his plank or beam,
The boatman singing what belongs to him in his boat, the deckhand singing
    on the steamboat deck,
The shoemaker singing as he sits on his bench, the hatter singing as he
    stands,
The wood-cutter's song, the plowboy's on his way in the morning, or at noon
    intermission or at sundown,
The delicious singing of the mother, or of the young wife at work, or of the
    girl sewing or washing,
Each singing what belongs to him or her and to none else,
The day what belongs to the day—at night the party of young fellows,
    robust, friendly,
Singing with open mouths their strong melodious songs.

                                     Walt Whitman

Nobody appreciates a support staff more than I—especially on Labor Day, the most vivid annual reminder to me of just how
much my job depends on my fellow workers. Labor Day is usually the
first week, sometimes the first *day* of classes at Colgate University, where

I teach; but because it is a national holiday, the support staff (though, for reasons that make sense only in the world of academia, *not* faculty and students) are given the day off. Year after year I dutifully show up on Labor Day morn to a pile of unsorted mail, unerased blackboards, unswept floors, and a men's room devoid of basic necessities, to teach my two Monday classes. Oh, how I miss my secretary and all those unheralded, underpaid keepers of old Lathrop Hall in whose company I pass most of my daylight hours! Labor Day's message to me is this: nobody makes it in the workaday world on his or her own. We all live in a society where we depend on one another perhaps more than we would like to admit. Our accomplishments are the result of a team effort. I learn this lesson by living it.

America's summer ends on Labor Day, three weeks before the autumn equinox, just as it begins on Memorial Day three weeks before the June solstice (or May Day in most of the rest of the Western world). Leisure done with as August draws to a close, we all look forward (usually with dread if we're schoolkids) to the week that follows—a time band headed by a day that has come to symbolize putting away our playthings and getting back to work. As a kid I remember asking myself: if fall doesn't begin until September 23, then what am I doing back in school when I should still be on summer vacation?

If Independence Day masquerades as our summer solstice, then Labor Day surely is our equinoctial "New Year." It signals the start of an anxious season, a short in-between time that is neither summer nor fall, but shares aspects of each. Labor Day is a conflict of interests. Nights are sharply cool and shorter days are warm. Fall colors betwixt green and brown are present for barely enough time to recognize them. The yet-to-reopen and the overripe dangle side by side on the vine. A host of new things we haven't seen for awhile intrude on us—thick fall fashion catalogs, long-sleeved shirts, new shows and exhibits.

Labor Day on the interstate means a parade of cars stuffed with weekend campers out for a last fling. It is a day when we think about closing up the summer place, watersealing the deck, and pulling in the lawn furniture. On Labor Day we charge up—for the final run in political campaigning, for the beginning of the football season and the beginning of the end of the baseball season—the "September stretch" that will culminate in the World Series.

I spend my summer "vacation" writing (Aristotle would approve), but Labor Day returns me to my regular job of teaching. I know that once I get into it, as I have at this season of the year on some forty previous occasions, I will once again revel in the classroom interaction with bright young minds that characterizes my work (is it fair to call it "work" when you're passionately in love with it?) in one of America's finest liberal arts colleges. Why, then, do I resist the thought of starting the cycle all over? Surely it isn't the discipline required to schedule and conduct classes. The rigor of the temporal bounds I attach to my own commitments to writing is an order of magnitude greater than what I confront in the academy.

I have thought a lot about this anxious period in my life and I think I have diagnosed my own case of Labor Day blues. It is a cousin of the temporal malaise related to the eve of New Year, or to any Sunday night in the week cycle—the problem of reinstituting beginnings, the difficulty of first footing. The problem with Labor Day is that I am forced, not of my own volition, to stop doing what I am doing and begin to do something else. Change structured by the outer world of the calendar is the culprit. Like moving from a wonderful main course to a fabulous dessert: I love both, but I don't like the waiter dictating when the time has come to move from one to the other.

Exclusively American, Labor Day emerges as an optimistic holiday (especially when the economy is booming), more in the spirit of Walt Whitman's "I Hear America Singing" (this chapter's epigraph) than Louis Untermeyer's "Caliban" (Chapter 6). On the surface less like May Day, which focuses primarily on worker solidarity, Labor Day has come to have more to do with celebrating labor's contribution. It reflects the dynamic character of our society by expressing confidence over the way diverse segments of America's commerce-oriented culture come together. Yet this holiday recognizes that the shoulders of our middle-class working men and women support the success of our economic system. These people deserve a day off after Sunday—with pay. As George Bernard

Shaw put it, "A day's work is a day's work, neither more nor less, and the man who does it needs a day's sustenance, a night's repose, and due leisure, whether he be painter or plowman."

The nation's first Labor Day was celebrated with a New York City parade sponsored by the Central Labor Union. The date was September 5, 1882, and the intention in choosing it had little to do with officially recognizing the end of the summer season. Peter McGuire, dynamic head of the United Brotherhood of Carpenters and an early architect of the eight-hour workday, delivered a fiery speech directed against the indignity accorded labor by the wealthy class. He pointed out that if we have days assigned to honor religious, military, and civic spirit, why not the industrial spirit—the vital force of the nation. He claims to have chosen the date because it filled a gap in our legal holidays, falling about halfway between the Fourth of July and Thanksgiving. Besides, this was "a most pleasant season of the year . . . to observe a festive day during which a parade through the streets of the city would permit public tribute to American industry."

Defying authority, ten thousand men left their jobs and paraded up Manhattan's Fifth Avenue from 14th to 42nd Street, ending the day with a picnic, a dance, and fireworks. The event was a big hit and celebrants repeated it again—and again and again. Five years later in 1887, Oregon became the first state to formally establish Labor Day: it was followed shortly by the District of Columbia. Thirty additional states quickly joined officialdom, and in 1894 Congress finally adopted Labor Day as a national holiday to celebrate the "joint partnership of capital and labor." Churches joined in the celebration in 1905 when the Presbyterians officially decreed the day before Labor Day as Labor Sunday.

But beneath the veneer of proudly parading workers celebrating a successful bond between labor and capitalism lies a turbulent history of Labor Day, one more equally suited to May Day, its matching bookend of travail situated at the front end of the summer of leisure. Remember Count Rumford's eighteenth-century utopian workers' community in Bavaria? It wasn't so different from the town of Pullman, Illinois, population 8,600 a year after its (1882) founding by railroad sleeping car magnate George Pullman. Like Rumford, Pullman took care of his people assiduously. The town's wide and handsome paved streets, named after great pioneers of industry such as Watt, Morse, and Bessemer, were bordered by townhouses and flats rented by the workers—with gas, water, indoor plumbing, sewage, and trash removal service. Market Hall near the town center served as the antecedent of the modern shopping mall. There was one bank (the Pullman Bank) one hotel (the Florence, named after Pullman's daughter), and one bar—all of it company owned and miles away from the disturbing moral and political elements in Chicago.

Pullman oversaw his subjects from his lofty place of business—a posh penthouse residence in the Florence that towered above the utopian workers' community. All the residents worked for his company, drew their paychecks from his bank, and had their rent automatically deducted. Nobody complained about the social confinements of this sort of paternalism until the 1893 depression, when the aristocratic overseer of the model town was forced to cut wages and lay off workers because of diminished orders. Railroad workers struck, pillaging Pullman cars and forcing President Grover Cleveland to send in federal troops to break the strike. The trying times of the struggle between exploited workers and their bosses that took place in the last two decades of the nineteenth century create a backdrop for the story behind why we celebrate Labor Day.

Labor Day's deeper roots emanate from the age-old struggle over the ownership of time—a battlefield we visited in Chapter 4 when we dealt with the question of claimants to history and the archaeological remains that give testimony to it. The story of who owns time as a *commodity* goes back to what I call the great medieval time wars, out of which emerged the first significant European clash between labor and management. The time wars pivot around the dawn of a great revolution in technology, particularly the invention and widespread use of the mechanical clock.

The flux of social change was truly enormous: there were upheavals in religion, in urban development, and in the very basic business of doing business. (Business derives from *busy* [German: *besich*], which means "to be engaged in something requiring time"; in other words, the opposite of *idle*, or having no activity in time.) God, the city, and commerce— in all three of these spheres human needs would encourage the establishment of the standards of time that ultimately led to the conflict between labor and management.

The revolution that defined this era involved neither a war nor an invasion, not even a new ideology. It was more a revolution in mentality. In a relatively brief span of years around 1300, virtually everything in the Western world became almost magically transformed into an essence to which a number could be assigned—a sea change in the very perception of reality. The quantitative revolution, to use historian Alfred Crosby's term, saw the first *portolano* marine charts (which allowed navigators to lay compass courses) and the invention of perspective painting to quantify geometrical space on a canvas. It also ushered in double-entry bookkeeping to quantify the economy, and polyphonic music to precisely mete out harmonious sound. Monetary standards, weights and measures—all were unleashed on the urbanized peasant turned commercialized citizen seven turns of the century ago. From that beginning point, Crosby argues that Western Europeans suddenly evolved a new, more visual and quantitative way of perceiving time, space, and material environment. The new way included the hourly wage and it gave our forebears their first taste of modern time consciousness.

At that seminal turn of that century, out of economic necessity, the hour was snatched from nature and confined to the hidden gear work behind the façade of a weight-driven machine. It happened between 1277 and 1340, as far as historians can document it. There had been timekeeping mechanisms of various kinds before—banded candles, sand hourglasses, water clocks powered by dripping liquid—but they were all too inaccurate or unwieldy for general use. Some unknown tinkerer's invention of the *escapement*, a mechanical device for regulating the uniform descent of a weight, suddenly enabled Europeans to make relatively reliable mechanical clocks. Time's dominion expanded. London got its first public mechanical clock in 1292, Paris in 1300, Padua in 1344. These public timepieces were not merely useful devices, but also symbols of civic status and progress. The Paduan clock, which included brass and bronze disks that pointed to the hours, the months of the year, and the signs of the zodiac, was renowned throughout Europe. It took sixteen years to build.

The historian and social critic Lewis Mumford has called the mechanical clock the world's single greatest invention. It was the machine that would objectively grind out a new temporal reality couched in a network of numbers. Mumford wrote that the clock disassociated time from human events. "[I]t synchronized human reactions, not with the rising and setting sun, but with the indicated movements of the clock's hands," thus helping to create the belief in an independent world of mathematically measured sequences: the special world of science. Ultimately, the escapement would entrap us.

I find particular irony in the historical fact that all the angst over the common sense of time was seeded neither in the marketplace nor in the hallowed halls of precise science. Rather, it was a child of the sixth-century Christian monastery. Many religions of the world call for regular times of prayer. Islam specifies five: sunrise, noon, sunset, evening twilight, and after dusk, while the Jew prays after daybreak, before sunset, and again after dark. Only in the Christian monastery were the times set by the hours—by the rule of an organized clergy whose duty it became to codify the schedule for prayer. Around A.D. 530, the rule of Saint Benedict specified when to "recite the hours": the Lauds, the prime, the terce, the sext, the none, the vespers, and the compline in the waking hours, and two more at night—the vigils and the matins. If we all pray to God together, the better will He hear our plea.

The precise measurement of time thus became a major concern as Christianity spread throughout Europe after the fall of Rome. But who would "stand watch" in the middle of the night to keep the observance of devotions on schedule? Who would keep the vigil? The clicking gear work of the verge-and-foliot escapement would ultimately become the sole sentry all supplicants could depend on.

The first mechanical clocks were little more than gravity-driven bells. They had neither friendly faces nor gesturing hands. In fact, the word *clock* derives from the French word *cloche*, or bell, a device to which the ears, not the eyes, were meant to respond. Remember Frère Jacques, the delinquent monk who slept through his matins? This temporally harassed figure in a children's song was one of the first people to feel the tyranny of the automatic alarm.

It happens that the mechanical clock arrived just as another unrelated development was sharply focusing the European mind on the fleeting nature of time. The Black Plague quickly spread northward from its introduction in 1347 by flea-bearing rats entering from the Levant at the port of Messina, Sicily. In three years, the pox decimated much of the continent (the Scandinavian countries and parts of northeastern Europe were spared), wiping out more than a third of the population. Be diligent in your prayer and in your daily acts, came the word from the pulpit. Watch the clock carefully: you could be experiencing your last hour! To avoid eternal death, one needed to prepare ever more diligently for salvation. Time flies! "It is sad that you do not employ your time better, when you may win eternal life hereafter," lamented a fifteenth-century preacher.

If the monastery was the midwife attending the birth of the mechanical clock, the city provided the ideal maternal community for that robot child to grow to adolescence. By 1298, the population of Europe was three times what it had been at the turn of the millennium. Venice, London, Basel, Paris: the city as we know it—a place where goods are assembled, processed, and traded—had been created. The new manufactured products and other goods moved from city to city and from city to country. Economic change bred more novelties: new, widely circulated currencies. Genoa and Florence minted the first genois and florin, respectively, in 1252, and Venice the first ducat in 1284. The establishment of a universal system of monetary exchange was yet another step toward abstraction. Increasingly, everything now had its price—including time.

Living in the city meant big changes in the rhythm of human activity. Thirteenth-century workers migrated en masse from the country to get jobs. There they could become shoemakers, weavers, textile workers, or dyers—and they could bring home a pretty good wage if they were well trained. But the urban workday was a far cry from the rural peasant's former daily schedule, which had consisted of a list of chores that began with feeding the chickens and ended with bringing in the cows—all accomplished alone and more or less in sequence, timed by the approximate rhythm of the sun in the sky.

Imagine starting work when it becomes light enough to recognize the difference between heads and tails on a coin, or paying your rent before sunset on the day after the first detectable crescent moon. These were viable subjective timing devices certified by nature in the not-so-distant Western past—until that ticking time bomb called the clock came along and provided a shock to the system of the migrating peasant.

Work in the city required collaboration and coordination among relatively large groups of people. The penalty for lost time was lost revenue. Piecework gradually yielded to the hourly wage, as church bells migrated first to shops, where they became work bells, then to the belfry at the center of town, where all manner of pealings, differing in pitch and duration, would impose discipline on those for whom the bells tolled—on masons and carpenters, wine makers, and linen cutters. The well-to-do likewise subjected themselves to a new discipline of time, egged on by Renaissance philosophers such as Leon Battista Alberti, who had a habit upon awakening of making a list of every activity he would engage in hour by hour for that day.

Regardless of where the laborers performed their tasks—whether in the vineyard or at the weaving loom, in the shipyard or the mine, whether in the home or at the bench in the shop—they came to resent the bells and mistrust those who rang them: the employer class who also ran the town government. Time seemed no longer to belong to God and man. It belonged to those who presided over this world.

But the medieval struggle over time between labor and management cut two ways. Clocks also gave workers the opportunity to master their own time, and they raised new and complex issues for employers and employees alike. It is a relatively simple matter to mark the length of a workday that begins at sunup and ends at sundown, but what of one that is measured in hours? Such questions about time management, which had never been raised before the advent of clock time, were bound to create conflict. There are many examples. In 1315, when they were required to handle fabric of a heavier weight, textile workers in the northern French city of Arras demanded higher wages. To increase their earning power, they further entreated to be allowed to exceed the length of the workday announced by the bells—the first overtime dispute. Management fought back: in the cloth trade, for example, sheep shearers, fullers, and washers who failed to obey the clothiers' bells were fined as follows: the equivalent of five British pounds for checking in after the morning bell, sixty for ringing it to call an assembly of fellow workers, the death penalty for ringing it to call for a revolt. Thus began the battle between management and the worker over who is really in charge of time.

"Time rules life" is the motto of the National Association of Watch and Clock Collectors. It is a credo borne out in the way we have organized everyday events, packaging them into precise, quantifiable bundles to maximize efficiency. We are always in a rush—always making haste. And we crave precision.

Like a football quarterback running out of time, the efficient worker forever battles the clock—a situation memorably parodied in Charlie Chaplin's 1936 film *Modern Times* (and again famously in an episode of *I Love Lucy* that found our heroine struggling comically to apply a chocolate covering to morsels on an assembly line). The assembly-line process was introduced in the United States early in the twentieth century. Mass production reflects many of the properties of scientific timekeeping that have become embedded in the Western way of life since the Industrial Revolution—sequentiality, consecutive change, and control.

In 1850, the average time per week spent earning a living was seventy-two hours on the farm, sixty-five in the factory. By 1900, time spent on the job was reduced to sixty hours a week. Our classic forty-hour week with Saturdays and Sundays free has predominated since the post-World War II boom began. But, paradoxically, the advent of a new techno-flex time has turned that curve around in the past two decades. Our cellular phones, pagers, Palm Pilots, and laptops make it possible to put in more hours talking to our bosses rather than our kids as we multitask our way through an even more extended "home workday." In 1987, Harvard economist Juliet Schor calculated that the average American worked 163 hours a year (an extra month!) longer than a generation earlier in 1969. Families put in 6.8 percent or more work hours in 1999 than they did in 1989, according to the union-supported Economic Policy Institute. Notice that I said "families," which implies that more members of the family are working to keep even (family income actually rose 9.2 percent in the same period). Black families work nine hours a week more than their white counterparts, Hispanic families thirteen hours more. There is also a gender disparity: husbands work one more hour, wives three compared with a decade ago. Much of the increase is mandated, particularly in the healthcare and service industries where companies avoid filling full-time jobs by requiring employees to work 5 to 10 percent overtime. Still, to stem the tide, a recent Maine backlash law called for a cap on overtime: eighty hours of total work per two-week period. Despite wanting to spend more time with the family, we feel the need to work more so that when we finally do get that long-awaited time together, we'll have acquired a quality environment in which to spend it—a backyard (preferably in-ground) pool, a cruise, or an exotic vacation place (pipe dreams for most working-class people).

But some specialized time counters paint a different portrait of the overworked American. Those who look into how we actually spend our waking hours think we waste a lot of the time new technology helps us save. We squander most of it watching TV. The average American spends three hours a day watching TV, one hour on the phone, four minutes filling out forms, four minutes having sex—and only six actual hours working; and the more hours people work the more they overestimate how much time they spend working. One group of Penn State researchers concluded that those who estimated that they worked fifty to fifty-four hours a week actually labored intensively for only 41.6 hours. In three hundred years we have progressed from believing that idleness will find employment in the hands of Satan to the notion that time off keeps us from getting the money we need to pursue the pleasures of leisure—which is why one in fifteen of us takes a second job.

Our downtime away from work is a blank space just waiting to be filled up. We think of it as whatever remains after we've done our work. And those of us who take leisure seriously sometimes overstructure it so that it comes off as a mere extension of work. "Saint Monday" was once the occasional holiday granted the exhausted worker by a generous employee—Memorial Day and President's Weekend Mondays, Boxing Day (the day after Christmas in the United Kingdom) and Easter Monday (largely in Europe) come to mind. If for no other reason than complete exhaustion we workers *deserve* our saintly September holiday.

Halloween:
Dead Time

Nothing underlines regularity so well as absurdity or paradox.

Victor Turner

Remembering where I was the evening of October 31 in any of my early adolescent years is easy. I and my pals would spend the afternoon gathering materials out of attic closets to make our disguises. An old sheet was a great starter for a ghost; torn pants, battered top hat, shoes with flapping soles, and a cigar would conjure up a hobo. Or we'd create a bank robber out of a plastic water pistol, black eye mask, and thug's hat. We all wanted to be social misfits: that was the main theme of our Halloween trick-or-treat masquerade. After supper three or four of my closest confidants would come by the house. Suited up, we'd grab our empty brown paper bags and flashlights and head out into the suburban surroundings for a solid three or four hours of masked ritual solicitation with but a single goal in mind: to acquire as vast a quantity of high-quality confection as possible. Lowest on the totem pole of excellence in the category of treats were popcorn balls, fresh fruit (like the ubiquitous autumnal apple), and donuts and cookies—never mind that these homemade and homegrown donations took more time to create and were better for us. They just weren't as highly prized as Tootsie Rolls, Pez, Jujy Fruits, Sugar Daddys, or Mary Janes (the adhesive power of the peanut butter taffy is still strong enough to extricate a molar). Highest on the hierarchy of delicacies were the full-size (three ounces before they shaved them down) Milky Way, Snickers, Three Musketeers, and Hershey bars.

Our peregrination began with a round of houses on our own Waldo Street and then proceeded to immediately adjacent and parallel Edgar and Victor Streets. Here were friendly faces who saw immediately through our disguises by the shapes of our bodies and the sounds of our voices. You could always count on them for a hefty hit of pure chocolate. (How well the people next door treat your kids is still a measure of status as neighbors.)

Next we'd move on to the twilight zone, the exotic territory of unfamiliar porches, doors, doorbells, and knockers more than a few blocks away—places we rarely saw except from a distance on our long walk to school. Dodge Avenue, a full quarter mile away across the vast Memorial Park ball fields, was a bonanza. It consisted of dozens of densely packed post-World War II Cape Codders that could be visited in short order with a minimum of wear and tear on the shoe leather. Dodge also featured the much anticipated and slightly more upscale (for blue-collar East Haven, Connecticut) #32—the blue house with white trim on the corner—a place where cold hard cash served as a sucrose substitute. The jolly cigar-chomping, beer-bellied man of the house (a used car dealer as I recall) would fling open the door to his hearth and parade clusters of trick-or-treaters to the front of the fireplace as soon as they arrived. Lining us up like some army general reviewing his troops, he would inspect each of our outfits and then engage in a serious monologue, using his wife as a sounding board and centering on the subject of who wore the best costume and why—a reasoned amalgam of originality, attention to detail, and raw spookiness. Then amid knocking by the next group of confectionary mercenaries, his decision rendered, he would pull out a handful of change from his pocket and proceed to deposit a nickel into the collection sack of all the runners-up. The winner he anointed with the gift of a quarter! Can you imagine how much 25 cents was worth in the 1950s—to a kid? At least a trip to a Saturday movie house matinee plus a two-hour box of Good and Plentys.

The exotic world beyond Dodge Avenue was a place where, under the pretense of being someone other than ourselves, we somehow acquired license to behave a little more outrageously. The further we roamed from the familiar turf where we all were subject to the social norms that guided us, the more outrageous our actions became. If anybody on more distant Hemingway Avenue failed to submit to our will—at least by forking over a popcorn ball—we would execute our "Trick" option by playing a prank on them. We'd either smash their carved pumpkin, soap their windows, or pummel the windshield of their car with raw eggs. With clear consciences, and assuaged by the belief that society tolerated, even condoned, such devilish demeanor (why else would our calendar keep a night devoted to this sort of antisocial madness?), we would consume most of the candy cache on the meandering stroll back to the safe fires of home, retelling exaggerated stories of narrow escapes from broom-wielding housewives provoked by our bravado.

Times have changed. The anarchy of today's Halloween is highly sanitized. Now the day is managed by grown-ups, and it is celebrated on the new turf of the shopping mall. Halloween has become a $2 billion annual business (second only to Christmas). It is a season that runs at least the entire length of the thirty-one-day month. Halloween 2000 was important enough to warrant a special issue of *Martha Stewart Living*, featuring Martha herself (she appears transformed into a black widow spider on the cover). The magazine contained recipes for ladyfingers (digit-sized pastries with red almond fingernails) and tips on how to transform an ordinary flashlight (for safety in crossing the street) into a ghoulish accessory. This year the Halloween shopping mania started particularly early. By August 15 a full aisle of our local drugstore was stocked with decorative items like "Frightening Frank" (enstein) who sings "Who Can It Be Now?" in synchro-motion, "Wicked Wolfgang" (the Wolfman) mouthing "I'm Your Boogie Man," Billy Bones singing

"Bad to the Bone," and "Witch Hazel" doing "Evil Ways." You can own one of these forty-two-inch-tall polyethylene wonders for only $29.95. Watch the handful of big box office movies from earlier in the year and, like picking Academy Award winners, you'll be able to predict with absolute certainty the costumes that will go on sale at Toys "R" Us the next October. For example, Freddy Krueger "the Slasher," was big in 1988, followed by Teenage Mutant Ninja Turtles, Mighty Morphin Power Rangers, Lion King, and Belle, who made the list in 1994. The Fall of 2001 featured action heroes like Xena Warrior Princess, Gladiator, Harry Potter, and a cadre of XMEN.

The parents who now orchestrate what once was a kids' holiday dedicate much of October's high-quality time with their offspring to creating original costumes—a Jeep, a toaster, an upside-down person, or a picnic (take a red checkered tablecloth, cut a hole in it, paste fake hot dogs, slices of cake, and wax cups onto it, and put your head through the hole. Glue a parade of plastic ants to the shroud for a special effect). According to one psychologist, parents can use Halloween to stimulate their child's creativity. It allows them to step outside of themselves and think in a different realm. Besides, what parent doesn't love sharing the magic of Halloween with their children?

The adult takeover (today nine out of ten kids between the ages of seven and twelve go trick-or-treating with their parents) began in the 1960s but it didn't really blossom until the mid-1980s, when the rise of the two-income family seized Halloween as a device for getting back in touch with the kids. The change was catalyzed by the widespread belief that sadistic adults (the real ghouls behind Halloween terrorism) were poisoning trick-or-treat goodies and that members of satanic cults were planning to kidnap and torture children. The earliest such case I know of involved Helen Pfiel, a Long Island housewife who was accused in 1964 of handing out ant poison buttons for candy. Investigators learned she did it as a joke because she got tired of giving away free candy to undeserving older teens. She claimed she was careful to label each package "poison." Nonetheless, her sick joke landed her a guilty plea for child endangerment (she got off with a suspended sentence). Three years later the first of the celebrated razor-blade-in-the-apple Halloween stories was born. A young New Jersey boy showed his parents a trick-or-treat apple he had bitten into, though not deeply enough to contact the blade. Within a week more than a dozen cases were reported up and down the eastern seaboard.

The satanic cult scare emanated from the midwest in the mid-1970s. It centered on the discovery of mutilated livestock allayed by a Missouri sheriff to devil worship. He suggested that it would just be a matter of time before hooded black-robed cult members sighted in the vicinity would seek a child victim—most likely a blue-eyed, blonde, unbaptized teenage girl. His warning, issued through the school system, caused something of a panic, which led to other worst-case scenario warnings such as "never go inside the front door of a house to accept a treat"; "never eat trick or treat goodies unless they are carefully examined by an adult"; "parents should allow trick-or-treating only between 1 and 3 P.M. on the Sunday before Halloween"; "use flameproof costumes"; "take along a flashlight"; "add reflective tape to your costume"; "visit only well-lit houses"; "don't allow children to wear a mask, but, if they must, insist that they remove it before crossing the street"; and so on. Nervous communities quickly barred all traditional Halloween celebrations and replaced them with events involving families and all age groups. Incidentally, not only was there never a single documented case of any Halloween related enticement to kidnap but also by 1982 all reports of booby-trapped apples were found to be hoaxes devised by children—or parents!

But all of this came too late to forestall the transfer of ownership of Halloween to the elder set. Consumerism replaced mythic sadism as parents got their kids off the street and into a Malloween, or Treat party where trustworthy merchant replaced sadistic neighbor as the principal donor to a new fancily decorated shopping bag (which sold for $4.99 in the store). Oddly enough, the forces of law and order took over sponsorship of the managed disorder that envelops Halloween. Some families turned their basements into haunting rooms where blindfolded children might be invited to put their hands into a bucket of squishy intestines (cold cooked spaghetti and salad oil) or eyeballs (peeled grapes). More elaborate rites included communal underwater pumpkin-carving contests and entire houses decorated in the style of the Addams family mansion. After a controlled haunting of trick-or-treaters who sign up on a list, the hosts invite both kids and their parents to dinner. Quite unlike Thanksgiving, which is traditionally confined to the family, or Christmas and Chanukah, which are religious holidays, as the first major holiday after the summer, Halloween comes at a time when the community is ready to regroup, so it makes sense that everyone in the neighborhood should celebrate together.

Adult Halloween has also become a platform for expressing New Age ideas and giving marginal members of urban society a voice. It is a time when neopagan associations and witches' covens defend their worship of nature against Christian persecutors. The annual Greenwich Village parade turns out artists and gays in outrageous camp costumes done up in bright colors: a cocktail, a gumball machine, a salad bar, a pink flamingo, and a hexagon of scantily clad transvestites linked by spider webs. At a recent parade one reveler showed up with an apparatus consisting of four 4-foot wooden sticks connected by ropes, all strapped to his head. From the ropes hung a very large brassiere, panties, and a few other unidentifiable unmentionables—a human clothesline! A disorderly affair unlike New York's other marches, this parade requires no registration form or fee. Its sinuous route is confined strictly to the local community whose members come together to act out their dreams in a seasonal time-out, when the rigid rules of organized society are temporarily relaxed.

Don't feel sorry for the kids. They once were usurpers too. The Halloweens of a few generations before mine didn't center any more strongly on impish pranksters of my 1950s ilk than today's version does on the same age set. The oldest reference to trick-or-treating—in the sense of either you pay me off or I'll pull a prank on you—dates back to the 1939 *Oxford English Dictionary*. Then it meant that the trick could be a handstand or a riddle. But the old pranks from earlier in the century and beyond, were far more elaborate; for example, removing something big and bulky to a place where it doesn't belong—like dismantling a farmer's wagon and reassembling it on the roof of his barn. Knocking down fences, tying doors shut—all constitute mass assaults on the domestic borders

of organized society by the disenchanted, whether they be alienated ado-
lescents or envious down-and-outers.

Dumping heaps of cowpies on one's front porch and knocking over
outhouses were once messier analogs of egg tossing. A 1920s story from
upstate New York tells of a group of teens who roped a privy belonging
to the town drunk who lived in an old shack at the edge of the community. As they began to pull it over they heard moaning sounds emanating from the throne within. It turned out that the drunk had dozed off
in the cabinet while paying a late night visit. The alarmed youngsters
peered through the defining half-moon hole cut in the door. Seeing that
their unwanted victim was still breathing, they dragged the compart-
ment to the town square and hoisted it up onto a gazebo. Next morning
when amused locals lowered the apparatus, they jarred the wino out of
his slumber. He staggered out into the bright daylight evidently never
realizing what had happened, though later he did confide to friends that
he was going to opt for modern indoor plumbing because the little old
outhouse just didn't seem as comfortable as he once remembered it.

This sort of nasty American pranksterism, like most
of our Halloween rituals, actually derives largely from mid-nineteenth-
century Irish customs that extend far beyond the childhood set. On
Halloween, Irish girls practiced the witchly art of resorting to spells to
divine for a husband. Or they pulled cabbages. Out into the fields they
went blindfolded until they stumbled over the first cabbage plant they
encountered. They would feel its head, big or little, and its stalk, straight
or crooked, the shape to conform to the "grand object of all their spells."
(The interpretation of Robert Burns's description is left for the reader.)
If any earth sticks to the root, the greater the fortune that comes with a
mate. The taste of the heart of the plant tells of his temper and disposi-
tion (I cannot imagine a positive omen derived from consuming the
deep innards of a raw cabbage!). Finally, maidens put the runts (stems)
over the door for good luck. We can easily see how spinsters creeping
through the kale patch could be displaced by derisive youths pulling
cabbages and using them as missiles to pelt the local establishments.

Blowing the smoke of burning cabbage stalks through key holes, battering doors with stolen cabbages, stopping up chimneys with cabbage heads—all were among the uses to which this versatile veggie, harvested in most locales in late October, was put in eighteenth- and nineteenth-century England and Ireland before it came to America.

In the "oracle of the nuts" a courting couple would each toss a nut into the fire. The course of their courtship would then be set by the way the nuts behaved. If they burn together quietly, a lasting and agreeable relationship, if they crackle and jump apart, so will you and your intended. Another fruitful form of divination called for peeling an apple, throwing the peel over your right shoulder and then examining its shape when it lands to discern the initial of your future loved one.

The Irish also brought over the habit of celebrating Halloween with huge bonfires to scare away the evil spirits who roamed the hills in the form of bats, black cats (a shape often taken by medieval Satan), and witches. Among the marginal members of the social stream, widowed women dressed in black have long served as archetypal witches. That the "weaker sex" was thought more susceptible to the ways of evil is clear in the ecclesiastical writings of male prophets going all the way back to the role of Eve in Genesis. One theory has it that feminine herbalists who dared ease women's pain in childbirth were interfering with God's plan, for He had considered it just punishment for Eve's sin. Also, because the number of widowed women living alone was fairly high in the Middle Ages and because women had little empowerment or legal influence, they became the logical scapegoats during the witch crazes.

Bobbing for apples and jack-o'-lanterns are Irish too. One of the most dangerous forms of bobbing for apples, a fruit in obvious abundance during the harvest season, finds its origin in seventeenth-century southern Ireland. A "snap apple" wheel with fifty-two spokes, one for each week of the year, is suspended at eye level from the hayloft. One out of every three spokes holds a lit candle, a second is sharpened to a point, and a third has an apple stuck at its end. Beneath the apparatus a stool is placed with a circle drawn about it. One person spins the wheel while each of the others takes a turn running around inside the circle fifty-two times, keeping one hand on the stool and rising as often as possible to bite an apple without falling prey to punishment by fire or perforation.

The jack o' lantern is named after a mythic Irishman who loved to play tricks on the devil. Having no place in heaven, he was condemned to wander around the world, going neither to heaven nor hell, always carrying a lantern to guide his way. Just as the groundhog substitutes for the badger on February 2, the pumpkin became a later New England stand-in for what originally was a hollowed-out turnip lit with a coal from the fires of hell.

Scary masks, spooky jack-o'-lanterns, witches, devils, and nighttime prowling—all signal an obvious connection with the deceased. And if we dig beneath the veneer of October 31 pop culture and its immediate antecedents, an ancient festival of the dead rises to the surface. Halloween is the modern-day version of Celtic Samhain, literally "when the summer goes." Its calendrical reciprocal, Beltane or May Day six months away, signals the start of summer.

Once the official first day of winter in early medieval Ireland, Samhain was ordained by practical considerations from past use—major seasonal transitions such as bringing in the cattle or witnessing the falling of the leaves. It was also a spiritually sensitive time, when the gates separating the world of the living and the dead were wide open to facilitate communication. On the eve of Samhain, the souls of the dead in Purgatory, that halfway world in space between eternal confinement in heaven or hell, would lurk about on the frozen landscape, begging to be allowed entry into our world. They hoped to revisit their homes, to soothe their frozen bones by the fire with their kin, to partake of a warm meal, and to petition their loved ones for prayers, before heading back to their graves for a long winter's nap.

Relatives would set communal bonfires on the hillside to beckon the dead back home—and in the bargain to encourage the sun on its course at a time when the lords of darkness seemed to be winning the never-ending war they annually waged on it. Druid priests once performed ceremonies honoring their sun god, while soothsayers cast omens for the forthcoming year: what would come of the farming, the hunting, and the gathering? Would there be storm, drought, or warfare? But others say the bonfires were meant to keep away the dead, for their behavior might threaten or persecute us. Dressing up as wild animals would scare them away, and, if that didn't work, gift bribes of food might be enough to get rid of them. Such is our uneasy and uncertain encounter with the afterworld.

Some of us may think our demise is the final act, but can we be sure? For most of human history death has been regarded as a rite of passage. As far back as third millennium B.C. Babylonia, the deceased were still considered participating members of the family. Even though the dead inhabited the underworld, the living were not absolved of responsibilities to them. People visited and cared for their dead relatives in their places of entombment, bringing them the necessary food to sustain themselves as they wandered about the world below.

The end of the year is not unlike the end of the month. Its last few days, when the waning moon fell into the arms of the rising sun god, marked that time when the two worlds met. Most of the festivals dedicated to the rites of dead spirits were conducted both at the end of the month and at the end of the summer. For example, the biggest one at Nippur, the Sacred Mound Festival, was celebrated at the end of the seventh month (which corresponds to our October). The City of Ur held a festival at the end of August (our time) dedicated to the underworld deity Ninazu. By then the grain had been fully harvested and the stubble on the freshly cut fields lay parched and lifeless in dwindling hot sunlight, not to be seeded until the rains arrived—a time between life cycles, one concluded and the next yet to begin. The dead no more severed their lifeline to the living than did the grain, which, though it had died, nonetheless retained the power to reseed.

These five-thousand-year-old Babylonian festivals were dedicated likewise to the return of the spirit for a brief visit to the family. Setting fires and lighting torches near the household guided the ghosts to the funereal meal that awaited them. A surviving royal text describes one such sacrificial offering, which was placed in an *apu* or conduit to the dead: "He will go and collect the blood in the *apu*, pour honey and oil into the apu; the king presents food to the spirits of the dead, the singer removes the meal from the table, places it in the apu, he pours honey, oil, beer and wine over it, the singer fills the *apu*, the king puts his foot over the apu; kisses the ground." (I am reminded of a recent Halloween night visit to a cemetery in New Orleans, where I witnessed heaping plates of real food being laid out directly on the gravesites.)

The Babylonians were no more certain than we when it came to dealing with the dead. How to carry on a dialog with the spirits presented a serious problem, for what the deceased experience is so thoroughly unknown to us. Surely we must respect them. But at the same time shouldn't we try to protect ourselves from any acquired evil they might transmit? A cuneiform text from the first millennium B.C. describing one of these occasions warns of evil ghosts and witches who sneak through the open gates of the underworld on these vulnerable occasions. Spell-casting ceremonies asking benevolent deities for protection were required to repel such uninvited visitors.

In Alexandrian Egypt, people fastened oil lamps to the eaves of their houses, where they burned all night long to commemorate the death of Osiris (which, timed by our calendar, would have occurred in mid-November). This nocturnal illumination on one night of the year ultimately became a commemoration to all the dead. Later, it too came to involve the laying out of food for the deceased.

Deceased Romans were considered no less touchy than their Babylonian counterparts over being dismissed to the Land of the Dead following their funereal meal. Roman Halloween took place on Lemuria, a three-day affair specifically labeled as All Souls' Days. Reverence and fear accompanied the unleashing of the spirits, who were thought to be quite capable of afflicting misery on the living. Supplicants would throw black beans at them in the hopes that the shades (as they called them) would accept them as substitutes for living members of the family whom they might otherwise carry off either out of envy or loneliness. Ovid tells us that an extra bean tossed into the open grave might alleviate the problem of any visitation in the first place:

When midnight has come and lends silence to sleep, and dogs and all ye
varied fowls are hushed, the worshipper who bears the olden rite in mind
and fears the gods arises: no knots constrict his feet; and he makes a sign
with his thumb in the middle of his closed fingers, lest in his silence an
unsubstantial shade should meet him, And after washing his hands clean
in spring water, he turns, and first he receives black beans and throws
them away with face averted: but while he throws them, he says: "These
I cast; with these beans I redeem me and mine." This he says nine times,
without looking back: the shade is thought to gather the beans, and to
follow unseen behind. Again he touches water, and clashes Temesan
bronze, and asks the shade to go out of his house. When he has said nine
times, "Ghosts of my fathers, go forth!" he looks back, and thinks that
he has duly performed the sacred rites.

Ovid goes on to tell the story of how Romans, preoccupied with waging
war, were punished for neglecting this devout seasonal observance:

for tis said that from that ominous day Rome grew hot with the funeral
fires that burned without the city. They say, though I can hardly think it,
that the ancestral souls did issue from the tombs and make their moan in
the hours of stilly night; and hideous ghosts, a shadowy throng, they say,
did howl about the city streets and the wide fields.

Tradition has it that the Christian takeover of this pagan festival of
the dead came about when saints replaced Roman deities and continued once Christianity was carried from the continent across the channel
to Britain. To the new religion the gods of the old faith would have been
considered to be evil and therefore especially unwelcome at a time of
danger for the soul of any good parishioner. This is probably why Christians suppressed the deadly rite and replaced it a day later (so as not to
be too suspect to the wise pagan holdout) with All Souls Day. A more
benign version of the night of spooks and spirits, this sanitized daytime
version of the old Roman rite involved a family graveside picnic accompanied by prayers and, as darkness fell, the lighting of ceremonial candles.
However, this scenario may not be strictly true according to historians
who have taken the trouble to dig out the medieval sources. Mid-fourth-
century Mediterranean Christians were already honoring saints martyred
under the old Roman emperors, but they did that in early May.

By A.D. 800 , a similar festival had been celebrated on November 1 in
central and northern Europe. Early medieval Irish Christians did the
same on April 15. We don't yet know why, but somehow by the tenth

century a date that was largely Germanic took hold. Honoring the dead at "Hallowtide" or "Hallowmas" did not become part of the picture until after A.D. 1000, when solemn masses for all Christian dead became linked with November 2, but not just because of the somber nature of the season. At home, attention was naturally focused on dying and decaying flowers and leaves. Old Halloween had as much to do with the widely held belief in Purgatory's halfway house, wherein the living could affect the course of the dead through prayer. The medieval saints were regarded as the principal intercessors on behalf of all souls on Judgment Day. Ironically (later Protestant) Germany, which tried to end such beliefs, ends up taking credit for setting the date.

English Protestantism forced yet another curious transformation upon Halloween. On November 5, 1605, papist conspirator Guy Fawkes was accused of attempting to blow up England's Houses of Parliament. He was duly drawn and quartered for his crime. But a year later Parliament declared that date a day of thanksgiving for the safety of the government and a general celebration by the Church of England of the triumph over a presumed Roman Catholic-directed plot. Now, because Halloween was strongly tied to the Catholic Church calendar and staid Protestants too felt the inner seasonal need to let off a little steam, many of its fun traditions were conveniently shifted over to Guy Fawkes Day. The night of the fourth became the traditional Mischief Night. Next day dummies known as "Guys" were set out on street corners to beg for money and that night they were all put to the torch in a huge bonfire. As a sign of the still great enmity of Protestant and Catholic forces in parts of Great Britain today, mock popes are paraded through the streets and pelted with rotten fruit while papal effigies are set aflame on Guy Fawkes Day.

Despite its twentieth-century American makeover, in many countries of the world modern Halloween is still imbued with the sacred tradition of honoring the dead. In Mexico for example, the first two days of November are called *Todos Santos* (All Saints) or *Días de los Muertos* (Days of the Dead). Their observance combines the solemn element of honoring dead relatives with the playful side of Halloween that dwells on encounters with the dead. Communities put on feasts, picnics, and plays, and families decorate their home altars with skulls and skeletons made of sugar. Tombstones of marzipan and "dead bread," baked figures of dead men and women lying in repose, with arms crossed, are all laid out for the dead spirits. Celebrants also attend religious services and pay a visit to the grave to refurbish and renew the abode of the dead. In the Tex-Mex and Cal-Mex borderlands the idea of dealing with the dead in such a direct manner, even though it promotes the solidarity associated with family values we hear so much about in our political campaigns, puts off many people, who mollify what they seem to regard as a too-pagan tradition by calling it the *Dia de los "difuntos"* (deceased) or *"finados"* (departed or finished). How many of us prefer to use the term "she passed away" or "he has left us" rather than starkly announcing "they died"? "Death" remains for us a frightening word.

At Halloween perhaps more than at any other spoke on the seasonal wheel of time we gape into the mirror of naked uncertainty and contemplate the mystery of death. On the one hand our secular culture teaches us to deny the supernatural except in the most profound divine sense. Only the preacher and the undertaker deal directly with the dead. Who is ever really comfortable at a wake or a funeral? We put the dead out of mind, remaining content (or so we say) to honor their memory—especially on the anniversary of their demise with a visit to the gravesite or an announcement in the local newspaper's obituary section. But the mysterious, irrational side of death never loses its grasp on us. When our annual Day of the Dead rolls around we behave erratically, allowing our kids to dress up as monsters. Is this our way of trying to come to terms with our fear of the unseen—to play with it, mimic and mock what we think it is? As grown-ups, we too need to overcome the fear of sudden change a brush with death brings. Can this be the motive behind the adult heist of October's last day?

The age and sex-role reversals we have noted in our other holidays, such as Carnival and New Year's Eve, and the general ascent to power of the marginal members of society such holidays bring for a moment, seem irrational too. The masks we wear—pirates, witches, burglars, goblins, and ghosts, even to some degree the action heroes—all signify anti-authority figures. Donning these rebellious faces gives us the anonymous right to behave the way *they* are supposed to behave—aggressively, anarchistically, precisely the way we conceive of the evil powers that threaten us. But such rituals of status reversal, occurring regularly and at pivotal points in the order of the seasons, only serve to strengthen existing social behavior. "Mask the weak in strength and demand that the strong be passive, so that they can sense whatever real aggression might be shown against them by their social inferiors," argues anthropologist Victor Turner. Recognizing the absurd restores social balance, as the chapter epigraph implies. What could be more emotionally satisfying to the disenfranchised members of society than the extravagance of being permitted to act out their illicit behavior? Listening to the plea of one's inferiors is a sign of acceptance.

Halloween lowers the high and raises up the low; it reaffirms the principle of hierarchy at precisely the time that it needs to be buttressed—when society feels threatened by the smell of decay that comes with the season. So gather the odd medley of topsy-turvy Halloween forces that attempt to cope with change. Seasoned with a touch of evil, we acquire the communal strength we all need to help the wheel of the seasons rotate.

Thanksgiving:
Transcending Pilgrims' Progress

MENU		
	Cranberry Juice	
Roast Turkey with Dressing		*Cranberry Sauce*
Sweet Potatoes	*Creamed Onions*	*Squash*
Pumpkin Pie	*Plum Pudding*	*Mince Pie*
	Milk	*Coffee*

Mamie Krythe

All vegetable gardeners share the ecstasy of plucking and eating that first ripe tomato or handful of sweet peas they nurtured from seedlings. In the North, the embryos that flourish in our gardens germinate in tiny boxes on windowsills, their occupants tenderly coddled before being sent to the wilds outside and set into rows to gain their legs. We keep a watchful eye, pruning, clipping, weeding, and worrying on their behalf.

Daily the beans saw me come to their rescue armed with a hoe, and thin the ranks of their enemies, filling up the trenches with weedy dead. Many

> a lusty crest-waving Hector, that towered a whole foot above his crow-
> ing comrades, fell before my weapon and rolled in the dust,

writes Thoreau of his relationship with the mile-long pole-bean rows he
comforted in solitude throughout the New England summer of 1846.
Too little sun, too much rain, invading crows, pesky groundhogs, an early
frost, a prolonged drought—over the long summer we gardeners deflect
the missiles of misfortune nature hurls at our adopted children from
the botanical kingdom as we count the days until we can savor that initial batch of early cherry tomato, savory squash flower, or crisp Bibb
lettuce—our first fruits.

Gardening is a creative act. That the human hand could deliver out
of a handful of tiny seeds such an abundance of sustenance to a table is
nothing short of a miracle. And all miracles deserve thanks—to nature,
to God. Complained Thoreau of husbandry:

> it is pursued with irreverent haste and heedlessness by us, our object
> being to have large farms and large crops merely. We have no festival, nor
> procession, nor ceremony, not excepting our Cattle-shows and so called
> Thanksgivings, by which the farmer expresses a sense of the sacredness
> of his calling, or is reminded of its sacred origin.

Every agrarian culture sets its own time of the year aside for
the purpose of giving thanks, usually at the beginning of the end of the
harvest season, which varies greatly according to climate. In early Europe the time to recognize the sacredness of simple farming was marked
by one of the four support pillars of the year. As we peel away the patterns in our modern calendar, we consistently discover a significant red-
letter day popping up in the old seasonal calendar about midway between
the pivotal points of the sun's journey—the solstices and the equinoxes.
Groundhog Day falls between winter solstice and spring equinox, May
Day between spring equinox and summer solstice. And, as we have just
seen, Halloween fills the gap between autumn equinox and winter solstice. The most obscure member of the quartet is Lammas, the halfway
point between summer solstice and autumn equinox.

I believe these quarter days of the seasonal year reflect our penchant
for symmetry—the need to geometrically divide the cycle of time the

way we quarter and eighth a circle of space. If you actually count days, you'll find that each of the quarter markers falls a few days before the midpoints of the seasons, probably a reflection of the old lunar way of reckoning the year by sighting first visible crescent moons after a given date of the year. Fixing Easter Sunday is a good example (see Chapter 5). Thus, there are 91¼ days in a quarter year but three months reckoned by moon cycles add up to only 88½ days. So, if you use visible moons to mark time, there's a slight backslide through the solar year. Maybe when it comes to timekeeping we are more insistent than nature on perfect symmetry.

Lammas, the first of August, used to be a red-letter day, but its color faded as we gradually strayed from agrarian life. The word means "loaf mass" in old English. It began as the opener in a chain of ninth-century English festivals celebrating the first of the harvest, when breads made from the season's first grain crop were blessed, broken, and ritually offered to the four corners of the domicile for protection. Our modern-day farmers' markets devoted to sharing the new abundance of the land are a vague remnant of the custom of displaying the first of the crops. Anyone who lives in my part of the world knows that when July gives way to August this is the most profitable time to visit them.

The spirit of Lammas resides in all of us who are there for nature's "firsts," whether we attend the Strawberry Festival in Plant City, Florida, the New Corn ceremonies of Native Americans of the northeast, the Asparagus Festival in Germany, or the celebration of the arrival of Beaujolais Nouveau in France. When we dine on new potatoes, native corn, the first salmon or oysters of the season, we collectively participate in the rite of bringing back the first of its kind in life's seasonal round.

If we count forward six months from Candlemas, we arrive at Lammas. At that time meadow fences put up at Candlemas were taken down to permit cattle to pasture after the hay crop had been taken in. The Irish celebrated Lughnasa, a festival of games dedicated to Lugh, the Celtic god of light who has left his name for us in European cities like Leyden and Lyons. Celebrants would make an offering of new corn to the deity by carrying it to a hilltop where it was buried. Following a meal made of newly harvested food, they would return to the hilltop to watch plays in which a Lugh impersonator banished the threatening monster of famine and blight.

Lammas remained significant throughout the Middle Ages. It was a time for holding fairs, paying rents, and electing officials. Our modern Election Day falls not too far from Thanksgiving—our own spin on a displaced Lammas. But there are far more ancient precedents. Jews celebrate the eight-day Feast of Tabernacles (Sukkoth) following the annual threshing and wine making; the Greeks held a nine-day affair honoring Demeter, goddess of agriculture. The Romans began the month of August by cutting straw, collecting leaves for fodder, and doing a second mowing of their irrigated fields—all under the protection of Ceres, goddess of the harvest. Ceres was to harvesttime what Flora was to springtime (see Chapter 6). We honor her name every time we eat our morning cereal. "Ceres and Earth discharge a common function: the one lends to the corn its vital force, the other lends it room," says Ovid.

Nineteenth-century theorists on religion argued that all primitive people attributed an animist function to the crop itself. If they thought trees were animated, why not wheat or corn? That plants might be endowed with mystical powers led people to deal with them out of fear and suspicion. This explained why farmers would cut the last sheaf of their grain crop blindfolded, warily throw their sickles from a distance at the last few standing stalks in the field, and take extraordinary care in handling the harvest, lest retaliating phyto-demons cast an evil spell on them. Today's historians are more inclined to regard the "last sheaf" ceremony as an expression of all the hard work of weeding, reaping, and threshing that went into nurturing it.

Harvest festivals like "last sheaf," which focus on the end point of taking in the crop, are a time for serious thought and the seeking of omens about what might lie ahead for next year's harvest. These Thanksgiving activities have always been attended by a variety of now long-forgotten magical procedures. For example, adept farmers would "read" the last sheaf of corn they reaped to acquire the information they needed—a variation of the "part-of-the-whole" divining principle mentioned in connection with Groundhog Day, and which we will see surfacing again in the twelve days of Christmas. To reflect the animate quality of the crop, the ultimate plant was often garbed in cloth and ribbon and fashioned into a harvest maiden. Wealthy landowners might resort to paying musicians to go into the fields to provide continuous all-day musical accompaniments to the last several days of harvesting—and not just for the harvesters. (Today the American cornfield is about the only place in the land that escapes the annoying background music that follows us from supermarket to mall.) If today's farmers behaved this way, we'd threaten to lock them up. But as members of a post-industrial society, it is difficult for us to appreciate the direct dependence our forebears once had on the whims of nature when it came to crop production, though prolonged droughts in the corn belt or deluges in the cotton belt occasionally jog our collective memories.

The idea of stuffing yourself at Thanksgiving has a long history too. The time for harvesting wheat, oats, barley, or corn was a particularly demanding period of the year for the worker. In medieval times he was typically a tenant farmer who needed help from every member of the family to perform the requisite low-tech, backbreaking labor for hours on end. On the last day of his travail his employer would duly reward him and his family with a bonus of a nourishing meal and plenty to drink. British poet Thomas Tusser writes in a 1573 treatise on farming:

> *In harvest time, harvest folke, servants and all*
> *should make all together good cheere in the hall.*
> *And fill out the black boule of bleith to their song*
> *And let them be merie all harvest long.*

When day was done, everyone—landowner, and laborer alike—got together to celebrate and to thank the forces of nature for their bounty. Workers were often presented with the gift of a goose from the "harvest home"—the antecedent of the end-of-the-year bonus turkey doled out to today's conscientious employee.

The Harvest Festival has always been a universal hub in the annual ritual cycle in practically all cultures. For example, as early as the seventh century B.C., the Chinese celebrated a festival variously known as the Great Cha. This was, above all, a feast of thanksgiving that came at the end of the agricultural year (the tenth lunar month in the Chinese calendar). On this occasion offerings were presented to the spirits, animals, and culture heroes connected with agriculture, among them the First Husbandman, founder of agriculture, and his cosmic counterpart, the Divine Husbandman. Cats (who eat mice) and tigers (who chase away wild boars) were among the animal crop protectors who received gifts of thanks. Like most other thanksgiving celebrations, Cha was also a food and drink orgy accompanied by music, dance, and masquerading. "The people of the entire state appeared as if mad," wrote one Chinese historian.

The advent of modern farming techniques and technology in the eighteenth century—the reaper, the baler, and other industrial tools—changed harvest time. For one thing these machines stretched the harvest season into September and beyond. It also diminished the sense of importance of the individual farm worker, now no longer bound to a fixed parcel of land as a tenant, but rather a hand hired by different employers as the volume of seasonal work warranted. Typically, itinerant groups of farm workers would show up where work needed to be done. On completing it, they were always offered plenty to eat and drink until the wee hours of the morning. Then they moved on to a neighboring farm for work on the next day—or as soon as sobriety attained equilibrium with the need to earn.

Our American version of Thanksgiving focuses on the end of the harvest. It derives directly from the old English custom of Harvest Home, and, like all the holidays we have examined, its many reinventions have been strongly motivated by the major needs and concerns of the day. In the 1620s the issue was survival in a strange land. The traditional Thanksgiving Day myth begins with the landing of the Pilgrims and the establishment of the Plymouth colony in Massachusetts in December 1620. Having lost more than half their company of 103, the remaining hardy souls were lucky to have made it through that first hard-scrabble New England winter. But, by the spring of 1621, the conclave had turned the corner. In the fall of 1621, with roofs over their heads and a bounteous harvest on the way, Governor William Bradford chose a date late in the year, when all the work was sure to be done, to celebrate their success with a feast and games. Hunters were sent out for wild turkey, ducks, and geese, while fishermen brought in eels and clams. Women baked hoe cakes and Indian pudding. Ninety local Indians honored an invitation to join the three-day feast. They brought deer and oysters, the latter a novelty to the new tenants of the eastern shore.

Two years later a drought coupled with the arrival of neighboring settlers, with whom the Pilgrims were compelled to share their now meager crop, nearly starved the lot of them out of existence. Governor Bradford resorted to fasting and ordered hours of prayer for salvation. God responded with late summer rains to save the crop—and so a second feast was called for in the autumn of 1623. Held on November 29, a Thursday, it was for the first time a religious as well as a social occasion. Bradford's proclamation on the occasion reflects the act of reciprocation that accompanies so many seasonal rites:

TO ALL YE PILGRIMS

Inasmuch as the great Father has given us this year an abundant harvest of Indian corn, wheat, beans, squashes, and garden vegetables, and has made the forests to abound with game and the sea with fish and clams, and inasmuch as He has protected us from the ravages of the savages, has spared us from pestilence and disease, has granted us freedom to worship God according to the dictates of our own conscience; now, I, your magistrate, do proclaim that all ye Pilgrims, with your wives and little ones, do gather at ye meeting house, on ye hill, between the hours of 9 and 12 in the day time, on Thursday, November ye 29th of the year of our Lord one thousand six hundred and twenty-three, and the third year since ye Pilgrims landed on ye Pilgrim Rock, there to listen to ye pastor, and render thanksgiving to ye Almighty God for all His blessings.

> William Bradford
> Ye Governor of ye Colony

The habit of fasting in somber reflection followed by bingeing is not so surprising when we recall that this is precisely what happens on so many of the other holidays (e.g., New Year's Eve, Christmas) that fall at the stress faults in the topology of the calendar.

Bradford might well have set some portion of that Thursday aside to thank the Native Americans whose land he had undertaken to call his own and who were helpful in guaranteeing the success of the intruder.

One Indian directly responsible for the Pilgrims' survival that first winter was Tisquantum, called Squanto, of the Patuxent tribe. Originally he was among a handful of so-called (in the proclamation) savages ("brutish men which range up and down [the East Coast], little otherwise than the wild beasts of the same") captured by the explorer Captain George Weymouth and taken to England as a curiosity to be shown to the wealthy English merchants who had backed his journey to North America in search of marketable resources. Unlike the others, the tale goes, Squanto was not only friendly but even desirous of traveling to England. His captors duly showed him off, taught him English, and in 1614 brought him back to America as a guide and interpreter. After a series of wild adventures that variously included being recaptured, nearly sold into slavery, and living for three years in a Spanish monastery (where he became educated in the Christian faith), Squanto returned home a year before the arrival of the Pilgrims. There he would help negotiate a treaty among local tribes as well as between the Pilgrims and the resident Wampanoag tribe.

It was Squanto who taught the Pilgrims where to catch fish and wild game, and how to fertilize their corn, all the while holding in check the local Indians, whom previous white visitors had inflamed by treating them with cruelty. Abusing his power (acquired through favoritism by the whites) by threatening local rulers with evil Pilgrim magic should they not do as he told them, Squanto antagonized Massasoit, the sachem of the Wampanoag, who demanded his return and prompt execution. But the Pilgrims, too dependent on Squanto's services, held out and the drama came to a surprise ending when Squanto died, ironically enough, of Indian fever. Sadly, no Indian other than "the savage" (and, incidentally, not a word about feasting) is mentioned in Bradford's first proclamation of a regularly scheduled Thanksgiving, dated November 15, 1636.

So goes the myth of the Pilgrims, whose perseverance, hard work, and humble beginnings gave rise to our American nation. But lately the pious Pilgrims have provided abundant fodder for the mill devoted to grinding up national mythologies. Revisionist historians characterize them as rather more human. Homosexuality, adultery, crime, and litigiousness were all a part of their social fabric. They drank lots of beer

and never ate much turkey. Moreover, say archaeologists, the record sug-
gests they didn't even land at Plymouth Rock.

In later seventeenth- and eighteenth-century colonial America, giving thanks at the end of the harvest developed into a sporadic religious
custom observed either in October, November, or even December (depending on where one lived in the colonies). Finally, to commemorate
the Pilgrims as well as to thank God for victory in the American Revolution (and thereby to strengthen the union), President George Washington declared Thursday, November 16, 1789, a nationwide holiday of
Thanksgiving. But the holiday was not established nationally as an annual affair until Washington finally proclaimed it in 1795. The careful
reader will note that while God is still in the picture in Washington's
proclamation, what He is being thanked for differs substantially from
the subject of the Pilgrims' prayers. The president wrote:

> and on that day to meet together and reorder sincere and hearty thanks
> to the great Ruler of nations for the manifold and signal mercies which
> distinguish our lot as a nation; *particularly for the possession of constitutions
> of government* which united and, by their union, establish liberty with
> order. (my italics).

Although Washington set aside Thursday, February 19, as the day of
public thanksgiving and prayer, the states stubbornly continued their own
end-of-the-harvest year customs. Thomas Jefferson was among the early
presidents who did not think the suffering of northern puritans was wor-
thy of official recognition by the entire nation, so it wasn't until deep into
the nineteenth century that Thanksgiving got transformed into not only a
religious and civic holiday but also one that returned the feast, now
reenvisioned as a family affair, to its present location in the calendar.

Nathaniel Hawthorne wrote in his 1842 *American Notebooks* :

> November 24th, Thursday
>
> This is Thanksgiving Day—a good old festival; and my wife and I have
> kept it with our hearts, and besides home made good cheer upon our
> turkey, and pudding, and pies, and custards, although none sat at our
> board but our two selves. There was a new and livelier sense, I think,
> that we have at last found a home, and that a new family has been gath-
> ered since the last Thanksgiving Day.

The menu I chose for this chapter's epigraph, already traditional by Hawthorne's day, dates from the early 1860s.

What Washington initiated as a way of bonding fledgling free colonies at the end of the Revolution, Lincoln would advance as a way of promoting unity in the midst of the strife of America's second generation—but Lincoln's action would take prompting by the iron will of an activist woman. Sarah Josepha Buell Hale (1788–1879), a home-schooled New Hampshire housewife and mother of four, emerges as a model of feminine independence at a time when the women's rights movement had only just begun to flicker to life. Talented, ambitious, and widowed at the age of thirty-four, she set up a millinery business and published a book of poems and a novel that dealt with the issue of slavery. In that work she also lauded the spirit of nationalism in Thanksgiving, which I think could apply to almost any red-letter day: "There is a deep moral influence in the periodical seasons of rejoicing," she wrote, "in which whole communities participate. They bring out . . . the best sympathies in our natures."

The book's popularity led her to the editorship a few years later of a new magazine devoted exclusively to women and specifically to furthering their education. Installing women as instructors at Vassar College and as overseas missionaries, along with raising funds to complete the Bunker Hill monument, preserving Mount Vernon, forming a Seaman's Aid Society—and establishing Thanksgiving as a national holiday—were among the social causes Hale addressed over a forty-year period in her *Ladies Magazine and Literary Gazette* (which later became *American Ladies Magazine* and finally, through partnership, *Godey's Lady's Book*).

In the late 1840s, Hale started petitioning state governors to establish a common day, the last Thursday in November, to celebrate a national Thanksgiving. By 1852 (a thousand letters later!), she was able to report in the July issue of her magazine that twenty out of thirty-one states (the strong objectors were Virginia, which had long expressed distaste for all puritans, and stubbornly independent Vermont) had agreed to celebrate the feast on the same day. In an 1859, editorial Hale entreated that if every state would join in a united Thanksgiving, war might be averted. Her November 1861 editorial for Thanksgiving as a day of peace implored (again unsuccessfully) the combating blues and grays to lay down their arms at least for that day. Two years later, Sarah turned to the White House. After making a patriotic plea for Thanksgiving in her September 1863 issue, she visited Lincoln himself and persuaded him to issue a proclamation (the second by a U.S. president) to be put into place by all the state governors. Addressed to them, Lincoln wrote, in part:

> And I recommend to them, that while offering up the ascriptions due to Him for such singular deliverance and blessings, they do so with humble penitence . . . commend to His tender care those who have become widows, orphans, or mourners, or sufferers in the lamentable civil strife in which we are unavoidably engaged, and fervently implore the interposition of the Almighty hand to heal the wounds of the nation, to the full enjoyment of peace, harmony, and Union.

An Englishman who visited the United States during the postwar period noted the newfound custom of feasting both on prayer and victuals: Everyone who joined the church, he wrote, would spend Thanksgiving morn listening to sermons galore followed by "a gigantic amount of eating and drinking." Even "the poorest of the poor, the meanest of the mean . . . were regaled with succulent white meat. The destitute and the infirm, the prisoners and captives were abundantly fed." Favored by God, America seemed, at least to this outsider, a land of plenty where no one went without sustenance. Even today the Thanksgiving Day TV evening news pays witness to the homeless and the starving who are guaranteed a full belly on the fourth Thursday in November. (What these people do for dinner the other 364 days of the year receives considerably less coverage.)

After a good turkey dinner, nineteenth-century urbanites would usually head out for a stroll or a ride in the family carriage. In New York, Broadway and its sidewalks were reported to be densely packed from Columbus Circle to Washington Square on Thanksgiving afternoon. Theaters and amusement places offered performances both in the afternoon and evening. And if you were still unsatiated, you could buy snacks or a good cigar from street vendors all along the route.

The Thanksgiving food of choice with which to stuff oneself is, itself stuffed, the turkey. What ham is to Easter and roast beef (it used to be goose) is to Christmas, so is turkey to Thanksgiving. The turkey is almost exclusively an American bird. The ancient Maya of Yucatan had feasted on it as early as three thousand years ago, long before the invading Spaniards took the wild turkey from Mexico to Europe and had it domesticated. Mole poblano (because it originated in the city of Puebla), a turkey simmered in a sauce of chili peppers and dark chocolate, is the traditional Christmas dinner in highland Mexico. Ecuadoreans consume the bird on New Year's Day. Because they interpret its gobblings as maledictions against the axe wielder in charge of the main course, the men in charge on execution day approach the turkey pen with a bottle of cheap *agua ardiente* and a rope. Before the poor bird has a chance to utter a response, one of the attendants grabs it by the neck while a second pours the firewater down its gullet. Held taut by the rope, the intoxicated turkey is then walked around in a circle by the rope until it falls to the ground in a drunken stupor. Thus anesthetized, the bird finally parts with its head.

Wishing on the wishbone after the meal as well as pavomancy—divining by watching turkey behavior when the birds take a noisy dust bath (to rid themselves of parasites)—are among the superstitions attached to our national November symbol. (Pay attention to how the dust flies, which way the down blows, and how long the bath takes—everything means something.) In northern climes they say that if the breastbone is light in color it will be a snowy winter; if dark (the color of the earth) there will be little snow on the ground.

The final adjustment in the placement of America's Thanksgiving day in the seasonal calendar emanates from the modern world of business and commerce—a fine tuning from the *last* to the *fourth* Thursday in November proclaimed by President Franklin Delano Roosevelt. The change came in response to complaints that late last Thursdays (like the 29th or 30th) encroached on Christmas, which could in some circumstances loom a mere three weekends ahead. At first not all states went along with his decree, but, being one of our more willful chief executives, FDR prevailed. His proposal was adopted as an Act of Congress in 1941 with the continued assurance that on this day people of our nation should reflect on the joys of our way of life, our rights and privileges, and our basic freedoms, by giving thanks to God. Seventeen years later,

President Eisenhower reinforced the religious aspect of the holiday by adding the worlds "Let us be especially grateful for the religious heritage bequeathed us by our forefathers" to his Thanksgiving Day message. In 2000, President Clinton's more secular, multicultural message added that despite our differences in background, age, politics, or race, we are all members of a larger American family and that, working together, there is nothing we cannot accomplish in this promising new century.

Despite a growing gap in the distribution of wealth (Bill Gates and Larry Ellison each earned a million times the median national income before the tech stock portion of the market fell back in 2002), the last third of the twentieth century and the entry into the new millennium have witnessed a marked decline in the religious aspect of November's fourth Thursday in America.

Today Turkey Day is devoted to TV sports, particularly football (an older generation can remember when people physically attended the local version of the game on Thanksgiving morning). Americans travel during Thanksgiving more than on any other holiday weekend, usually to the home of parents, grandparents, or one of the family elders who still manages to cook or cater a bird-centered feast. Grandma and Grandpa represent for us a kind of mythic American Adam and Eve, speculates one anthropologist. I can still remember singing "Over the river and through the woods…" with the kids excitedly bouncing around in the back seat and repeatedly asking "Are we there yet?" Gridlocked on the thruway on Wednesday the 26th, my four-year-old asked me: "Daddy, are *all* the cars going to see their Grandma and Grandpa?"

Whether we get Friday off usually determines how far we'll transport ourselves and how long a stay our time budget will allow. Those of us who need to travel by air find the trip increasingly stressful as airport congestion and security shows no tendency to wane. The morning after Thanksgiving also brings with it the added strain that comes with the unveiling of the consumer's Advent calendar, which tallies the official number of shopping days 'til Christmas. It kicks off the busiest weekend of the year for retailers (over 65 million consumers visited the malls on "Black Friday" last year).

The big gender split in our own family Thanksgiving holiday usually occurred when the women and young children were left at the table to discuss family issues, while the male members of the clan adjourned to the living room and plopped themselves in front of a TV screen (which seemed to increase in diameter about two inches per year) to watch football. Most spectators were fast asleep by halftime. National Football League fans are still treated to a half-time view of popular sports TV announcer John Madden's answer to the multifaceted problem of "Who ate all the drumsticks?" or "I'm not really a turkey fan." His "Terducken," a six-drumstick amalgam of the anatomical parts of turkey, duck, and chicken, cleverly pieced together, emerges as the ultimate choice table fare characterizing twenty-first-century American freedom of choice, prosperity, and downright uncompromise when it comes to getting what we want.

We may have replaced the traditional morning church service with the local high-school football game and that in turn with the distant view through a window of somebody else playing games, but we still dutifully (and usually punishingly) stuff ourselves, revisiting the excess behavior of Harvest Home, New Year's Eve, and Mardi Gras—marks of the many seasonal breathing points we number in red on our calendars.

Christmas:
From Resurrection To Rudolph

I used to take part in smiling at the Sun with only one side of my
face. When the Sun first came back it seemed to be stretched out
on the horizon. So when someone saw it for the first time we all
rushed out so that we could smile at it. . . . With the introduction
of Christianity these practices were discouraged . . . But the
practice of smiling at the Sun did not change with the new
religion.

John MacDonald

For the Inuit who live in the Canadian Arctic, what happens on
the winter solstice (December 21) is far more dramatic than any comparable cosmic phenomenon those of us who live in temperate and tropical latitudes witness. Christmas time there doesn't just bring lengthier
noontime shadows and longer nights. It is a time of total darkness—
both day and night.

Cold November begins with the bright orange sun spiraling its way
downward as it circles daily around the sky on a track nearly parallel to
the horizon, its disk gradually encroaching on the bare tundra. By the

middle of the month, the sun's lower limb reaches down and begins a bumpy ride over the hilltops. Round the cardinal points of the horizon it goes from north to east to south to west, then north again. A few rounds later, when it manages a peek through the clouds, the pale red disk has sunk noticeably into the snow. Gradually it flattens out like a deflated tire and vanishes, making a few brief reappearances through deep divots between the low rolling hills and in rare mirages. By month's end it is gone. The lord of the day has disappeared—replaced by a long, slowly diminishing twilight as bright stars joined by fainter ones proclaim the arrival of the long Arctic night.

People of the Northwest Territories call it Tauvikjuag—the seven weeks between late November and mid-January when the sun is gone. We don't know how their ancestors behaved during this period, for early explorers acquired no records, even though the settlement has been inhabited for two thousand years. White strangers didn't seem to care much about Eskimo customs anyway. We can only imagine what went through the minds of the early inhabitants of this frigid region when the long darkness overtook the daytime at this vital seasonal turning point. Will the lord of light who has abandoned us now restore himself and start back on his course toward humanity, bringing with him an end to the menace of the dwindling daylight hours and a return to greater warmth and longer light? How can we help?

Today in Inuvik and Barrow, Alaska, people party, eat, dance, and drink—"get legless" as the locals say. They do it communally, playing games such as finger pulling and high kick— games that test their strength and endurance—or dancing in the skins of the animals they honor, such as the fox and the wolf. They look outward as they celebrate not just with family and friends but farther outside the household into community hall and church. At winter solstice, people turn inward as well. They reflect on who they are and what it means to be a physically strong hunter.

This feeling of deep concern that accompanies the winter solstice is no less appreciated in other cultures. Bronze Age Stonehenge was probably built not only with its main axis pointing to midsummer sunrise but also to fix the midwinter full moonrise, which appears close to the same point on the horizon, thus marking the days of the year when two celestial luminaries were needed to bear continuous light into the world from dawn to dusk and back to dawn again. Seasonal festivities taking place there might have included a sharing of food, gossip, old stories, and, I would guess, some serious concern expressed in ritual form about the sun's apparent demise.

Built-in solstice registers abound in neolithic architecture. For example, in the Orkney Islands the passage grave of Maes Howe, a third-millennium B.C. tomb, has a long narrow aperture over the entrance that allows sunlight into the interior only at winter solstice. Several *cursus* monuments (long rectangular enclosures surrounded by banks) in southern England have their axes aligned with the midwinter sun at the horizon.

The architectural reckoning of the annual southern solar standstill extends well beyond prehistoric societies. At the peak of their civilization in the eighth century, the classic Maya of Yucatan registered the shortest day of the year in their city plans. Writing and sculpture excavated at one of their great cities tell an engrossing winter's tale of death and resurrection.

What time is more critical in the smooth operation of organized society than a change of president or the death of a ruler? Any discontinuity is unsettling—a kink in the circle of time. How would the people know that once their leader was gone, an offspring would possess the same powers? What guarantees it? For the Maya the bloodline proclaimed the principle of immortality through a divine link to heavenly ancestors. At the ruins of Palenque in the interior of Mexico's Gulf Coast, a stucco inscription in the Tablet of the Cross (so called because of the presence of a Maya tree of life once thought to resemble a Christian cross) tells us that the son of the deceased ruler Pacal (Shield Bearer), Chan Bahlum (Lord Jaguar), is his reincarnated spirit. The myth of Maya creation says that when the old gods who created the world died, they passed through the underworld and reemerged in the east as celestial bodies—the sun and Venus are often prominently mentioned. And so it was for the kings. After Pacal underwent his apotheosis in the underworld, his powers were reborn in his son. Like the coming of spring after a long dark winter, the old ruler reemerges invigorated in the body of his son.

Maya architecture provided an elaborate stagecraft to serve as a backdrop for the celestial reenactment of this resurrection myth. If you travel to Palenque on December 21 and climb to the top of the tower in Chan Bahlum's palace, you can still watch the winter solstice sun dive directly into the Temple of the Inscriptions where Pacal is interred—an architectural hierophany like the descending equinox serpent at Chichén Itzá (see Chapter 4). In the Palenque hierophany the plunging sun is Pacal. He begins his descent into the underworld as he takes his first steps on the temporal road to resurrection. The effigy of the dying king is portrayed falling into the abyss on the lid of his own sarcophagus. The message cast in writing, sculpture, and architecture plays on the Maya philosophy of cyclic time. Death is the force of creation that propels life and leads to birth. Chan Bahlum is his own father, a re-envisioned version of his predecessor by blood in the great solar transformation. Among the surviving (and now largely Christianized) Maya, Christ is still depicted as a sun god with rays of light emanating from this crown.

Many archaic winter solstice themes are deeply imbedded in our modern celebration of the Christmas holiday. Even though the Christmas season is connected with the Nativity, biblical texts offer us no reliable information on precisely when Christ was born; spring or summertime turn out to be better guesses than the winter solstice. As for the Star of Bethlehem, no single cosmic event we can generate with modern astronomical computer software—be it a comet, a supernova, or the close encounter of planets—offers any help in pinning down the date. My opinion is that the story was *midrash*, a Hebrew term meaning the arrangement of a mixture of truths to tell a story—in this case the story of the Gospel. The good news of imminent salvation is a theme that resonates with the ambience of winter solstice.

The earliest record that places the Nativity on December 25 comes from a calendar dated to A.D. 354. The fourth-century writer, a scribe named Syrus, tells us that the Romans lit candles on this day to celebrate the sun's birthday. Because Christians participated heavily in the ritual, officials of the young Church talked it over and, impressed with the symbolic potency of the ritual of bringing back light into the world that accompanied this time of year, they decided to officially solemnize Christ.

Interestingly, pagan Rome itself had sacralized the day only a little more than a century earlier. In A.D. 273, Emperor Aurelian had officially designated December 25 as the Roman winter solstice festival, the Birthday of the Unconquered (or Unconquerable) Sun (*Dies Natalis Solis Invicti*), so called because of what actually appeared in the sky on that occasion. (Though they couldn't measure it with any accuracy because the sun advances very slowly along the horizon as it nears the solstices, the Romans nonetheless reckoned December 25 to be the longest day.) Our switch to December 21 (or 20) is in part due to the backshift of the calendar resulting from the Gregorian reform of 1582 when an attempt was made to readjust the calendar to fit the course of the sun.) The sun's birthday celebrated the belief that time would not be at an end. The sun God Apollo (a spinoff of the earlier Persian deity Mithras) would not vanish on his southward winter course but instead would return to the world to achieve victory over darkness. When the fourth-century Emperor Constantine made Christianity the official religion of the Eastern (Holy) Roman Empire, it didn't take long for the feast to be adopted as the celebration of the *Dies Natali* (he deleted the words *Solis Invicti*) with Christ, the Savior, officially displacing the sun as the herald of time's rebeginning.

If we back up still further, we find that the solstice also collides with the notorious Roman Saturnalia, a festival that lasted several days before and after the solstice, though it gave no particular emphasis to the actual solstice date. More like our New Year celebrations, this was a festival dedicated on the one hand to the formal completion of the cycle of the seasons and on the other to preparations for a new one. All businesses, schools, and civic places were shut down as a carnival atmosphere of noise and revelry took over the capital. Everybody surrenders to pure pleasure, the Roman writer Libanius tells us. There is even a hint of the commercialism that modern Scrooges attach to the holiday season: "The desire to spend money grips everybody. . . . A stream of presents pours itself out on all sides," he wrote. Roles were reversed as masters waited on their servants. Pranks were played; masks were donned and a mock king—old Saturn himself, god of the underworld—was elected to preside over the revelry and license. He was ritually sacrificed at the end of the feast, just as Jupiter, benevolent king of the gods, had once dethroned him from his mythical earthly reign. A feeling of wild anticipation, not unlike what we observe in the Inuit (or imagine in neolithic Stonehengers), pervaded the season. Old fires were put out in the temples and Vestal Virgins kindled new ones, adorning the doorways of the temples with new foliage (the antecedent of our Christmas mistletoe) to open the season of farming.

The Roman writer Lucian fantasizes about what he would do were he king of Saturnalia: tell someone to shout insults to himself, order another to dance naked, another to pick up a woman and twirl her about the dance floor acrobatically. Like Halloween, Saturnalia relieved the tensions of the season by relaxing norms—the elite would let their hair down and the unholy would be accorded a temporary claim to status. Saturnalia strengthened the social hierarchy.

Christmas was never more popular than in the Middle Ages, a time when Christianity rose to become the dominant religion in Europe and much artistic endeavor was spent to express its new essence. In 1058, the feast acquired its modern name of "Cristes Maesse." The four-week Advent, the period of anticipation leading up to the celebration of the Nativity offered a panoply of Christmas events. Some began the season as early as St. Martin's Day (November 11). (He was a fourth-century son of a Roman military tribune who had had a vision of Christ after dividing his cloak and giving half of it to a scantily clad, shivering pauper.)

So many of our standard symbols of Christmas—the Yule log, holly, and caroling—radiate out of eleventh- to thirteenth-century northern Europe. The burning of the Yule log (from *Hiaul* or *Huul*, Old English words for wheel or sun, likely derived from the Scandinavian word *jol* or *jul*, which gives us our word "jolly") may be a remnant of a rite in which celebrants once set huge bonfires to beckon winter's holy light to return to the sky. Hence the custom of saving the biggest log for the fire, which must last all day and into the longest night. To connect rituals from one cycle to the next a part of the Yule log must be kept to kindle next year's fire. Traditionally, the whole bottom trunk of a tree was cut and dried on the previous Candlemas, which ended the last Christmas cycle. Evergreens were the logical choice for they are symbols of everlasting life. The prickly leaves and branches of holly also portend the promise of a fertile earth brought about by the newborn sun. Their nettles serve as his protector, their bright red berries warning of imminent danger from evil spirits who might stifle the sun's delicate awakening and fragile early ascent up into the heavens. (Christ is often pictured in crèche scenes nestled amid such protective bushes.)

The custom of caroling became immensely popular after the late eleventh-century Norman Conquest. Groups of singers would go around the neighborhood striking up melodies heralding the heavenly birth and all the comfort and joy that will follow in its wake. Chilled carolers would be invited in and rewarded with a warm cup of cheer and a snack as testimony to the general goodwill that attaches itself to this communal season. Some considered it unlucky not to offer sustenance at length to the first chorus that appeared at the door. At times the jovial sing-along atmosphere took on an air often accompanying Halloween's trick-or-treat ceremonies, with gifts duly anticipated and bad fortune descending on those who balked at the rite. An unidentified early-seventeenth-century Scrooge wrote: "Our ears are saluted with the dissonant screaming of Christmas carols, which the miserable creatures sing who travel from house to house with the vessel cup" (a container with an image representing Christ).

One of our most popular weather superstitions—predicting the weather for the months of the succeeding year based on what happens meteorologically on each of the twelve days of Christmas—is also a product of the Middle Ages. Farmers were careful to record the weather on each of the days that followed the shortest day, like so many steps upward in time from the nadir of the sun's course. They would mark each day with a circle of chalk, leaving it blank like a new moon if the weather was good, filling it in like a full moon if the weather was bad and partially filling it (like a crescent or quarter) if the day was mixed. The phase of the moon on Christmas night was another prognosticator—a waxing moon foretold a good year, a waning moon the opposite. Out of these practices developed our modern *Farmer's Almanac*, which, with the exception of adding recipes and tips on household management, still operates on the same principle. We have encountered this regenerative concept of time before (remember Groundhog Day?)—the future is contained in the past. Likewise the year cycle repeats in miniature the whole cycle of creation.

I think the twelve days of Christmas, over which the most intense celebration of Christ's birth occurs, are the remains of the uncounted days that occur at the end of a twelve-moon phase cycle of approximately 354 days—a bundle of time that must be added onto the end of the old lunar year to round out a full cycle of the sun. Here we need to remember that farmers tend to be intense moonwatchers. For some peasants of central Europe, these exceptional 12 days between the Nativity and Epiphany (January 6) were actually thought to lay outside the year—signifying a deliberate halt to life's chain of events—a time for recollection and reconsideration of the past as well as prognostication for the future.

Moonwatching also lies buried in Chanukah, the Jewish "Feast of Lights," which Gentiles think of as "the Jewish Christmas." What Passover is to the equinox, Chanukah is to the winter solstice. It moves about the calendar from year to year because it is a lunar-based holiday. Hebraic tradition fixes it on the 25th day of the month of Kislev, but because the moon phase cycle and our seasonal year of the sun do not fit neatly together, it can land anywhere between late November and late December in the modern calendar. In tune with solstice phenomena of major turnarounds, this holiday is all about the weak triumphing over the strong, a theme typical of much of the Old Testament literature that tells the story of the persecuted Israelites. Chanukah specifically celebrates Jewish independence from second-century B.C. Syrian oppressors. It culminated in the recovery of their temple, which the enemy king had defiled, and the rekindling of the eternal lights within it. The eight-day celebration commemorates the miraculous burning of the lamps that, though devoid of oil, nonetheless continued to light the temple, thus enabling the devout to fully restore their altar. Jewish households today feature a lighting of the menorah, one candle for each of the eight days, accompanied by traditional dishes, games, and an exchange of gifts.

Mistletoe and caroling live on in the traditional twenty-first-century American Christmas even though many of us complain that the light of the spirit of Christmas has been diminished, even extinguished, by the shadow of commercialism. The myth of the capitalist takeover of the Yuletide season originates in the advertising boardroom. It funnels into the mall, and empties out its goods on the home hearth. The case of one of Christmas's most beloved characters, Rudolph the red-nosed Reindeer, is a good example.

Rudolph, a member of one of the world's most beloved species, is a rejected deer. As in the tale of the ugly duckling, playmates make fun of him because of his luminous red nose (like big ears, a protruding proboscis is a universal object of derision). In a stroke, Rudolph's stigma is converted to a timely talent when Santa Claus, stumbling around in the foggy darkness while attempting to make his annual deliveries one Christmas Eve, notices a glow of light emanating from Rudolph's house. He awakens the deer and asks him to lead his team. With the light from the deer's nose illuminating street signs and house numbers, Santa's meteorological crisis is averted and kids all over the world get their presents. On the return trip Rudolph whirls the sleigh around amid those who had made fun of him. Wild applause by all the neighborhood deer kids prompts Santa to dub him the best reindeer ever and to invite him aboard as a regular.

Long before Johnny Marks wrote the song in 1949, Robert L. May, a Montgomery Ward ad department employee, penned the story. Mail order company execs had assigned May the task of creating an animal story to head a promotional "giveaway" during the Christmas season sale campaign of 1939. Two and a half million copies of May's storybook were distributed that Fall and when the item was resurrected in 1946 and went commercial in 1947, Marks got the idea to write the song.

What is it about the Rudolph story that made him so enduringly popular with children? Given a break, a kid with a stigma can be transformed into a hero. This theme also resonates with the idea that a seemingly disadvantaged child can help solve a grown-up's problem. Present too is the popular notion of a special animal guiding humans to safety in the face of great danger—like Lassie and Rin-Tin-Tin.

Who knows better how to create popular trends (with commercial benefits) for kids than the advertisers? The upbeat ending of the Rudolph story—"Happy Christmas to all and to all a good night"—features a closing line May borrowed from Clement Clark Moore's "Account of a Visit from St. Nicholas." It comes about as a result of all the packages and presents—no doubt purchased through the Montgomery Ward catalog—getting to their ultimate destination. It is indeed a Happy Christmas when we all end up with the material goods we so passionately seek. (By the way, one modern literary gumshoe, in the contemporary spirit of debunking legends, has recently declared Moore to be as phony as the Pilgrims—a plagiarist who borrowed verse, meter, style, and vocabulary from an earlier source.)

To trace the roots of the story of the modern takeover of our most popular holiday by greedy capitalists, we need to back up to nineteenth-century Britain and America. After a half-millennium wave of popularity, Christmas fervor had become greatly diminished. Christmas in mid-seventeenth-century puritanical America was outlawed by Protestant reformists as another one of those idol-worshipping religious festivals well worth expunging. Fines were levied on workers who took the day off. It was only in the early nineteenth century that the migrations of liberal German and Dutch Protestants to U.S. shores led to a restoration of its holiday status to the calendar.

Dickens is the figure most responsible for striking a nerve in the (early) Victorian revival of Christmas. His famous story, which first appeared in 1843, was nothing less than a frontal attack on the growing greed and self-centeredness, which he portrayed as endemic to a newly industrialized urban society. Dickens's anxious response to the discontent over rampant social decay stressed that Christmas should be a festive occasion, with good cheer, generosity—and plenty. All of us—rich, *nouveau riche*, and middle class alike—should enjoy the wealth of the nation.

The same story line rings loud and clear in "How the Grinch Stole Christmas," a takeoff on Dickens's "Bah, humbug!" Ebenezer Scrooge character from "A Christmas Carol." The Grinch is an activist antihero who deliberately contrives to stop the transmission of goods in their tracks by stealing every item from every hearth that smacks of the spirit of gift giving. Then, for inexplicable reasons, his hard-hearted spirit undergoes instant meltdown when he confronts a tearful little waif in front of the Christmas tree he has just pilfered. In the Scrooge story we encounter the same born-again conversion of a penny-pinching miser. (Ebenezer, appropriately enough, means "stone"—an apt description of his heart.) The good spirit of Christmas swells the Grinch's heart and he ends up not only returning all the stuff but also overseeing its redistribution. For this he is accorded a place of honor at the communal dining-room table, where he gets to carve the roast beast.

One last enduring Christmas story in this genre (there are many) is the more adult-oriented, Oscar winning *Miracle on 34th Street*. Challenging skepticism about Santa Claus, this story centers around the rivalry between two big city department stores, a rivalry that becomes intensified when one of the stores happens to hire the real Kris Kringle (a corruption of the German *Christkindlein*, or Christmas bringer of gifts to kids) to portray Santa. Price-conscious Kris naively advises some customers to shop in the competitor's store—an intolerable commercial disadvantage to his employer. After variously being put on trial and locked up in a psychiatric ward where he is probed and pronounced disillusional, Kris, with the help of a little girl who never stops believing in him, succeeds in instilling all those who surround him—including the little girl's unbelieving bottom-line mother and the managers of the rival stores—with the true spirit of Christmas. Faith and imagination conquers all, even the greedy profit takers. Our young heroine ends up with the dream post-World War II gift of a brand new house in the suburbs—an ironic outcome given the movie's slant against consumerism.

The paradox of Christmas today lies in the confrontation of the strong materialist sense of the consumer and the decidedly nonmaterialistic values of the religious celebrants, for whom we suppose the holiday was originally intended. Last year Christmas retail sales added nearly $200 billion to our economy—more than the gross national product of a majority of world nations.

Gifts used to be personal possessions. When you gave a gift, you sacrificed a portion of yourself by giving up something dear to you. It might be a verse you wrote, flowers you grew, or a picture you painted. Gift giving was a transaction in which the giver, in a spirit of reciprocity, also expected to play the role of receiver of a similar precious possession: "It is better to give than to receive." That all changed when gifts became impersonal goods with the coming of the nineteenth-century industrial age. As Emerson lamented, "It is a cold lifeless business when you go to the shops to buy one something that does not represent your life and talent."

The nineteenth was also the century of Santa Claus. Before he became the bearer of gifts as goods, Santa started as a mask for Christmas in the face of Protestant criticism of the feast. When Ben Jonson introduced him as "Christmas His Masque" in 1616, he was a character who promoted games and feasts, not presents. Bearded, but not particularly rotund, he wore a tall hat, white shoes and long stockings, and a furry gown. He took on the name of St. Nicholas, the red-robed patron saint of children during the romantic Victorian era, after having variously been referred to as Father Christmas and Sir Christmas. Santa didn't balloon to popularity as the jolly old fat elf who coursed across the sky in a reindeer-driven sleigh until the American Clement Clark Moore (allegedly) wrote his famous 1822 poem.

The Christmas tree, which brought together the perfect midwinter combination of green and light, was a German innovation that picked up on the discarded tree symbolism (see Chapter 6). It took firm root in the United States of the nineteenth century as the designated place where Santa dropped his bountiful load. There is a big dispute about who set up the first Tannenbaum on U.S. soil. One claimant, Charles Follen, says he put a candle-lighted tree in his Cambridge, Massachusetts, home in 1832. The Christmas card, part of the old custom of sending blessings on the New Year, also grew immensely popular in the second half of the nineteenth century ($6.9 billion in retail sales last year, or three to one over its nearest rival, Valentine's Day).

With industrial capitalism growing in post-Civil War nineteenth-century America, the home became the refuge of the family, a quiet place away from the indifferent machine clatter of the world outside. Home was the place where affectionate gift giving was supplemented by feasting. Like gift exchange, the traditional Christmas dinner is an outgrowth of the feast of plenty that marks the turn of the year. Turkey, roast beef, and ham (replacement for the traditional boar's head, baked peacock, and goose of earlier ages) all have the distinction of being cuts of meat large enough to share among an extended family group.

All the gluttony that goes with the main meal is sanctioned by the "Spirit of Christmas Past" in Dickens's tale. His description of the Christmas meal is excessively obscene by modern lean cuisine-oriented standards: "Heaped upon the floor . . . were turkeys, geese, game poultry, brawn, great joints of meat, suckling pigs, long wreaths of sausages, mince pies, plum puddings, barrels of oysters . . . and seething bowls of punch, that made the chamber dim with their delicious steam." Like many of the old transitional points in the framework of seasonal time, Christmas remains, even in the face of our professed fitness consciousness, a time band devoted to excesses. (Despite all our pronouncements on the evils of food, America in the first decade of the new millennium is fatter—and more unrestrained—than ever.)

America's overindulgence exhibits a curious inversion when it comes to income class. Why is it that some of the poorest looking homes in my neighborhood invest in the highest wattage of blinking baubles at Christmas time, many of which remain up—and lit—year round? When I pass by these same places two months earlier, their lawns are overcrowded with spooky Halloween "graveyards" and ghosts and spiderwebs made out of magic-markered old bedsheets and "angel hair" hanging in the trees. Three months later the same trees are studded with plastic Easter eggs; and I would wager that were I invited in for Thanksgiving Day dinner I would probably confront the biggest turkey money can buy. The people who live in these places seem to be saying: "We may not have much, but we're sure going to flaunt whatever we've got." The holidays are times when we binge as a way of calling a temporary halt to agonizing over our troubles. And the poorer we are the more we need a break. The better to let it all hang out—it relieves tension. We have witnessed this periodic letting off of steam at other stress points in time's framework—for example, at Carnival and Mardi Gras and New Year's Eve.

There is scarcely a holiday when we don't live beyond our means at least for a little while.

Today there are many American Christmases, each reflecting a component of the ethnic makeup of our emerging society. Latin American Christmases are manifold in their variety of customs. Those in the Southwest are accompanied by *Los Matachines* (grotesque figures). Their Christmas dance ceremony is dedicated to the silly extreme behavior that often characterizes end-of-a-cycle rituals. Men don masks and tight-fitting colorful costumes; they make weird gestures at one another. To the timing of a drumbeat they proceed to beat each other over the head with air-filled bladders and wooden swords, ritually killing one another. Scholars have puzzled over the origin of *Los Matachines.* The word may be Arabic (*nutawajjihin*), Italian (*mattacino*), or even Spanish or French. It may be connected to the morris dances mentioned in Chapter 6, or possibly even an old Aztec satirical play, as evidenced by the Yaqui Indian *matachin* dances practiced just south of the border.

Long lost in the limelight of Christmas, the lighting of the Chanukah candles has undergone a resurgence, especially since the Holocaust, the strengthening of Zionism, and the establishment of the State of Israel. Today it emerges as a mechanism for ethnic solidarity among all Jews. Chanukah has become Christmasized, a sort of "Judaism Lite," that allows celebrants with varying degrees of devoutness to savor the day in whatever proportions best suit them. Like its Christian counterpart, it has its commercial element. The customary small cash gifts have been replaced among the wealthy class by cars, ski vacations, and myriad appliances. As one Chanukah historian writes, "America's Jews have reacted to their exclusion from Christmas the way they typically react to their exclusion from a country club, by building a better one of their own."

Although it originated two thousand years later, the African-American festival known as Kwanzaa also focuses on the idea of the liberation of oppressed people. A 1966 invention of social anthropologist Maulana Karenga, Kwanzaa (a Swahili word meaning "first fruits") was intended, as firebrand politician Al Sharpton once put it, "as a way of de-whitizing" the Christmas season. In the socially turbulent 1960s Kwanzaa also embodied a reaction against consumerism and commodi-fication of the holiday social ills African-American people had acquired from their white capitalist oppressors. Time, however, has dulled the blade of protest. By the 1990s, the holiday acquired all the earmarks of White Christmas. Case in point: three hundred exhibitors, ranging from Pepsi and J. C. Penney to Anheuser Busch and Hallmark, turned up at a 1993 Kwanzaa expo in New York, offering items for sale ranging from Kwanzaa cards to teddy bears in African clothing.

Borrowing heavily from the Jewish model, devout Kwanzaa cel-ebrants light one candle on each of seven days (December 26–January 1)—the traditional Christmas day is excluded. Each candle honors a cultural rather than a religious principle toward which believers pledge to strive: unity, collective work and responsibility, creativity, faith, and so on. Today, like Latinos and other minorities, more than twenty mil-lion American blacks refashion Christmas into a holiday that has mean-ing for them. Like all the other holidays before it, Christmas is a reinvented tradition. Our capacity to change its meaning to suit the times is the force that keeps it alive.

"What Goes Around . . ."

Human culture is the great processor of time. Like other
creatures of the biological world, our ancestors began simply by
sensing the rhythms of natural time—the beat of the tides, the
coming of the rains, the on-and-off stroboscopic flickering of the
full moon's light, the comings and goings of swallows, locusts, the
red tide, and El Niño. But once we grabbed hold of the controls,
we changed the order. We manipulated time, developed and
enhanced it, processed, compressed, and packaged it to conform
to our perceived needs.

Anthony Aveni

This is the story of our love affair with time—as I characterized it
in an earlier work. Those red-letter days that mark the resting points,
the reflective moments in our journey around the annual wheel of time,
follow this temporal rondo. We have celebrated the year's ebbing and
flowing, key notes in its musical strain, its moments of tension followed
by relaxation, the returning themes of life and death, germination, and
harvest that guide us through the seasons in various guises. What have
we learned?

Nature is where time begins. We have discovered that nature's diverse and ever-changing forces gave the year a rhythm writ in a variety of scores. Pagan polytheism converted the holidays to occasions for honoring the deities who personified those forces: wind, sun, moisture—even highly specialized powers, like the one that causes mold to appear on the grain crop. Christianity further transformed the natural world to pay homage to its saints. Each step in the evolution of the year further diminished the direct contact between the human condition and the rhythm of nature. Today the secular taming of the tenets of organized religion joins the forces of mercantilism to further obscure the original meaning we once attached to each of our holidays.

Our journey around the circle of seasonal time that binds us is but one kind of natural rhythm we experience. We find throughout history a kind of quaint amusement, a sense of the unique magic that comes with each special day; but above all our encounter with the seasonal cycle tells us a lot about ourselves—how we've changed. Our forebears seem to have assumed an attitude toward the pace of the seasons that we no longer share—the notion of living a life *in* time, rather than despite it. They actively participated in singing nature's song; they conducted rites they thought impacted the way the forces of nature actually would behave. Our contemporary performance on the holidays is starkly passive by contrast. Sometimes we forget what we're singing about, what we're celebrating—let's sleep in, then go shopping. Can there yet be deeper meaning in these days for us?

From a practical point of view, having completed our look back at the days we hold dear, we also learn that the way people create seasonal calendars depends less on any measure of the native intelligence of time's users and more on who is in charge of time and what purpose its owners would have it serve. The way we imprint seasonal cycles with formal calendars turns out to have much to do with controlling activities in the society in which we live—how we eat, how we proliferate, how we labor to sustain ourselves. We have found that many of the older calendars were fastened firmly to the agrarian economy at the points of deepest concern—the bad as well as the good times when we look to powers that transcend, powers with whom we need to conduct a dialogue—a discourse that will enable us both to survive and thrive. The farmer's crisis always seems to occur at planting time, yet when the great moment of tension recurs it never seems quite the same—for what holiday is an exact repeat of itself? Neither is the anxiety of the harvesters who measure out the store of grain to feed the populace, nor the sigh of relief when those responsible finally can feel assured there will be plenty for everyone (which doesn't always happen). Then comes the release—the thank-yous, halle-lujahs, and hurrahs. Festivals for paying debts to the gods always seem positioned strategically in between work time and rest time.

Business calendars, social calendars, religious calendars—all are com-ponents of seasonal time in more highly organized societies, and each serves different interests. In state and imperial societies such as classical Rome, bureaucratic rulerships tried to harness time by merging schedules into a single, all-encompassing calendar, one capable of addressing all in-terests. The success of the empire demanded that everyone must be given their time due—their season. For the Western world especially, the cul-tural taproot that underlies the organization of the year has grown out of economic determinism, though Judeo-Christian religion still plays a major role in the holidays we keep. Timekeeping may have begun with a religious motive, but modern consumerism—the idea that time is money—originated in medieval mercantilism. Today the rigid control of human time is powered largely by the business of making money in a highly in-dustrialized, techno-world that creates its own seasons—and stresses. We have seen the profound effects of these forces on the transformation of Christmas, Easter, Halloween, and most of the other holidays.

We never cease to improvise the melody that accompanies the rhythm of the seasons. Some holidays survive only to become revitalized by con-venient substitutions that slightly alter their meaning. Others fade into obscurity as the significance once attached to them seems no longer ten-able. For example, Pan American Day is still celebrated on April 14, though it is scarcely recognized. It was established in 1930 by the Pan American Union to honor the first International Conference of Ameri-can States (1890), with the stated purpose of promoting peace, com-merce, and friendship among the countries of North and South America. But its initiation, housing in, and domination by the United States (the

U.S. Secretary of State and representatives of the various nations based in Washington, D.C., oversaw all the presiding officers) caused it to lose popularity among most member republics. American Indian Day (the fourth Friday in September), instigated by Native American tribes, never caught on either, perhaps because its founding document, though it honored Native American philosophy and social institutions, also evoked an image of guardianship by framing its goals in the need to struggle for "enlightenment and competency that is consistent with American citizenship."

Children's Day and the once pivotal Lammas have expired too. Their demise, coupled with the institution of new holidays that have begun to stick, gives us a sense of the dynamic quality of the seasonal calendar and what it will look like in the future as the structure of society and the public rituals that attend its requirements remain in constant flux. The rash of American patriotic holidays instituted in the mid-nineteenth to mid-twentieth-century war-torn years from the Civil War to World War II, Korea and Vietnam, has been followed by a tide of special days that recognize the multiethnic components of a newly emerging society. Martin Luther King Jr. Day is the most recent example. There are others less well known: for example, Rizal Day (December 30) honors the death of Jose Rizal, a martyr of the 1890s Philippine Independence movement. Alhough it was organized a century ago, Filipino students and workers have since taken it over and employed it as a means of sustaining national identity and pride amid an engulfing American society. Rizal Day's charter evokes the same tension between a people's need to perpetuate their heritage and the inevitable forces that seek to immerse it in a pluralistic society. Today's West Indian Carnival Day, Chicano Day, Cuban Day, and Puerto Rican Day parades join those of St. Patrick's and Columbus's that served the same purpose for earlier waves of immigrants.

Ringing in new festivals alongside revivified older ones is not a modern invention. It happened when the exotic cultures of the Middle East came into contact with the Roman Empire, when the Aztec and Inca states enveloped the Americas, and when Spain in turn engulfed them. Cultures do not die. Like the colors on the painter's palette, they blend together to create new hues. The seasonal calendar is a reflection of the creation process. It has been and always will be an ordered list of "time due," an expression of the needs we anticipate for our survival, both as individuals and as a society.

The old musical score that once made up the song of the seasons may seem in tattered condition. Alhough it has lost many chords—in the archaic gleanings of Halloween, in the dim image of Lammas's first fruits resurrected at Thanksgiving time, in newly sanctioned Labor Day and resanctioned May Day, in all the days of tarnished scarlet tint—we continue to hum the tune. And in the amended notes that make up the improvised melody of time we rediscover not just a continuous history of our repeated encounter with life's forces, but also the wonderful story of who we were before we became ourselves.

Notes .

While putting my own spin on the seasons I was greatly influenced by a number of texts, some of them classics. Far from outdated, Martin Nilsson's 1928 *Primitive Time Reckoning* is a gold mine of resources on calendar making in a variety of ancient cultures. The more recent *Oxford Companion to the Year* by Blackburn and Holford-Stevens (1999) has become the encyclopedic reference on what we celebrate day-by-day throughout the seasonal cycle. I found no better history of the seasons than Ronald Hutton's brilliant and thorough work *The Stations of the Sun*, which captures the changing essence of many of the calendrical rites derived from the English-Scottish tradition. Two of the resources on holiday magic and omens I found myself consulting repeatedly are Kingsbury et al.'s *Weather Wisdom* (1996) and Opie and Tatem's *A Dictionary of Superstitions* (1989). In my view, historian of religion Leigh Schmidt has written the best recent work on the nineteenth- and twentieth-century commodification of the holidays: *Consumer Rites, The Buying and Selling of American Holidays* (1995). Finally, Jack Santino's two books *All Around the Year* and *Halloween and Other Festivals of Death and Life* (both 1994) helped give me a sound sense of the role the holidays play in contemporary middle-class America. Specific reference to my epigraphs, quotes, as well as other notations follow.

Chapter 1

Epigraph: Nilsson, p. 46.
"The need to be identifiably different . . . ," Frake, p. 284.

Chapter 2

Epigraph: Eliot, T. S. "Four Quartets."

"To this day the Indians . . . ," Don Juan Pio Perez in Stephens, Vol I, p. 280.

Moon of worms, etc. . . ., I offer a lengthy discussion of moon-based calendars in *Empires of Time*, Ch. 3.

On the installation of the Roman calendar, see Astin, and York, for the various conflicting accounts that place the change of the starting date of the year (from March 15 to January 1) between 153 B.C. and 133 B.C.

"Omens are wont. . . ," Ovid I: 179.

"Here's to thee old apple tree . . . ," Hutton, p. 46; dates to 1791.

"Here's to thy pretty face . . . And next year, if we live, we'll drink to thee again," ibid., p. 50.

"Take out then take in . . . ," Opie and Tatem, p. 284.

"God send you plenty . . . ," ibid.

Chapter 3

Epigraph: Barrow, Henry, *The Writings of Henry Barrow,* 1587–90, pp. 462–63, cited in Thomas, p. 60.

"We believe in the wisdom of the groundhog . . . ," Krythe, 1962, p. 34.

"Let the scientific fakirs gnash their teeth . . . ," Krythe, 1962, p. 35.

"When ducks are driving . . . ," Kingsbury et al., p. 126.

"When swallows fly low . . . ," Kingsbury et al., p. 390.

"Wanns uf Aller . . . ," Fogel, p. 231.

After Candlemas day . . . etc., Kingsbury et al., p. 53.

"But when Zeus . . . ," Frazer, *Hesiod*, pp. 126–27, lines 564–69.

"Evil return to the one . . . ," Memory Paterson, p. 87.

"All lessons . . . ," Aristophanes, p. 61.

"For this was sent . . . ," Chaucer in Robinson, p. 366.

"Oft I have heard . . . ," Herrick—reprinted in Bliss, p. 48.

"I wouldn't have got rid . . . ," Opie and Tatem, p. 419.

"Mr. Blossom was my man . . . ," Hazlitt, p. 610.

"A magic spell . . . ," DeLys, p. 357.

"You old henpecked wretch . . . ," Schmidt, p. 81.

"If you'd lasso a real live man . . . ," Santino (*All Around the Year*), p. 74.

Chapter 4

Epigraph: Eliade, *Patterns in Comparative Religion*, p. 309.

". . . and having arrived there . . . ," Landa, p. 158.

"They said ... that ... ," ibid.

"... an architectural assemblage ... a spectacular hierophany ... ," Rivard, p. 52.

The earliest recognition of the phenomenon goes back much further (see Carlson).

"Man becomes aware ... ," Eliade, *Patterns*, pp. xii–xiii.

"To the ancient peoples ... ," Rivard, ibid.

"Marvelous pyramidal geometry," Arochi, p. 59.

"It was just ... ," Castañeda, pp. 190–91.

"His erect and perfect form. ... ," Emerson, *Miscellanies*, Vol. II, pp. 50–51.

Lindsay Jones's book and John Carlson and E. C. Krupp's papers on the serpent hierophany have also contributed to material used in this chapter.

Chapter 5

Epigraph: web-holidays.com, 2001.

"I eat only grass ... ," Harley, p. 60.

"But how can this be ... ," Anderson and Dibble, p. 7.

"The One Who Looks at the Moon," Bredon and Mithrophanow, p. 406.

"The practical argument ... ," *Nation's Business*, p. 26.

"At first the infant ... ," Shakespeare, As You Like It (II, 7).

"The afternoon and evening ... ," Carnival in Rome, 1843. *Barclay Fox's Journal*, pp. 310–11 (London, 1979), quoted in Blackburn and Holford-Strevens, p. 604.

"The farmer holds high ... ," Fat Tuesday in Cajun Louisiana, as reported in the *Washington Post*, Mar. 7, 1984, quoted in Santino (*All Around the Year*), p. 95.

"Between maturity and birth ... ," York, p. 229.

Nemontemi, Sahagun, op.cit. Book 2, Ch. 19.

"... then there is a thing ... ," Hutton, p. 152.

On reversals of behavior, see e.g., Babcock, pp. 196–97.

A wide variety of Easter decorations are pictured in Schmidt, Ch. 4.

Chapter 6

Epigraph: Hobsbawm, "Man and Woman ... ," p. 133.

"Fire! Fire! ... ," Hutton, p. 219.

"March will search ... ," Opie and Tatem, p. 241.

"I shall never forget ... ," Krythe, *Holidays*, p. 115.

"thorn means scorn, ... family away," Hutton, p. 231.

"... men of great gravity," ibid., p. 228.

"riotous assemblies ... I think it ... ," Blackburn and Holford-Stevens, p. 185.

"a heathenish vanity ... ," ibid., p. 186.

"frisking ... madd Bacchinalians," Santino, (*All Around the Year*), p. 185.

"God, we don't like to complain . . . ," Untermeyer, p. 306.
"Young children were stolen . . . ," Larsen, p. 58.

Chapter 7

Epigraph: Potosi, Bolivia, *El Diario*, on-line newspaper, ninaja@usa.net, June 16, 1998, author's translation.
"And the Inti . . . under the sun," ibid.
". . . they regarded as an indication . . . ," Cobo, p. 27. Geography buffs will recognize the error of Cobo's ways: June 21 is in fact the first day of winter in the southern hemisphere. The Inti Raymi festival more appropriately fits the other seasonal turning point in the sun's course, December 21, and may be more akin to our Christmas.
". . . and the sacrifice . . . ," ibid.
"This afternoon the Eskimos . . . ," MacDonald, p. 131.
"But when you see . . . one part of wine," Frazer, *Hesiod*, pp. 127–28, lines 582–95.
Academy of Leisure Sciences, see www.eas.ualberta.ca/elj/als/als2.html
"I place my shoes…," Opie and Tatem, p. 352 (significant probably because the shoes are the point of contact between the feet and the ground).
"under both of them . . . ," Ovid, VI: 267.
"mightily drives away . . . ," Opie and Tatem, pp. 336–37.

Chapter 8

Portions of this chapter were drawn from my article "Time's Empire," *Wilson Quarterly* (1998) xxii (3):44–57.
Epigraph: Walt Whitman, "I Hear America Singing," Untermeyer, p. 40.
"A day's work . . . ," Krythe, *Holidays*, p. 177.
"a most pleasant season . . . ," Santino, (*All Around the Year*), p. 140.
"joint partnership . . . ," ibid.
A detailed description of Pullman, Ill. and the strike is given in Smith, Ch. 9.
"quantitative revolution . . . ," Crosby, Ch. I.
"it synchronized . . . ," Mumford, p. 286.
"It is sad . . . ," Landes, pp. 90–91.
See James Gleick's entertaining diatribe on the paradox of wasted time in *Faster, the Acceleration of Just About Everything*, Barker, *Aristotle*, p. 317.

Chapter 9

Epigraph: Turner, p. 175.
"never go inside . . . street", etc., Santino (*Halloween*), pp. 30–32.

"grand objects of all their spells," Mooney, p. 408. The Irish origins of many of
   these Halloween customs are explored in Mooney and in Sewell Johnson.
"He will go and . . . ," Cohen, p. 459.
"When midnight has come . . . ," Ovid, Fasti, V: 428–54.
". . . for tis said . . . ," ibid., II: 545–55.
"Mask the weak . . . ," Turner, pp. 175–76.

Chapter 10

Epigraph: Krythe, *Holidays*, p. 237.
"Daily the beans . . . ," Thoreau, p. 100.
"It is pursued . . . ," ibid., p. 102.
"Ceres and Earth . . . ," Ovid, Fasti, I: 674.
"in harvest time, . . . ," Hutton, p. 332.
"The people of the entire state . . . ," Bodde, p. 71.
"to command solemn days . . . ," Bradford.
"Inasmuch as the great . . . ," Krythe, *Holidays*, p. 235.
"brutish men . . . ," Bradford, p. 26.
On the history of the pilgrim settlements, see Deetz and Deetz.
". . . and on that day . . . ," Blackburn and Holford-Strevens, p. 655.
"This is Thanksgiving Day . . . ," ibid., p. 656.
"There is deep moral influence . . . ," users.erols.com/va42nd/thanksgiving.html
"And I recommend to them . . . ," Krythe, *Holidays*, p. 237.
". . . the poorest of the poor . . . ," ibid.
"Let us be . . . ," Krythe, *Holidays*, pp. 239–50.
See also President Clinton's Proclamation, printed in the *New York Times*, Nov
   18, 2000.
On Grandma and Grandpa as mythic Adam and Eve, see Santino (*All Around
   the Year*), p. 177.
Statistics on shopping from www.retailindustry.about.com

Chapter 11

Epigraph: MacDonald, p. 112.
"The desire to spend money . . . ," Libanius, quoted by Hutton, p. 123.
"The desire to spend money . . . ," Hutton, p. 123.
"Our ears are saluted . . . ," Opie and Tatem, p. 57.
On Moore's so-called legacy, see Don Foster's *Author Unknown*.
"It is a cold, lifeless business . . . ," Emerson (1844), p. 94.
Christmas card statistics from www.magicmoments.com
"America's Jews have reacted . . . ," Schwarz, p. 88.

"... as a way of de-whitizing," Schmidt, p. 301.

For more on *"Los Matachines,"* see Cantú in Gutiérrez and Fabre, pp. 57–67.

"Heaped up on the floor . . . ," Dickens, p. 94.

Chapter 12

Epigraph: Aveni, "Times Empire," *Wilson Quarterly* (1998) xxii(3):44–57.

Other defunct holidays can be found by leafing through the pages of Krythe's *Holidays*, or for more ambitious readers, the *Oxford Companion to the Year*.

For more on Rizal Day, see Guyotte and Posadas in Gutiérrez and Fabre, pp. 111–28.

References

Anderson, Arthur and Charles Dibble (eds.), *Bernardino de Sahagun, Florentine Codex, General History of the Things of New Spain, Book 7* (Santa Fe, N.M., and Provo, Utah, 1953).

Argüelles, José, *The Mayan Factor: Path Beyond Technology* (Santa Fe, 1987).

Aristophanes. See Fitts.

Aristotle. See Barker.

Arochi, Luis, *La Pirámide de Kukulcan: Su Simbolismo Solar* (Mexico, 1976).

Astin, A. E., *Scipio Aemilianus* (Oxford, 1967).

Aveni, A., *Empires of Time, Clocks, Calendars and Cultures* (New York, 1989).

Aveni, A., *Behind the Crystal Ball, Magic, Science and Religion from Antiquity to the New Age* (New York, 1996).

Aveni, A., "Times Empire," *Wilson Quarterly* (1998), xxii (3): 44–57.

Babcock, Barbara (ed.), *The Reversible World, Symbolic Inversion in Art and Society* (Ithaca, N.Y., 1978).

Barker, Ernest (ed.), *The Politics of Aristotle* (Oxford, 1946).

Barnett, James, *The American Christmas* (New York, 1976).

Batchelor, Mary, *The Everday Book* (New York, 1982).

Blackburn, Bonnie and Leofranc Holford-Stevens, *The Oxford Companion to the Year* (Oxford, 1999).

Bliss, Frank, *In Praise of Bishop Valentine* (London, 1893).

Bodde, Derek, *Festivals in Classical China, New Year and Other Annual Observances During the Han Dynasty 206 B.C.–A.D. 220* (Princeton, N.J., 1975).

Botkin, B. A. (ed.), *A Treasury of Western Folklore* (New York, 1951).

Bradford, William, *Of Plymouth Plantation 1620–1647* (Introduction by Francis Murphy) (New York, 1981).

Bredon, Julie and Igor Mithrophanow, *The Moon Year, A Record of Chinese Customs and Festivals* (reprinted) (New York, 1966).

Brewster, H. Pomeroy, *Saints and Festivals of the Christian Church* (New York, 1904).

Carlson, John, "Pilgrimage and the Equinox 'Serpent of Light and Shadow' Phenomenon at the Castillo, Chichén Itzá, Yucatan," *Archaeoastronomy: The Journal of Astronomy in Culture,* xiv(1) (1999): 136–51.

Castañeda, Quetzil, *In the Museum of Maya Culture, Touring Chichén Itzá* (Minneapolis, Minn., 1996).

Chippindale, Christopher, *Stonehenge Complete* (London, 1983).

Cobo, B., *An Account of the Shrines of Ancient Cuzco* [1651?] John. H. Rowe (tr. ed.), *Nawpa Pacha* 17 (Berkeley, Calif., 1979): 1–80.

Cohen, Mark, *The Cultic Calendars of the Ancient Near East* (Bethesda, Md., 1993).

Crosby, Alfred, *The Measure of Reality* (Cambridge, 1997).

Deetz, James and Patricia Deetz, *The Times of Their Lives: Life, Love and Death in Plymouth Colony* (New York, 2000).

DeLys, Claudia, *A Treasury of Superstitions* (New York, 1997).

Dickens, Charles, *A Christmas Carol* (Philadelphia, Pa., 1918).

Eastman, George, "The Importance of Calendar Reform to the Business World," *Bulletin of the Pan American Union* 61(1927): 655–66.

Eliade, Mircea, *Patterns in Comparative Religion* (New York, 1958).

Eliade, Mircea (ed.), *The Encyclopedia of Religion* (New York, 1987).

Emerson, Ralph Waldo, *Essays, Second Series, "Essay V: Gifts"* (Boston, Mass., 1844).

Emerson, Ralph Waldo, *Miscellanies* (Boston, 1878).

Eliot, T. S., *Four Quartets* (London, 1960).

Fitts, Dudley (ed.), *Aristophanes: The Birds* (New York, 1957).

Fogel, Edwin, *Beliefs and Superstitions of the Pennsylvania Germans* (Philadelphia, Pa., 1915).

Foster, Don, *Author Unknown* (New York, 2000).

Frake, Charles, "Lessons of the Mayan Sky: A Perspective from Médieval Europe" in *The Sky in Mayan Literature*, ed. A. Aven, (New York, 1992), pp. 274–91.

Frazer, James, *The Golden Bough, A Study in Magic and Religion* (New York, 1922).

Frazer, R. M. (ed.), *The Poems of Hesiod* (Norman, Okla., 1983).

Gleick, James, *Faster: The Acceleration of Just About Everything* (New York, 1999).

Goold, G. P., *Ovid in Six Volumes*, v. Fasti (2nd ed.) (Cambridge, Mass., and London, 1989).

Gutiérrez, Ramón and Genevieve Fabre, *Feasts and Celebrations in North American Ethnic Communities* (Albuquerque, N.M., 1995).

Harley, Timothy, *Moon Lore* (London, 1885).

Hazlitt, W. Carew, *The Popular Antiquities of Great Britain* (New York, 1965).

Hesiod. See R. M. Frazer.

Hobsbawm, Eric, "Man and Woman in Socialist Iconography" *History Workshop*, vi (1978): 121–38.

Hobsbawm, Eric (ed.), *The Invention of Tradition* (Cambridge, 1983).

Hutton, Ronald, *The Stations of the Sun, A History of the Ritual Year in Britain* (Oxford and New York, 1996).

James, E. O., *Seasonal Feasts and Festivals* (London, 1961).

Jones, Jacqueline, *A Social History of the Laboring Classes* (Oxford, 1999).

Jones, Lindsay, *Twin City Tales, A Hermeneutical Reassessment of Tula and Chichén Itzá* (Niwot, Colo., 1995).

Kingsbury, Stewart, Mildred Kingsbury, and Wolfgang Mieder, *Weather Wisdom: Proverbs, Superstitions, and Signs* (New York, 1996).

Krupp, Edwin, "The Serpent Descending," *Griffith Observer* (1982) v 46(9): 1–20.

Krythe, Mamie, *All About the American Holidays* (New York, 1962).

Krythe, Mamie, *All About the Months* (New York, 1966).

Landa. See Tozzer.

Landes, David, *Revolution in Time, Clocks and the Making of the Modern World* (Cambridge, Mass., 1983).

Larsen, Egon, *An American in Europe, The Life of Benjamin Thompson, Count Rumford* (New York, 1953).

MacDonald, John, *The Arctic Sky, Inuit Astronomy, Star Lore, and Legend* (Toronto, 1998).

Martha Stewart Holiday, Halloween, *Martha Stewart Living* (special issue) (New York, 2000) October.

Matteker, Philip, "A Fixed Date for Easter," *The Christian Century* (22–29 March, 1989): 300–01.

Matthews, Leonard, "The Hibernation of Mammals," *Smithsonian Report for 1955* (Washington, D.C., 1956): 407–17.

Memory Paterson, Jacqueline, *Tree Wisdom, the Definitive Guidebook to the Myth Folklore and Healing Power of Trees* (London, 1996).

Miller, Daniel (ed.), *Unwrapping Christmas* (Oxford, 1993).

Mooney, James, "The Holiday Customs of Ireland," *Proceedings of the American Philosophical Society* (1889) 26 (130): 377–427.

Mumford, Lewis, *The Myth of the Machine* (New York, 1966).

Nation's Business, "Sound off Response: Anchoring Easter-Pro and Con" (June 1972): 26–28.

Newall, Venetia, *An Egg at Easter, A Folklore Study* (London and Boston, 1984)

Nilsson, Martin, *Primitive Time Reckoning, A Study in the Origins and First Development of the Art of Counting Time Among the Primitive and Early Culture Peoples* (Lund, 1920).

Opie, Iona and Moira Tatem (eds.), *A Dictionary of Superstitions* (London, 1989).

Ovid. See Goold.

Richards, E. G., *Mapping Time, The Calendar and Its History* (Oxford, 1998).

Rivard, Jean Jacques, "A Hierophany at Chichén Itzá" *Katunob* (1970) 7(3): 51–57.

Robinson, F. N. (ed.), *The Complete Works of Geoffrey Chaucer* (New York, 1933).

Sahagun. See Anderson and Dibble.

Santino, Jack, *All Around the Year, Holidays and Celebrations in American Life* (Urbana and Chicago, Ill., 1994).

Santino, Jack, *Halloween and Other Festivals of Death and Life* (Knoxville, Tenn., 1994)

Schmidt, Leigh Eric, *Consumer Rites: The Buying and Selling of American Holidays* (Princeton, 1995).

Schwarz, Frederic, "Merry Chanukah," *American Heritage* (January 2001): 84–88.

Scullard, H. H., *Festivals and Ceremonies of the Roman Republic* (Ithaca, New York, 1981).

Sewell Johnson, Helen, "November Eve Beliefs and Customs in Irish Life and Literature," *Journal of American Folklore* (1968) 81: 133–42.

Sickel, H.S.J., *Thanksgiving, Its Source, Philosophy, and History with All National Proclamations and Analytical Study Thereof* (Philadelphia, 1940).

Smith, Carl, *Urban Disorder and the Shape of Belief* (Chicago, 1995).

Stephens, John Lloyd, *Incidents of Travel in Yucatan* (2 vols.)(New York, 1843).

Thomas, Keith, *Religion and the Decline of Magic* (New York, 1971).

Thoreau, Henry, *Walden* (New York, 1987 [1854]).

Tozzer, Alfred (ed.), *Landa's Relación de las Cosas de Yucatan* (Cambridge, 1941).

Turner, Victor, *The Ritual Process, Structure and Antistructure* (Chicago, 1969).

Untermeyer, Louis, *Modern American Poetry, Modern British Poetry* (New York, 1919).

Watts, Alan, *Easter, Its Story and Meaning* (New York, 1950).

Wicke, Charles, "The Mesoamercan Rabbit in the Moon: An Influence of Han China," *Archaeoastronomy, The Journal of the Center for Archaeoastronomy* vii (1–4): 46–55.

York, Michael, *The Roman Festival Calendar of Numa Pompilius* (New York, 1986).

Index

*Note: Page numbers in **bold** *refer to entire chapters.*

Academy of Leisure Sciences, 97–98
Adams, John, 105
Adler, Victor, 89
Advent, 154
advertising, 157–58
agriculture
    animism and, 138
    crop fertility, 99–100
    fall festivals, 137
    fire and, 103–5
    labor and, 139
    "last sheaf" ceremony, 138
    modern farming techniques, 140
    sacrifices, 94
    Samhain, 127–28
    Thanksgiving and, 135–36, 136–40
    time measurement and, 166–67
    weather prediction and, 155–56
Akitu festival, 67
Alaska, 150
Alberti, Leon Battista, 115
Alfred P. Murrah Federal Building, 8
Algonquin culture, 17
All Around the Year (Santino), 171
All Souls Day, 14, 38, 129, 130
Alta Vista, Mexico, 57–58
American culture. *See also* Native American culture
    American Indian Day, 168
    "antipodal man," 59–60
    Easter celebrations, 77–78
    Groundhog Day, 29–34
    "I Hear America Singing" (Whitman), 107, 109
    Labor Day, 2, 4, 12, 107–18
    Mesoamericans, 15
    Pan American Day, 167–68
    Pilgrims, 140–41, 142–43
    President's Day Weekend, 118
    Thanksgiving and, 140–47
American Notebooks (Hawthorne), 143
Anatomie of Abuses (Puritan manual), 84
animism, 138
Anna (Biblical), 35

anthropology, 76
"antipodal man," 59–60
aphrodisiacs, 43
Apollo, 153
April Fool's Day, 18–19
apu, 128–29
architecture
    as calendars, 93–94
    cursus monuments, 151
    Mayan, 151–52
    monuments, 59–60
    pyramids, 47–58, 93
    solstice registers, 151
    Stonehenge, 59, 94–95, 150–51
Arctic regions, 150
Argüelles, Jose, 55–56
Aristophanes, 41
Aristotle, 97–98
Arochi, Luis, 52–58
art, xii
As You Like It (Shakespeare), 70–71
Ash Wednesday, 71–72
astrology, 6
astronomy
    architecture as calendars, 47–58, 93–94, 151
    computists, 68–69
    measuring solstices, 92–93
    seasonal passage of sun, 18
    solar zenith, 14–15
    springtime constellations, 37
    Stonehenge and, 150–51
Aurelian, 153
Aveni, Anthony, 165
Aztec culture, xii, 23, 56, 60

Baal, 80
Babwende, 2
Babylonian culture
    Easter origins and, 67–68
    moon watching, 12
    New Year's Day, 22
    religious syncretism and, 102–3
    view of death, 128–29

Bacchanalia, 6
Bacchus, 6–7
Bacon, Roger, 6
badgers, 34
Baldus, 72
baptism, 102
Barrow, Henry, 29, 35
baseball, 13, 109
bears, 36
Beltane, 80, 127
Bennu bird, 66
Bible, 35
birds, 41–42
Birthday of the Unconquered, 153
birthdays, xii. *See also* Christmas
Black Plague, 114
bonfires. *See* fire
Boxing Day, 118
Bradford, William, 140–41
Brahmin, 64
Branch Davidians, 8
British culture, 23
Buddhism, 65
Burns, Robert, 125
business. *See* economy and commerce

cabbage, 125–26
Caesar, Julius, 19–20
calendars
     architecture as, 93–94
     Celtic, 1, 37–38
     Chinese, 16
     fiscal, 12
     Gregorian, 15–16, 20, 37, 153
     "intercalated" time, 16–18, 73
     Jewish, 16
     leap-years, 20
     Mayan, 73
     as representation of time, xiii
     Roman, 17–18
     saints' days, 5–6
     seasons represented by, 1–2, 166
     types of, 167
"Caliban in the Coal Mines" (Untermeyer),
     87, 109
Cancun, Mexico, 52
Candlemas, 34–39, 46, 80, 137
Carnival
     behaviors associated with, 72–73
     Christmas compared with, 161–62
     Fat Tuesday and, 76–77
     Halloween compared with, 132
     immigrant cultures and, 168
caroling, 155, 157–59
Castañeda, Quetzil, 56
Castillo at Chichén Itzá, 47–58, 61
Catholicism, 90. *See also* Christianity
Cato the Younger, 83
cave art, xii
Celtic culture. *See also* Irish culture
     bifurcated year, 13–14

calendar, 37–38
     Druids, 59, 127–28
     Lughnasa, 137–38
     seasonal calendar, 1
     solstice day and, 98
     Stonehenge, 94–95
Central Labor Union, 110
Ceres, 138
cesium clocks, 20–21
Chalchihuites, Mexico, 57–58
Chan Bahlum, 151–52
change, 5
Chanukah, 8, 124, 156, 162
Chaplin, Charlie, 116
Charles IX, 18–19
Chaucer, Geoffrey, 41–42
Chenango Valley Music Fest, 104
Chicano Day, 168
Chichén Itzá, 3, 47–58, 58–61
Children's Day, 78, 100, 168
Chinese culture
     calendar, 16
     Chinese New Year (Yuandan), 16, 20, 25
     fall festivals, 139–40
     fertility rituals and, 41
     moon's role in, 64, 66
     solstices in, 4, 95–96
Chippindale, Christopher, 59
chocolate, 43–44
Christianity. *See also* Christmas
     Advent, 154
     "antipodal man," 59–60
     Ash Wednesday, 71–72
     baptism, 102
     Bible, 35
     bird symbolism and, 66–67
     Branch Davidians, 8
     Candlemas, 34–39
     Church of England, xiii
     Easter, 63–78
     Eastern Holy Roman Empire, 15
     Epiphany, 71
     Good Friday, 7, 72
     Gregorian calendar, 15–16, 20, 37, 153
     Holy Roman Empire, 15
     Holy Week, 72, 77
     integration of pagan festival, 130
     Jesus Christ, 7, 66–67, 71, 152
     John the Baptist, 102–3
     Lent, 67
     May Day and, 90
     Michaelmas, xii
     Nativity, 15, 152–53
     Palm Sunday, 72
     Pentecostalism, 6
     prayer times, 113
     Protestantism, 34, 131, 158
     religious syncretism, 102–3
     Roman traditions and, 152–53. *See also*
          Roman culture
     saints, 5–6, 166
     Simeon (Biblical), 35

Star of Bethlehem, 152
Virgin Mary (Mary, mother of Jesus), 3, 34–35, 39
Christmas, **149–63**
"Christmas His Masque," 160
consumerism, 45, 157–59, 159–62
dinners, 146
foods, 161
Halloween compared with, 124
magic and, 7
Nativity, 15, 152–53
Santa Claus, 157, 159, 160
symbols of, 157–59
transformation of, 5
trees, 160–61
twelve days of, 156
Yule logs, 154
Church of England, xiii, 131
cities, 114–15
Civil War, 5, 144–45
Claudius II, 40
Cleveland, Grover, 111
Clinton, William Jefferson, 147
clocks
business and, 111–12
cesium, 20–21
economics and, 111–16
standards for time measurement, 12
cockfighting, 75–76
College of Augurs, 19
Columbine High School shooting, 8
commercialism. *See* consumerism; economy and commerce
communism, 86
computists, 68–69
Constantine, 153
Consumer Rites: The Buying and Selling of American Holidays (Schmidt), 171
consumerism
Chanukah, 156
Christmas, 45, 157–59, 159–62
Easter, 77–78
greeting cards, 27–28, 44–45, 160–61
Halloween, 5, 45, 122–23
Mayan hierophany, 54
Saturnalia, 153–54
Thanksgiving, 146, 147
timekeeping and, 167
Valentine's Day, 43–45
costumes, 119–22, 127–28. *See also* role reversal
Council of Nicaea, 69
Count Rumford, 88, 110–11
courtship, 99
creation myths, 151
crescent moons, 12
Crosby, Alfred, 112
Cuban Day, 168
Cupid, 43, 45
cursus monuments, 151
cycles of time, 26

death
All Souls Day, 14, 38, 129, 130
Black Plague, 114
Días de los Muertos, 131–32
Halloween and, 127–28, 131–33
honoring the dead, 5, 131–32
Land of the Dead, 129
various interpretations of, 128–32
Demeter, 138
Diario de Yucatán, 53
Días de los Muertos, 131–32
Dickens, Charles, 158, 161
A Dictionary of Superstitions (Opie and Tatem), 171
Dies Natali, 153
Dionysus, 6–7
diurnal cycles, 12
divination. *See also* folklore; magic
dowsing rods, 99
dreaming bannocks, 100
at Halloween, 126
omens, 19
"oracle of the nuts," 126
"part-of-the-whole" principle, 138–39
plants and, 100
weather prediction, 25, 29–34, 35–36, 155–56
wishbones, 146
Divine Husbandman, 140
Dog Star, 13
dowsing rods, 99
dreaming bannocks, 100
Druids, 59, 127–28
dry seasons, 2
dumb cake, 100
Dzibilchaltun, 57

Earth-Mother Goddess, 91
Easter, **63–78**
in America, 77–78
Easter Monday, 118
fixing the date, 3–4, 69, 137
Gregorian calendar, 20
lunar cycles, 63–66
origins, 67–70
season, 70–77
symbolism, 66–67
Economic Policy Institute, 117
economy and commerce. *See also* consumerism
calendars and, 12
Christmas and, 45, 157–59, 159–62
clocks and, 111–16, 117–18
Industrial Revolution, 88, 116
Kwanzaa and, 162–63
money, 24, 114
poverty, 88, 145
Saturnalia celebration, 153–54
Thanksgiving and, 146
tourism, 52
eggs, 66–67

Egyptian culture
    gods' birthdays celebrated, xii
    Isis festival, 21
    mummification, 21–22
    Nile river cycles, 13
    Ramses II, 59
    view of death, 129
Eighteen Rabbit (Mayan ruler), 59
Eisenhower, Dwight D., 147
Election Day, 138
Eliade, Mircea, 47, 51–52, 58
Eliot, T. S., 11, 25
Elizabeth I, 28
Emerson, Ralph Waldo, 60, 160
Engels, Friedrich, 89
English culture, 24, 42
environmental issues, 82
Eostre, 67. *See also* Easter
epacts, 69
Epiphany, 71
equinoxes, **47–61**
    as beginning of spring, 38
    Easter and, 67–70
    ownership of time and, 3
    as seasonal markers, 1
    solstices compared with, 93
escapements, 112–13. *See also* clocks
ethnicity, 8, 162, 168
European culture, 99–103

Fabergé eggs, 67
farming. *See* agriculture
Fasti (Ovid), 18
Fat Tuesday, 76
Father's Day, 78, 100
Faunus, 39–40
Fawkes, Guy, 131
Feast of Tabernacles, 138
feasts. *See* foods
feathered serpent, 47–58
Februa, 39
February holidays, **29–46**
fertility
    agricultural, 99–100
    birds as symbol of, 41
    controlling, xi
    magic to enhance, 39
    May Day and, 89
    rabbits as symbol of, 65–66
    seasons associated with, 13
fire
    fire jumpers, 99
    guiding ghosts, 128
    Halloween, 126, 127–28, 131
    purification, 80
    solstice celebrations, 98–99, 103–5
    Yule logs and, 154
fireworks, 4
"first footing," 23
First Husbandman, 140
"firsts," 3
fiscal calendars, 12

Flight of the King, 74
Flora, 138
Floralia, 83
folklore. *See also* divination; magic
    dowsing rods, 99
    ghosts, 128–29
    Halloween, 126
    omens, 19
    "oracle of the nuts," 126
    "part-of-the-whole" principle, 138–39
    plants, 100
    rabbits, 65–66
    wishbones, 146
    witches, 83, 129
Follen, Charles, 160
foods
    chocolate, 43–44
    Christmas dinner, 161
    dumb cake, 100
    Fat Tuesday, 75–76
    feasts, 68, 145
    Mole poblano, 146
    overindulgence, 27
    pumpkins, 7
    turkeys, 145–46
football, 13, 75–76, 147–48
Fortuna, 102
Fourth of July, 4, 104–5, 108
Frake, Charles, 5–6
Friar Tuck, 85
full moons, 12

gardening, 135–36
Geb, 66
Gelasius, 40
Gennep, Arnold van, 89
German culture, 79, 98
ghosts, 128–29
gift-giving
    Chanukah, 156
    Christmas, 45, 157–58, 159–62
    New Year, 27–28
    Valentine's Day, 42–45
globalization, 89–90
Gnosticism, 56, 60
goal of book, 2, 9
Gobbler's Knob, 30
gods, xii. *See also* specific deities
Good Friday, 7, 72
Great Cha, 139–40
Greek culture
    fall festivals, 138
    solstices in, 4, 97
    time cycles observed by, 26
Green George, 82
Greenwich Village parade, 124
greeting cards, 27–28, 44–45, 160–61
Gregorian calendar, 15, 20, 37, 153
Gregory XIII (pope), 20
Groundhog Day
    Celtic calendar and, 1
    groundhogs, 3, 36

Imbolc compared with, 38
as springtime marker, 46
substitution principle and, 7
Thanksgiving compared with, 136
weather prediction and, 29–34
Gulf Stream, 37
Guy Fawkes Day, 131

Hale, Sarah Josepha Buell, 78, 144
Hale-Bopp comet, 55
Halloween, **119–33**
Celtic calendar and, 1
consumerism, 45
as "half-New Year," 14
inversion principle and, 7
May Day compared with, 80, 84
Saturnalia compared with, 154
symbols associated with, 4–5
Thanksgiving compared with, 136
*Halloween and Other Festivals of Death and
Life* (Santino), 171
Hamilton, New York, 104
Han China, 41, 95–96
Hancock, John, 105
Harmonic Convergence, 55–56
harvest day, 15
Harvest Festival, 139
Harvest Home, 148
harvest moons, 16–17
Hawthorn tree, 81
Hawthorne, Nathaniel, 143
Heaven's Gate cult, 55
hedgehogs, 37
Henry VIII, 35
Herrick, Robert, 42
Hesiod, 37, 97
hibernation, 33–34
hierophany, 51–58, 61, 152
Hindu culture, 64, 86
hmeen, 93
Hobbes, Thomas, 83
Hobsbawm, Eric, 86
holly, 155
Hollywood, 85
Holy Roman Empire, 15
Holy Saturday, 72
Holy Week, 72, 77
Horus, 73
Hottentots, 64–65
House of the Seven Dolls, 57
"How the Grinch Stole Christmas" (Dr.
Seuss), 158–59
Howland, Esther, 44
Hunbatz Men (Maya spiritualist), 56
Hunter's moons, 16–17

"I Hear America Singing" (Whitman), 107,
109
I Love Lucy (television program), 116
Iglulingmiut culture, 96
Imbolc, 37–39, 46
immigrant groups, 168–69

immortality, 82
Inca culture
fall of, 60
solstices and, 4, 92, 93–94
indentured servitude, 86–87
Independence Day, 104, 108
India, 86
Industrial Revolution, 88, 116
"intercalated" time, 16–18, 73
International Conference of American
States, 167–68
"International Day of Action Against Capi-
talism," 89
International Festival of the Arts, 104
Inti Raymi festival, 14, 92–94
Inuit culture, 4, 96–97, 149–50
inversion principle, 7
Irish culture. *See also* Celtic culture
Halloween and, 125–26, 130–31
solstice day and, 98
springtime, 38
Irving, Washington, 82, 85
Ishtar, 102
Isis, 13, 21–22, 73
Israel, 162. *See also* Judaism

Jack-in-the-Green, 82
jack-o'-lanterns, 127–28
Janus, 19
Jarvis, Anna, 78
Jefferson, Thomas, 27, 105, 143
Jesus Christ
bird symbolism and, 66–67
depicted as sun god, 152
Easter season and, 71
substitution principle and, 7
Jewish calendar, 16
John the Baptist, 102–3
Johnson, Ben, 160
Johnson, Lyndon, 78
Juarez, Benito, 54
Judaism
Chanukah, 8, 124, 156, 162
fall festivals, 138
Kabbalah, 82
Passover, 68
rebirth symbolism, 102–3
Rosh Hashanah, 7, 16, 22
Torah, 22
Yom Kippur, 16
Zionism, 162
Judgment Day, 131
Juneteenth, 105
Juno, 39, 40
Jupiter, 154

Kabbalah, 82
Kao Mei, 41
Karenga, Maulana, 162
Kelley, J. Charles, 57–58
Kepler, Johannes, 69
Kinich Ahau, 93

Krythe, Mamie, 135
Kukulcan temple, 48–51, 55
Kwakiutl culture, 17
Kwanzaa, 8, 162–63

La Paz, Bolivia, 91
*La Pirámide de Kukulcan—Su Simbolismo
    Solar* (Arochi), 53
labor
    clashes with management, 111–12
    clocks and, 115–16
    indentured servitude, 86–87
    Labor Day, 2, 4, 12, 107–18
    May Day and, 87–90
    mine workers, 87
    slavery, 105
    strikes, 88
    Thanksgiving and, 139
    unions, 88–89, 110–11
Ladies Magazine and Literary Gazette, 144
Lake Titicaca, 92
Lammas, 1, 136, 137–38, 168
Land of the Dead, 129
Landa, Diego de, 50
"last sheaf" ceremony, 138
leap-years, 20
leisure, 97–98, 104–5
Lemuria, 129
Lenin, Vladimir Ilyich, 89
Lent, 67
Libanius, 153
Liberty, 89
Lincoln, Abraham, 78, 144, 145
Little John, 85–86
London, England, 82
Los Matachines, 162
love, 39–46
Lucian, 154
Lughnasa, 137–38
lunar cycles, 15–17. *See also* moon
lunar hierophany, 54. *See also* moon
Lupercalia, 39
Lupercus, 45

MacDonald, John, 149
Macedonian culture, 15
Madden, John, 148
Maes Howe, 151
magic. *See also* divination; spells
    in Babylonian culture, 129
    dowsing rods, 99
    fire associated with, 98–99
    Halloween and, 125
    love spells, 43, 100–101
    New Age mysticism and, 38–39
    purification rituals, 35
    solstices and, 96
    spells, 38–39, 43, 100–101
    sympathetic magic, 7
    witches, 83, 129
Maid Marian, 86
Maní (Mayan town), 50

maps of cultures, xiii
Mardi Gras
    behaviors associated with, 4, 72–73, 74–
        75
    Christmas compared with, 161–62
    inversion principle and, 7
    Thanksgiving compared with, 148
Marduk, 22
Marks, Johnny, 157
Mars, 17
Martha Stewart Living, 121
Martin Luther King, Jr. Day, 168
Marx, Karl, 88
Mason-Dixon line, 37
Massasoit, 142
Mater Matuta, 101–2
mathematics, 112
mattacino, 162
Maundy Thursday, 72
May, Robert L., 157
May Day, 79–90
    Celtic calendar and, 1
    as "half-New Year," 14
    as marker of springtime, 36–37
    "Maying," 81
    northern latitudes and, 2
    renewal themes, 7
    rituals associated with, 4
    Roman Catholicism and, 90
Mayan culture
    calendar, 73
    collapse of, 55, 60
    contemporary myths, 3
    Hunbatz Men (spiritualists), 56
    solar zenith, 14–15
    spring equinox celebration, 47–58
    summer solstice, 4, 93
    turkey and, 146
    winter solstice and, 151
*The Mayan Factor: The Path Beyond Tech-
    nology* (Arguelles and Swimme), 55
"Maying," 81
maypoles, 81–84
McGuire, Peter, 110
Memorial Day, 104, 108, 118
mercantilism, 167
Merry Mount Plantation, 84
Mesoamericans, 15
mestizos, 56
Metonic cycle, 68
Mexican culture, 131–32, 146
Mexico City, Mexico, 57
Michaelmas, xii
Middle Ages, 126, 154
midrash, 152
millenialism, 61
mine workers, 87
Miracle of 34th Street (film), 159
Mischief Night, 131
mistletoe, 157–59
Mithras, 153
Modern Times (film), 116

Mole poblano, 146
money, 24, 114
months, 16–18
monuments, 59. *See also* architecture
moon
   agriculture and, 156
   in Babylonian culture, 12
   in Chinese culture, 64
   Easter and, 63–66, 69
   harvest moons, 16–17
   Hunter's moons, 16–17
   lunar cycles, 15–17
   lunar hierophany, 54
   Native American culture, 16–17
   New Year and, 69
   phases, 2, 12, 15–16, 18
   rabbit figure in, 63–67
Moore, Clement Clark, 158, 160
Morris Dance, 85
Morton, Thomas, 84, 85
Moselle Valley, 98
Mothering Sunday, 78
Mother's Day, 100
movies, 31, 85
Mumford, Lewis, 113
mummers, 26–27, 77, 85
mummification, 21–22
Murrah Federal Building, 8
Murray, William Breen, 57
"Mystic Krew of Comus," 76

National Association of Watch and Clock
   Collectors, 116
National Bureau of Standards, 12
National Geographic, 31
National Institute of Anthropology and
   History (INAH), 49
Nation's Business, 70
Native American culture
   Algonquin culture, 17
   "antipodal man," 59–60
   Christianity and, 59–60
   five seasons recognized by, 2
   Judaism and, 60
   lunar cycles and, 16–17
   "noble savage" image, 60
   Thanksgiving and, 140–42
   Yaqui Indians, 162
Nativity, 15, 152–53
nature's relation to time, 6–7, 166
nemontemi, 73
Neo-Aztecs, 56
Neolithic cultures, 4
Nephthys, 73
New Age mysticism
   blackthorn tree, 38–39
   equinox celebrations and, 55
   Gnosticism and, 60
   Halloween and, 124
   Harmonic Convergence, 55–56
   Heaven's Gate cult, 55
   millenialism, 61

serpent of light myth, 47–58, 61
   spring equinox celebrations and, 49
New Corn ceremonies, 137
New Fire ceremonies, 50–51
New Haven, Connecticut, 104
New Orleans, Louisiana, 74–75, 76, 129
New Year's Eve and Day, 11–28
   behaviors associated with, 4
   Christmas compared with, 161–62
   Halloween compared with, 132
   Inti Raymi festival, 92
   inversion principle and, 7
   Labor Day compared with, 109
   moon and, 69
   resolutions, 19
   Thanksgiving compared with, 148
New York City, 21, 22–23, 110, 145
Newton, Isaac, 84
Nile River, 13, 21–22
Nile Valley, 59
Nilometer, 13
Nilsson, Martin, xiii, 1
Ninazu, 128
Nippur, 128
Northwest Territories, 96
Nut, 66, 73
nutawajjihin, 162

Oklahoma City bombing, 8
Old Testament, 16
omens, 19
"oracle of the nuts," 126
Orkney Islands, 151
Osborne, Dorothy, 42
Osiris, 13, 21–22, 73, 129
overindulgence, 27
Ovid, 18, 101, 129–30, 138
Oxford Companion to the Year (Blackburn
   and Holford-Stevens), 171
Oxford English Dictionary, 124

Pacal, 151
Pachacuti, 92
pagan religions, 166
Palenque ruins, 151–52
Paleolithic culture, xii
Palm Sunday, 72
Pan, 39–40
Pan American Day, 167–68
parades
   Greenwich Village parade, 124
   Labor Day, 110
   Rose Bowl Parade, 26
Passover, 68
Pater Noster, 29
patriotism, 8, 168
pavomancy, 146
peacocks, 66–67
Pennsylvania Dutch, 33–34, 66–67
Pentecostalism, 6
Pfiel, Helen, 122
phallic symbolism, 83

phenyl ethylamine, 43
Philippine Independence movement, 168
phoenix, 67
Pilgrims, 140–41, 142–43
Pisté (town), 55
Pizarro, Francisco, 92
plant divination, 100
Playboy, 66
Pliny the Elder, 18
polar regions, 96–97
politics, 59, 108, 167. *See also* labor
The Politics (Aristotle), 97–98
polytheism, 166
poor houses, 88
pop culture, 61, 127–28
Porter, Cole, 42
Portillo, José Lopez, 54
Pottier, Eugene, 79
poverty, 88, 145
pranksterism, 125–27. *See also* trick-or-
    treating
prayer times, 113
presents. *See* gift-giving
President's Day Weekend, 118
Priapus, 83
Primitive Time Reckoning (Nilsson), 171
Protestantism, 34, 131, 158
Puerto Rican Day, 168
Pullman, George, 110–11
Pullman, Illinois, 110–11
pumpkins, 7
Punxsutawney Ground Hog Club, 30
Punxsutawney Phil, 30
Purgatory, 127, 131
purification themes
    Christianity and, 35
    fire and, 80
    solstices in, 96
    water and, 102–3
purpose of book, 2, 9
*The Pyramid of Kukulcan—Its Solar Sym-
    bolism* (Arochi), 53
Pyramid of the Sun, 57
pyramids, 47–58, 93

Qoricancha, 14
quantitative revolution, 112
Quiangalla, 94
Quintilis, 17

Ra, 73
rabbits, 63–67
railroads, 110–11
Ramses II, 59
reality-based holidays, 8
rebirth symbolism, 34, 48–49, 92, 102–3
redemption, 71
"red-letter days," xiii–xiv
Regifugium, 74
religious syncretism, 102–3
Remus, 39

renewal themes of holidays, 6–7, 28. *See
    also* rebirth symbolism; resurrection
    themes
resolutions, 19, 24
resurrection themes
    Easter and, 71, 77
    in Mayan culture, 151–52
    mummification, 22
    phoenix, 67
Rivard, Jean Jacques, 51
Rizal Day, 168
Robigalia, xii
Robin Hood, 85–86
role reversal, 25, 132, 153–54
Roman Catholicism, 90. *See also* Chris-
    tianity
Roman culture
    agriculture, 18
    calendar, 17–18
    Christianity and, 68
    Easter season and, 73
    fall festivals, 138
    fertility goddesses, 83
    gods' birthdays, xii
    Janus, 19
    pantheon, 6
    St. Valentine and, 40–41
    summer solstice, 4, 101–2
    sun's birthday, 152
    view of death, 129–30
Romulus, 39
Roosevelt, Franklin Delano, 146
Rose Bowl Parade, 26
Rosh Hashanah, 7, 16, 22
routines, 11
Rubio, Alfredo Barrera, 49
Rudolph the red-nosed reindeer, 157–58
rulers, 59, 167
Russian culture, 22

Sacred Mound Festivals, 128
sacrifice, 65, 94
Sahagun, Bernardino de, 65
saining, 24
"Saint Monday," 118
saints
    calendar development and, 5–6, 68, 166
    St. Benedict, 113
    St. Brigid, 37
    St. John, 14
    St. John's wort, 103
    St. Martin Day, 154
    St. Michael, xii
    St. Nicholas, 160
    St. Patrick, 7, 168
    St. Valentine, 3, 39–46
Sakkria, 64
Samhain, 80, 127
Sanskrit, 64
Santa Claus, 157, 159, 160
Satan, 35
satanic cult scare, 123

Saturnalia, 7, 101, 153–54
Scandinavian culture, 36
Schor, Juliet, 116–17
Scottish culture, 22, 23
seasons. *See also* specific seasons
    importance of understanding, xi–xiv
    inversion principle and, 7
    magic associated with, 96
    May Day and, 80
    politics and, 92
    represented by calendars, 1–2
    wet seasons, 2
secularism, 166
September 11 terrorist attacks, 8
serpent of light myth, 47–58, 61
Seth, 73
sex and sexuality
    aphrodisiacs, 43
    love spells, 43, 100–101
    May Day and, 81, 82–84
    phallic symbolism, 83
    Venus, 13, 102
Sextilis, 17
shadows, 20
Shakespeare, William, 70–71
Sharpton, Al, 162
Shaw, George Bernard, 109–10
Shrove Tuesday, 74
Shrovetide, 75
Simeon (Biblical), 35
Sirius, 13
sköl, 23
slavery, 105
Slumbering Groundhog Lodge, 30–31
snakes. *See* serpent of light myth
"snap apple" wheel, 126–27
socialism, 89
Sol Invictus, 18
solar zenith, 15
solstices
    Chinese New Year and, 20
    Christmas and winter solstice, 5
    fire symbolism and, 103–5
    importance of, 4
    Inca culture and, 14
    measuring, 92–93
    in polar regions, 96–97
    as seasonal markers, 1
    solstice pillars, 94
    solstice registers, 151
    summer solstice, 4, **91–105**
    winter solstice, 5, 18, 149–52, 152–63
Sosigines, 20
Sothis, 13
South America, 91
spells
    in Babylonian culture, 129
    Halloween and, 125
    love spells, 38–39, 43, 100–101
sports
    cockfighting, 75–76
    Labor Day, 108–9

May Day, 84–85
New Year's Day, 12–13, 26
    solstice day, 99
    summer celebrations and, 105
    Thanksgiving and, 147
spring
    eggs and, 66
    May Day as marker of, 36–37
    spring equinox, 3, **47–61**
Squanto, 142
Star of Bethlehem, 152
The Stations of the Sun (Hutton), 171
Statue of Liberty, 4
sterility cures, 39
Stonehenge, 59, 94–95, 150–51
Stonehenge Complete (Chippindale), 59
strikes, 88
substitution principle, 7
Sukkoth, 16, 138
summer solstice, 4, **91–105**. *See also* solstices
sun gods, 7, 14–15, 152
superstition, 81, 82, 155–56. *See also* divination; folklore; magic
Swedish culture, 79
syncretism, 102–3
Syrus, 152

Tablet of the Cross, 151
Tannenbaums, 160
Tarquins, 74
Tauvikjuag, 150
tax returns, 12
Taylor, John, 75
Taylor, Sarah, 86–87
technology, 140
Tecuciztecatl, 65
television, 117
Temple of Kukulcan, 48–51
Teotihuacan, 57, 58–61
terrorism, 8
Thanksgiving, **135–48**
    American version, 140–47
    creation of, 78
    evolution of, 5
    Halloween compared with, 124
    New Year's Day compared with, 26
Thompson, Benjamin, 88
Thoreau, Henry David, 136
Tiahuanaco, 91, 92
Tiber river, 102
time
    clocks and, 111–16
    ownership of, 111–12, 165–69
    relation to nature, 166
    routines, 11
Times Square, 21
Tisquantum, 142
Tlaloc, xii
toasting, 23
Todos Santos, 131–32
Torah, 22
Totonac Indians, 54

tourism, 52
traditions, invention of, 86
travel, 147
trees
    Blackthorn tree, 38–39
    Christmas trees, 160–61
    Hawthorn tree, 81
    maypoles, 81–84
    Tree of Liberty, 86
trick-or-treating, 119–22, 124–25, 155
turkeys, 145–46
Turner, Victor, 119, 133
Tusser, Thomas, 139

Uaxactun, 93
unions, 88–89, 110–11. *See also* labor
United Brotherhood of Carpenters, 110
Untermeyer, Louis, 87, 109
Ur (Babylonian city), 67, 128
urbanization, 114–15

"Valentine Writers," 44
Valentine's Day, 7, 39–46
Valhalla, 72
Venus, 13, 102
Vesta, 101
Vestal Virgins, 154
Vestalia, 101
Victorian England, 66. *See also* English
    culture
Virgin Mary (Mary, mother of Jesus), 3, 34,
    35, 39
voladores, 54
Voltaire, 61

Walber, 82
Washington, D.C., 37

Washington, George, 27, 143–44
wassail, 23
water, 102
weather prediction, 25, 29–34, 35–36, 155–
    56. *See also* divination
Weather Wisdom (Kingsbury), 171
weddings, 100
West Indian Carnival Day, 168
wet seasons, 2
Weymouth, George, 142
Whitman, Walt, 107, 109
wildlife, 31–32
Wilson, Woodrow, 78
Wind Rose, 92
winter solstice, 5, 18, 149–52, 152–63
wishbones, 146
witches, 83, 129
women
    summer solstice celebrations and, 99–
        100
    widows, 126
    witches, 83, 129
    women's rights movement, 144
woodchucks, 32–33
Works and Days (Hesiod), 37
World Anarchist Federation, 89

Yaqui Indians, 162
yin and yang forces, 41, 96
Yom Kippur, 16
York, Michael, 73
Yuandan (Chinese New Year's Day), 16
Yucatan peninsula, 48
Yule logs, 154

Zionism, 162